The MINUTES Of
SALEM BAPTIST CHURCH

The MINUTES Of
SALEM BAPTIST CHURCH

HAMILTON COUNTY, TENNESSEE
1872–1915

Transcribed with History 1835–1941

Daniel L. Roark

iUniverse, Inc.
New York Lincoln Shanghai

The MINUTES Of SALEM BAPTIST CHURCH
HAMILTON COUNTY, TENNESSEE 1872–1915

iUniverse books may be ordered through booksellers or by contacting:

iUniverse
2021 Pine Lake Road,Suite 100
Lincoln,NE 68512
www.iuniverse.com
1-800-Authors (1-800-288-4677)

ISBN-13:978-0-595-35657-7 (pbk)
ISBN-13:978-0-595-67256-1 (cloth)
ISBN-13:978-0-595-80135-0 (ebk)
ISBN-10:0-595-35657-5 (pbk)
ISBN-10:0-595-67256-6 (cloth)
ISBN-10:0-595-80135-8 (ebk)

Printed in the United States of America

To the stalwart members of Salem Baptist Church who,
like the Apostle Paul, fought the good fight, finished their course,
and, most importantly, kept the faith.

Contents

List of Photographs

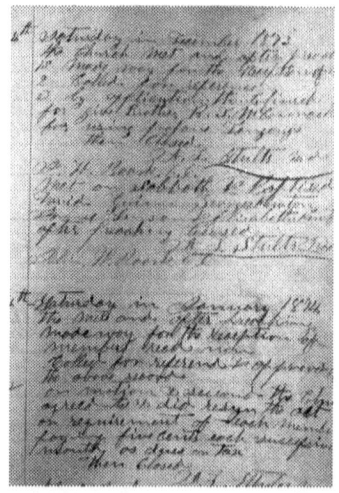

Church Book of Salem Baptist Church
Top: Bound church book.
Bottom: Original page of church book

Preface

"For where two or three are gathered together in my name,
there I am in the midst of them." Matt. 18:20 KJV

A church in the 1800s would, if possible, obtain for its records a book of bound blank pages. The business of the church would be noted in this bound volume which would be called the "church book." The church book could also be a sheaf of papers bound by a piece of string or in another manner. The church took the care of its book quite seriously. Paper was not yet in ready abundance. Space in the book was guarded carefully, using each page as judicially as possible. The surviving minutes of Salem Baptist Church were found in such a book.

Transcription of a text, particularly a text from a previous century, is a task wrought with trepidation. It is more than a simple matter of typing written text. Research is required throughout the entire process. Transcribing church minutes from a previous century requires that the transcriber understand the events, attitudes, and convictions of the people involved at the time the minutes were written. The transcriber must, at least temporarily, acquire those attitudes and convictions.

In the past two years, I have found myself sitting in Salem Baptist Church, sweating from the heat of a mid-summers day, patiently listening to a sermon from a preacher who was approaching middle age one hundred years before I was brought into this world. I sat with the church clerk as he wrote the minutes of the day's meeting by candle light following baptism at Moon's Landing. I have felt the joy of being accepted into the church and the agonizing, soul searching pain of being excluded from a religious community.

Although any mistakes in the transcription of the minutes must rest entirely upon my shoulders, I have, at all times, tried to remain true to the original text, which was no easy task. The education of the members of Salem Baptist Church varied, though they were largely uneducated by today's standards. Fortunately, due to the minimal qualifications for church clerk of simply being able to read and write, the job of clerk naturally fell to the members who could do so. Often the clerk would be someone who held a civil service position such as A.L. Stulce who was Deputy County Court Clerk.

A recurring difficulty was caused by the habit of one clerk spelling a surname differently than another clerk, neither of which would be correct. To make family research easier, I have tried to list all possible spellings in the index. However, in some instances it is possible that, regardless of additional research, I was never able to ascertain the correct original spelling.

In addition, modern software stubbornly refuses to accept misspelled words and would often automatically correct my purposeful misspellings, causing me to re-type it until the software accepted it the way it was spelled in the minutes. This same problem also affected capitalization and other punctuation. And while rearranging the minutes to fit into the text in order to keep the book at approximately 300 pages, I have tried to remain true to the original minutes.

The history of Salem Baptist Church is based on the minutes and other available church documents from Salem, its sister churches, and East Tennessee Baptist associations, with additional research to confirm dates, to connect events and people, and to add additional information on events surrounding Salem Church. When the minutes are quoted in the text, proper English and punctuation are used without continual reference to the minutes.

As I made progress on the minutes and came to know the members of Salem Baptist Church, the project became not only a labor of love, but the impetus for a journey that encompassed soul searching, religious reflection, and introspection. Researching and writing a history of people and times past requires one to come to grips with his or her own mortality, causing a reevaluation of the author's life, purpose, and contribution to reflection by future generations. Transcribing the minutes and writing a history of a church necessitates a confirmation of the author's religious beliefs, attitudes, and convictions. It is impossible to delve into the history of a religious institution, much less one which one's ancestors attended, without reexamining one's beliefs.

I would like to thank my father for sending me on that journey and accompanying me along the way and my mother for her unwavering support all of my life. I would like to thank my wife, Cyndy, for her perseverance and patience. Cyndy put up with hours of my not being entirely in the present and listened patiently to endless stories of another time and place. I would also like to thank my children: Jennifer, Conner, Cameron, and J.D. Jennifer for allowing me to be a father and the three boys for putting up with their father's times of distraction and impatience.

It is necessary for me to thank Howard Scott for his reminiscence of the last days of the Salem Baptist Church and for editing the integration of his story into the text. Thanks go as well to Darwin Lane and David Roark of the Roark-Conner Association for their support and encouragement. Sadly, David Roark passed away before the book was published. He does, however, reside now with the Lord and the ancestors he so meticulously noted in his books of the Roark-Conner lineage.

As for the journey, it is ongoing. The essence of the journey, however, lies within these pages. It is my hope that readers will accompany me on the journey, not only learning about Salem Baptist Church, but also experiencing church life on the frontier in the nineteenth and twentieth centuries.

Maxmillian Haney Conner

Maxmillian Haney (M.H.) Conner, arriving in the Salem area in the early 1835, was one of the trustees of Salem Baptist Church when title to the church property was established. M.H. Conner would remain an active and faithful member of Salem Church until his death.

Chapter One
Salem Baptist Church
1835–1872

Sunrise in the wilderness of East Tennessee in the early 1800s would bring a shine to the leaves, a sheen to the dew covered grasses, and the sound of horse hooves pounding the ground, echoing through the trees across the hillside. The horse's rider would be wearing the closest thing to a "Sunday-go-to-meeting" suit he could afford, with an overcoat if not summer. The saddle bags would hold a well worn Bible. In the rider's hand, and laid across the saddle in front of him, was a rifle, armed and ready.

The rider would be a minister on his way to one of his churches or to an area in need of a church. If he met anyone on the trail, where there was a trail, it would most likely be another minister, a farmer on the way to the nearest town or settlement, or Indians, hopefully friendly. The rifle was for unfriendly Indians, thieves, and ne'er-do-wells, as well as predatory animals. The church to which he was on his way would be on his mind as he thought of, or went over, his sermon. The minister would not be picturing a white washed building with benches, a pulpit, and bell in the tower. His churches were the people themselves meeting in places of convenience. One church would meet in a particular grove of trees. Another might meet in someone's cabin.

The pioneers of his churches would be anxiously awaiting his arrival. In some areas, he would be their link to civilization. The minister would bring news from surrounding areas, a Bible story, and guidance for their salvation. The infrequent services helped them to keep their faith alive in trying circumstances. In East Tennessee, it would be common for Cherokee Indians to attend the church, or for the church to be at a mission in a sparse Cherokee village. The whites in the area coexisted with the Cherokees, occupying land with permission from the Indian tribe.

To endure the hardships of the frontier took more than a determined pioneer spirit. It required a faith that everything would work out for the best—that something more was to come other than the meager crops they scratched out of the earth. The minister brought them a renewal of that faith as well as reaffirming that they were not alone. Ministers were often linked closely with the education level of their congregations and small communities. Many families would rarely read anything but the Bible and church literature. Church meetings were the social activities of these communities which oftentimes did not have a school or other social center.

In the early 1830s, all land south of the Tennessee River and the Hiwassee River had been reserved to the Cherokee tribes by the Calhoun Treaty of 1819.[1] What was to become Chattanooga was then Ross's Landing. Prior to the execution of the Calhoun Treaty, the Cherokees had struggled to relate to the new nation and its people and by 1820 the Cherokee Indians were well on the road toward the white man's culture. The course of the Cherokee education and development was accelerated in the 1820's by the invention and acceptance of a syllabary by Sequoyah, son of a Cherokee woman and a white trader. This made possible the writing and printing of the Cherokee language and a large number of the Indians learned to read and write in their own language. There was probably less illiteracy among the Cherokee than among the whites living in the same states.[2] Considerable credit for the advancement in education among the Cherokees can be attributed to the influence of Christian missions.

Missions, churches, and even schools, in new and frontier lands were formed and services or classes held, around campfires, by the river, in groves of trees, wherever deemed suitable, without benefit of a stationary structure. And so it was when a group of men and women met on a tract overlooking the Tennessee River in Cherokee Territory on May 23, 1835—the fourth Saturday in May—and formed Salem Baptist Church.

A unique characteristic of the Salem congregation was their immediate desire and commitment to build a church building. The founding members and their parents had grown up in western Virginia and North Carolina during the time of the "great religious awakening" on the western frontier. It had been a time of itinerant preachers and camp meetings but with few organized churches and even fewer church buildings. Populations were sparse, families were on the move to find free land, and church buildings were not a high priority. Religious services had been held irregularly depending on the availability of a circuit-riding minister on horseback. Planned camp meetings, where families camped for several days, had provided what little Biblical instruction was available beyond the family.

But then, on that fourth Saturday in May 1835, on a creek near the Tennessee river, the Salem congregation committed to erecting a church building, not a campground—here they would regularly meet as a church body and here they would teach their children the words of the Lord. They had come to stay. A short time later a log structure was erected as a meeting house for the church on land near the Blue Springs Ferry operated by James T. Gardenhire, white son-in-law of Cherokee leader, Path Killer.

Founding fathers of Salem Baptist Church are unknown but probably included James Gardenhire, George Irwin, and Maximilian Haney Conner. George Irwin and M.H. Conner "and their successors" were later named as trustees when title to the church property was formally established. M.H. Conner was twenty-nine when the church was founded and had arrived in the Ocoee territory in January 1835. He was to remain an active member of Salem Church throughout the remainder of his life. Both Conner and Irwin were listed on the 1836 tax list of Civil District 10 of Hamilton County, which had by that date extended its jurisdiction to the south bank of the Tennessee River.

Pioneers in the community that made up Salem's congregation during the first few years of the church included the Conners, Roarks, Smiths, McCallies, Gardenhires, Hixons, Johnsons, Crosses, Webbs, Haneys, Killians, Richeys, Friddells, Gambles, and McCormicks. No complete roster of the original members is now available. Not all of these families were represented in the charter membership, but many of them were.[3]

As the men and women met to form the first Baptist church in the Ocoee area, President Andrew Jackson was working with leaders of the Cherokee Nation for their relocation to lands beyond the Mississippi. Two months before, in March 1835, the U.S. Senate had approved a buy-out offer to the Cherokees, and in April President Jackson had published a letter to "the Cherokee Tribes of Indians East of the Mississippi River" explaining the financial offer and urging its acceptance by the Cherokees.

T.J. Campbell, a former member of Salem Church, born in the last year of the Civil War in Hamilton County, in his address on the history of the church at the one-hundredth anniversary of Salem Baptist Church on Sunday, May 26, 1935, described the church's founding as follows:

> When a group of God-fearing men and women assembled in this community to organize Salem Church, Andrew Jackson was president of the United States. Victoria was a sixteen year old girl being prepared to become Queen of England. The Church of the Holy Sepulchers, which was the occasion of a great war, had not been erected in Jerusalem. Cleveland and Chattanooga had not yet appeared on the map. Birchwood was a spring and a birch tree or two. There were only scattering white families in this part of the country which was still in possession of the Cherokee Indians. These pioneers, however, while

striving to establish homes for themselves and their children in the wilderness, thought it also well to plant and propagate the religion of their fathers.[4]

There was, at that time, bitter division among the leaders of the Cherokee Nation on how to respond to government pressures. Opinions were divided between those of Cherokee leaders Major Ridge, with his son, John Ridge, who advocated peaceful acceptance of the Senate's offer and that of John Ross, who strongly suggested opposition. As the founding fathers met to form Salem Church, meetings were being held at the home of John Ross at Red Clay to decide the response of the Cherokee Nation.[5] Unfortunately, within three years the trail of tears for the Cherokees would begin at Blythe's Ferry.

With the opening of the Ocoee Land District by the Tennessee Legislature in 1838, the area around Salem Church began to grow in population, having become part of Hamilton County in 1836. In September 1844, when Salem Church was nine years old, the members moved to acquire title to the tract on which the church meeting house was located. The dedicatory deed provided by George W. Gardenhire read as follows:

> For the love and affection I entertain for George Irwin and M.H. Conner, Trustees for the Salem Church, I do hereby give, transfer, and convey to them and their successors my tract of land in Hamilton, Tennessee, District Number Ten, containing by estimation two acres and bounded as follows to viz Beginning at the North West [sic] Corner on a post oak tree, thence North East [sic] twenty poles, thence South East [sic] sixteen poles, thence South West [sic] twenty poles, thence North West [sic] sixteen poles to the beginning including two acres to have and to hold the same to the said George Irwin and M.H. Conner and their successors [and] assigns forever I do covenant and agree for myself and my heirs to warrant and defend the title to the said tract of land to the said George Irwin and M.H. Conner and successors [and] assigns against the lawful claim of all persons whatever.
> This 24th Sept. 1844
>
> G. W. Gardenhire   Seal
>
> Attest
> C.C. McKeehan
> Robert McCallie[6]

As the number of Baptist churches grew in a given area, a Baptist Association would soon be formed to bring the churches together. Associations were intended to be autonomous, subject to votes among the delegates of member churches. The earliest Baptist Association was formed in England in the 1650s. Philadelphia spawned the first Baptist Association in America in 1707. The Charleston Association in South Carolina was the first Baptist association in the South in 1751.

Of the fifteen associations stemming from the Tennessee Association that was formed in 1802, the closest geographically were the Hiwassee Association, formed in 1821, and the Primitive Ocoee Association formed in 1841. When the Ocoee Baptist Association was formed in 1859, the rules of the Hiwassee Association were used at the meeting and part of the Hiwassee Association was absorbed into the Ocoee Association. For this reason, the Ocoee Baptist Association is attributed to the Hiwassee Association.

Salem Baptist Church was fundamental in its Christian faith and, in 1842, aligned itself with the Primitive Ocoee Baptist Association, the first and only Baptist Association available to Salem at that time. While the Ocoee Baptist churches did not participate directly in the Great Revival, which had run its course by 1815, they were involved in the subsequent controversies developing from that movement, particularly as to missions, baptisms, and Sunday schools. One of the immediate results of the Great Revival was the expansion and impetus given the missionary movement among the Baptists and other denominations.

The promotion of missionary activity, however, was far from unanimous and a large anti-mission element also developed. This group objected to the centralization of authority and to an educated and paid ministry. All missionary societies and similar man-made organizations were contrary to the Scriptures, it was held. Anti-mission sentiment was strongest on the frontier and, as late as 1847, there was a large anti-mission group in Tennessee.

Indicative of this spirit was the Primitive Ocoee Baptist Association organized in 1841, four years before the Southern Baptist Convention was founded at Corinth Church in Augusta, Georgia. Little is known about this Association except that it was formed out of the Tennessee Association, and that it existed until 1860, a year after the Ocoee Association of Missionary Baptists was organized. The Primitive Ocoee Association, by 1848, consisted of between eight and thirteen churches all located south of the Tennessee River in Hamilton and Bradley counties. In this period, several attempts were made to unite the Missionary and Primitive groups or to admit the Missionary Churches into the earlier Primitive Ocoee Association. Harrison Church, representing the missionary element, made advances for union and cessation of "fighting in the Church of Christ." Agreement was finally reached, for after organization of the Ocoee Baptist Association in 1859, "the ole one was dissolved."

A few words should be given to the explanation of the term "Primitive Baptist," as well as to state that both the former and latter Ocoee Associations were primitive in nature. The term "Primitive Baptists" is, at the same time, a misleading yet appropriate term. Primitive Baptist ancestors have been called by various names over the ages. The name Primitive Baptist became popular in the early 1800s when the term primitive conveyed the idea of originality rather than backwardness. Accordingly, Primitive Baptists claim to maintain the doctrines and practices of the original Baptists, who claimed to be the New Testament church. Primitive also conveys the idea of simplicity. This well describes the Primitive Baptists, whose church services consist of nothing more than preaching, praying, and singing.[7]

Using the terms loosely, the stance of the Primitive Ocoee Baptist Association was "Orthodox Primitive," while the later Ocoee Baptist Association would be viewed as "Conservative Primitive."

The former association was anti-missionary, did not have Sunday schools, and did not believe in training. Such Primitive Baptists believed that Bible study and worship should involve the entire congregation as a whole and segregation of the church into age groups was against the teachings of the Bible. Likewise, the Holy Spirit did the teaching which mortal man could not do.

The Ocoee Baptist Association felt that it was a church's, and its association's, responsibility to spread the gospel outside a church's physical borders, to provide separate Bible study to children in order to help them fully understand the word of the Lord, and to train teachers and missionaries for the task for which they felt chosen. Outside of the few differences, both associations maintained the same beliefs, principles, and practices such as referring to ministers and church leaders as elders, requiring elders to be male, foot washing during communion, and baptism by immersion. "The appointment of two men to 'ride as missionaries' revealed a great interest in carrying the message of Jesus Christ to the 'destitute portions of the Association.' The subject of missions, and that of Sabbath Schools, became very familiar in the annual sessions of the Ocoee Baptist Association."[8]

By 1850 Hamilton County had a population of just over 9000 while the area south of the river and north of Old Harrison had a population of almost 1000.[9] With an increase in population and commerce comes change, even in the churches and their associations. When change comes, the populace is split between those accepting, and those rejecting, change. The churches were not exceptions.

In 1856, while Salem Baptist Church began to feel the rumble of change, the church meeting house burned. The building and all of the previous records were destroyed. Rather than rebuild in the same location, the church voted to relocate away from the river and closer to what was the center of the Salem community. A new meeting house was built on what is now Birchwood Pike adjacent to Grasshopper Creek on land owned by Joseph Roark. It would serve as a church and school.

Just when they were getting settled into the new church house and setting about reconnecting the members in a new location, the world began to change drastically for Salem, her sister churches, and the south. The missionary movement began to take hold in East Tennessee as well as the feeling that Sunday schools were needed to pass the work of the Lord to the increasing number of children. Both ideals were met with hesitation from church and association members, even those who would eventually resolve to accept the changes. Echoes of the Great Revival were calling them to reaffirm their commitment to keep the mission effort within the church and refrain from having Sunday school in order that church members of all ages could hear the word of the Lord together as churches did in biblical times.

In either case, both sides struggled with a difficult question. From the outset, both held the belief that theirs was the true path to a heavenly reward and that the other group was disillusioned. Yet these were not nameless and faceless people they were condemning. These were people they had known for years, some close friends, and in some cases, family. Although it could scarcely be spoken, at some point doubts would have to form as to which might actually be the proper path and why God would have them condemn people they knew were God-fearing.

Salem Baptist Church did not attend the meeting in 1859 that was to be a planning meeting for the new Ocoee Association. They would, instead, attend the twentieth anniversary meeting of the Primitive Ocoee Association. The change would not be easy for Salem Church. It is not known how many members would leave Salem to remain with a Primitive Baptist Association. At the meeting of the new association, the name Ocoee Baptist Association was adopted. At the second meeting in 1860, at which Salem Church would be represented, the Primitive Ocoee Baptist Association would be dissolved.

The constitution of the Ocoee Baptist Association provided that each member church would be entitled to three messengers, that no person should be eligible to election as moderator for two years in succession, that the Association was not a legislative body and had no power over the churches as far as their independence and discipline were concerned. It was merely a paternal conference "to learn each other's state, to cherish brotherly sympathy and union, and advance each other in the faith, love, and hope of the gospel."

The Ocoee Association was organized in response to a call published in The Tennessee Baptist, on July 2, 1859, advocating the formation of a new association from the Hiwassee, State Line, and Sweetwater Associations. The boundary set forth in the proposal began "at the State line on the southwest corner of Hiwassee Association, then making the line between Tennessee and Georgia the southern boundary line, until it includes Polk County, Tennessee, then making the Hiwassee river the northern line until it intersects the Tennessee river, thence including all that portion of Hiwassee Association southwest of the junction made by the Hiwassee and Tennessee Rivers, together with any contiguous churches at any point too remote for any other Association." It covered the present area of Bradley, Hamilton, and Polk Counties and that portion of Meigs County south of the Hiwassee River. Elders William McNutt, Jonas Burk, and Lewis Mitchell signed the call. The Ocoee Association was designed to unite the missionary and anti-mission churches, and replace the Primitive Ocoee Baptist Association.[10]

While the churches of the Ocoee Baptist Association were reeling from the unsettling division of Baptists in East Tennessee, the rumble of conflict would steadily grow. Even those churches not affected internally were concerned about their troubled brethren at sister churches. Their faith was about to be shaken to its roots. The movement for the abolition of slavery had been encouraged by the Great Revival as it came to an end in the early 1800s, and the slavery question entered even the controversies of the southern Baptists. Emancipation sentiment was not as strong in Tennessee as it was in Kentucky, but East Tennessee was more abolitionist than the rest of the state, probably because of the fewer number of slaves in that region. Until the Civil War, churches in East Tennessee counted a few slaves among their members—among the first licentiates of the Ocoee Association in 1859 was Ephriam, a "col'rd brother." While in 1867 the First Baptist Church of Chattanooga granted letters of dismissal to two "colored members," Candies Creek Church had the previous year admitted several "colored persons" to membership.

April 1861 and the fall of Fort Sumpter at Charleston saw the beginning of the Civil War, which, in East Tennessee more than any other area in the country, divided brother against brother and family against family. Families were equally divided and long-time friendships were severed. The Ocoee Baptist Association ceased to function and no meetings of the Association, with its fourteen member churches, were held between 1861 and 1865.

As both armies, North and South, maneuvered to position for the battles of Chickamauga and Chattanooga in late 1863 and early 1864, the area around the Salem Church building was subject to devastation. Horses and other livestock were taken by the subsistence officers of both armies. Rail fences disappeared as camped armies sought wood for campfires. Rich and cultivated farm lands were made worthless by the trampling of thousands of horses and men. Following the battle of Chickamauga, the beloved meeting house of Salem Church was used as a hospital for the Confederate wounded. Through the agony of war, fought at its doorstep, through the sorrow from loved ones killed in battle, through the tears of defeat, and through the bitterness of a divided community, Salem Baptist Church survived, as did the church building itself.

An example of Unionist sentiment held by some of the Ocoee Baptists may be found in the 1864 statement from the Candies Creek Church to the Ocoee Association that the members of the church thought "'it necessary to spread on record the cause of this long space of Eleven months between Church meetings the Cause is this there arose a rebellion people in force and arms against the country and drove the male members nearly all from their homes and throwed the country in such a deranged condition' and that it was best not to have meetings. In 1865, a member of the church was reprimanded for calling another a 'confounded copperhead.' Thus did the churches take sides in the Civil War."[11]

With the surrender of the Confederate armies, the congregation of Salem Church began to experience the extended suffering of the Reconstruction era. Old and deep animosities engendered by years of conflict were not easily forgotten. Salem Church struggled to adjust. Money was scarce and the returning veterans of both armies, many of whom were unable to work because of war wounds, found their farms difficult to cultivate in the ravaged countryside. The suffering and deprivation of Reconstruction was to last ten long years.

In 1865, the "Ocoee Association was preparing for a session with the church at Cookson's Creek in Polk County, Tennessee. One interesting note of the fourth annual session [1865] was the fact that eighteen letters were received from churches, an increase of four over the first annual associational meeting."[12] Salem was one of the four additional churches being represented that were not at the first meeting. The "interesting note" comment illustrates the association's joy at having that many churches active at the height of Reconstruction. It was also reported at that meeting that various areas within the geographical boundaries of the Association had no regular services or preachers.[13]

Divisiveness caused by the war could have easily split the church asunder, but, in spite of the remnants of the war, Salem Church survived. A brief statistic illustrates the potential for conflict within the church. By August 1872, the earliest date for which church records are available, Salem Baptist Church had 162 members. Of the 35 men of the church between the ages of twenty-three and fifty-five (the ages most likely to have seen military service during the Civil War), almost half had served in the war—eight for the Union forces and eight for the Confederacy.[14] Still, while animosities doubtless continued elsewhere, the extent minutes of the church reflect no war-related difficulties within the church.

Rules of Decorum of Salem Church

Article 1.   The Church meetings shall be opened and closed by prayer.

Article 2.   One person only shall speak at the same time who shall arise fro his seat and address the Moderator when he is about to make his speach.

Article 3.   The person speaking shall not be interrupted in his speach bny any person except the moderator untill he is done speaking.

Article 4.   The person speaking shall strickly adhere to the Subject under consideration And shall in nowise Either reflect on or make any unfriendly remarks on the Imperfection of the person who preceeded him But shall farely state the case and convey his Ideas on the Subject as concisely as posible.

Article 5.   No member of the church shall abruptly absent himself from the church without leave from the Moderator.

Article 6.   No member shall speak more than three times on any one Subject with out permission from the Church.

Article 7.   No person shall have liberty of laughing during the time of business in the church nor of whispering in time of public speaking.

Article 8.   The Moderator shall not interrupt any member of the church when speaking until he is done unless he violates the rules of this church.

Article 9.   No member of the church shall address an other in any other appellation than that of Brother.

Article 10   The members of the Church shall consider it their duty to attend their Church meeting once in Each month unless providentially hidred.

Article 11   Any member of the Church who shall knowingly violate any of the rules of this church shall be reprooved by the church as may be thought proper.

Article 12   All business of the church shall be done by a majority Except the reception of members which shall be done by the unaninous voice of all the members present.

Article 13   All motions made and seconed shall be attended to unless with drawn by the person who made it.

Joseph Roark

Joseph Roark finalized the donation of a portion of his land to Salem Baptist Church in 1872 for the new meeting house. His wife, Juda Ann Carr, was a member of the Church at that time. Joseph would be baptized and join Salem Church in December of 1873, three years before his death. His sons and their families would be an integral part of Salem Baptist Church throughout the remainder of its existence.

Chapter Two
Salem Baptist Church
1872–1879

The surviving minutes of Salem Baptist Church begin in 1872. It is not known what records were kept by the church, if any, from the end of the Civil War until 1872. Ironically, the surviving minutes illustrate the activities and feelings of the Church during its most important years of growth. The minutes begin with the meeting on the fourth Saturday in August. The next month, probably under circumstances relating to Reconstruction and the formation of James County in 1870, the Church formalized its land title September 28, 1872, with a deed signed by Joseph Roark to the Trustees of the Salem Baptist Church:

State of Tennessee, James County

I, Joseph Roark, for and in consideration of respect that I have for the cause of religion and education Do give and bequeath to the trustees of Salem Baptist Church a certain tract or parcel of land containing by estimation one acre be the same more or less situated in the Third Civil District of James County and bounded as follows embracing the land where the meeting house now stands running in every direction from the house so as to include an acre outside my fence which land the said Trustees and their successors are to have and to hold as long as the same is used for Church and Educational purposes but no other then the same returns back to me as giver or donor of the same

This the 28th day of Sept 1872

Joseph Roark

Attest A.L. Stulce
John W. Roark
State of Tennessee
James County

Personally appeared before me A.L. Stulce, Special Deputy County Clerk of said County of James, Joseph Roark the maker of the within Deed a man with whom I am personally acquainted and acknowledge the within Instrument for the purposes therein contained.

    Witness my hand at office in Ooltewah the 22nd day of March 1873

A.L. Stulce

Special Deputy County Court Clerk

State of Tennessee

James County   Register's Office, April 1st 1873

    Then was the foregoing deed received for registration with certificate and is now of record in Book 1, Page 136

    Witness my hand at office the day and date last above written

J.G. Ruston

Register

Salem Church was not racially divided in the 1870s. The church rolls for 1872 and 1874 contained the names of African-American members. The African-American members were listed last on the church roll when it was reconstituted in 1872 and 1874. Their names included: Thomas Eldridge, Mary Moon, Arnold Mangrum, and Caty Mangrum.[1] The African-American members of Salem Baptist Church were full members, appointed to committees and participating in meetings. There is no record of them on the rolls after 1874. As freed men and women began to gather for mutual support, they would start their own churches and communities.

The surviving minutes are an illustrative personal account of church life in the latter part of the nineteenth century, and the first part of the twentieth—a picture of the community life that would not be available elsewhere. Witnessing to, and conversion of, non-believers was done in the confines of the church. In the community, one was judged by his/her citizenship and personal character. In the church, he or she was judged by the quality of their religious character.

Meetings at Salem Baptist church were held on the fourth Saturday with preaching on the Sunday following. Usually, a meeting followed services on Sunday and the church would often "adjourn to meet at night." Sabbath school, or Sunday school, would not begin until November 1873 when Salem Baptist Church "Resolved herself into Sabbath School to meet each successive Sabbath." There is no evidence in the minutes that Sunday school was held every Sunday, but records of "children's day" exist outside the minutes. Salem Church would agree to preaching on the second Sunday in 1873. Since they did not change the meeting times to the second weekend of each month until 1878, it can only be assumed that, in 1873, the church agreed to have preaching on both the second

Sunday and the fourth Sunday, with business meetings on the fourth Saturday. The church would change back to the fourth weekend in 1879.

The delay in beginning a Sunday school until thirteen years after joining the Ocoee Association illustrates the reluctance of former primitive churches to make the transition to evangelistic theological church practices, in addition to the historically slow rate with which churches and religious bodies accept change. With religion so intrinsically a part of a person's life, it is understandable that change in that religion would not elicit immediate acceptance. Sunday school and missions were the main reasons for the new Ocoee Association's split from the primitive, or anti-missionary, association. However, although Sabbath school began at Salem Church in 1873, it would be many years before the minutes of the meetings mentioned missions, with one exception.

In May 1873, the Church "took up a collection for the Ministry." At the 1872 Ocoee Association meeting, the association emphasized not only Foreign Missions, but the Committee on Systematic Benevolence recommended to "the churches of this association" a quarterly collection "commencing with the month of December, 1872, March, 1873, June and September, 1873, for Home Missionary purposes..." The collection in May appears to be taken for the June quarterly payment. Salem Baptist Church consistently heeded the urging of the association, but struggled to maintain its financial support of the association's purposes. It was difficult to collect even enough to keep up the meeting house and pay the pastor's salary. Although the members of Salem Church would continue to contribute what they could throughout the life of the church, it was rare for the members to be able to meet their apportionment to the association.

The anti-missionary view held that time and money were better spent within the home church and local sister churches. This Salem Church did faithfully, even after they later adopted the larger mission view. On September 26, 1873, Salem Church dismissed twenty-four of its members for the purposes of constituting a new church in the growing community of Birchwood. The members leaving Salem Church to form the First Baptist Church of Birchwood were: Mack Conner, Margaret Conner, James Madison Conner, Jane Bare Conner, M.M. Gross, Latisha Gross, John Gass, Lee Lane, Sarah Lane, William Curton, Mary E. Curton, George Campbell, Catherine Smith, Jacob Baker, Elizabeth Baker, John B. Roark, Nancy Roark, James Cameron Sr., James Cameron Jr., Lena Dickson, Hose Gross, Duke Kimbrough, Burton Holman, and T.J. Leonard.

John (J.H.) Gass would return to Salem Church in 1890 when he was elected pastor. It is not known when or where J.H. Gass was ordained. Most likely, he was not ordained at Salem. If he were an ordained minister when Birchwood began, he would not have needed to be "dismissed." Not having been the pastor of

Salem at the time, he would have simply been elected by the Birchwood Church. Upon his death in October 1896, J.H. Gass was buried in the Birchwood Baptist Cemetery. His headstone reads "Asleep in Jesus."

Another unique member of the delegation sent to form the new Birchwood church was Duke Kimbrough. Although he was not a preacher, his son, I.Z. (Isaac Zachariah) Kimbrough carried on the East Tennessee legacy of Baptist ministry begun by the patriarch of the ministerial "clan." I.Z. Kimbrough had been pastor of Salem Baptist Church from 1866 through 1871. He would return as pastor in 1883. Duke's grandfather and namesake, the elder Duke Kimbrough was the head of a family producing a line of distinguished Baptist preachers, beginning with the elder Duke himself.

In the 1866 Ocoee Association minutes, I.Z. Kimbrough was not only listed as pastor of Salem Baptist Church, but also as supply pastor for "Corinth, M.C." There is also a "Corinth, B.C." listed. Ostensibly, the initials stand for Meigs County and Bradley County. With the poor economy brought on by the war and Reconstruction, many churches were having considerable trouble paying their pastors, including churches of the Ocoee Association. The association would appoint supply pastors to be called if the church had no pastor available for their monthly services. The supply pastors for the churches in the association were primarily associational pastors, but also included other current pastors of churches in the association.

In 1869, the Ocoee Association recommended "Elder I.Z. Kimbro and J.W. Wilson…to ride as Missionaries of this Association the coming year."[2] In that year, Rev. I.Z. Kimbrough was pastor of Salem Baptist Church. Although the association would appoint missionaries to travel to different areas for a specific purpose, all pastors in the association were urged to minister to other areas when not tending to the duties of their church. The associational missionaries (those that were appointed) were required to make a report at the end of their term, listing the churches, Sunday schools, and business meetings they had attended. They were also to keep a log of the miles they traveled and a record of expenses.

Rev. I.Z. Kimbrough would preach at Salem and assist in presiding over communion meetings into the 1880s when he was again elected as pastor of Salem Baptist Church in 1883 and 1884. He would see his father's cousin, the Rev. I.B. Kimbrough, at association meetings. As a pastor in the association he would spend much of his time traveling from church to church, preaching and supporting the association. Rev. I.Z. Kimbrough would continue his family's distinguished tradition for many years.

In 1869, Rev. A.L. Stulce was listed in the Ocoee records as Supply Pastor for Salem Church. He became pastor of Salem Baptist Church in 1871. Although Ocoee Association records indicate that Stulce was the pastor through 1880, the church minutes indicate that he was the pastor only through 1876. However, he continued to represent Salem as a delegate to the association through 1880, being listed in Ocoee records as pastor of Salem Baptist Church. Rev. Stulce moved his membership to another church and would be given a letter of recommendation in 1881, but it would be 1898 before his name would cease to appear in Salem Church minutes as preacher, clerk, or moderator for the day.

The minutes of the Hiwassee Association in 1865 show A.L. Stulce to be a delegate from Friendship Baptist Church. In the minutes of Salem Baptist Church, Friendship Church was one of the sister churches Salem would periodically invite to participate in a communion season. The church would invite nearby churches "to seats" with them regardless of their association affiliation. Pastors were permitted to preach where they were needed at churches of the same faith and order.

Stulce would also be colporteur of the association in 1890, and did "a noble work, considering his adversity and limited funds."[3] The colporteur would travel throughout the association in a missionary capacity, selling Bibles and religious literature. Stulce would attend the association's pastor's conference in 1899. He was last listed in the Ocoee records in 1901 when he was nominated for Moderator of the Association, but was not elected. A.L. Stulce was not only a definitive member of the Salem Church community, but also a distinctive resident of the newly formed James County (1871) serving as Special Deputy County Court Clerk. A perusal of court records and marriage records of Hamilton and James counties through the 1870s will find a frequent recurrence of the name A.L. Stulce. The Church Rolls note that A.L. Stulce died December 22, 1910.

Salem Baptist Church would elect R.T. Howard as pastor in 1876. Howard would be elected pastor again in 1883, and once more in 1886. While he was pastor of Salem Church from 1876 to 1878, he was also clerk and missionary for the Hiwassee Baptist Association. Reverend Howard would retire from the association in 1882 having served as clerk for thirty years—never missing a meeting while also serving as missionary for twenty-seven years. In the minutes of the Hiwassee Association meeting in 1865, R.T. Howard is listed as clerk for the meeting and as ordained minister from Washington Baptist Church along with J. Howard. It is not known from the minutes whether R.T. Howard was pastor of Washington Church at that time. Prior to the Hiwassee meeting in 1865, he was Chaplain of the 19th Tennessee infantry regiment of the Confederate Army for three and a half years during the Civil War.[4]

S.J. Blair would be pastor of Salem Church from 1878 to 1879. Blair had been an associational pastor with the Ocoee Association since its inception in 1859. At the original 1859 meeting in which it was agreed that the new association would be called the Ocoee Baptist Association and the Primitive Ocoee Baptist Association would be dissolved, Elder S.J. Blair was not only listed as an ordained minister of the association, but as supply pastor of Pleasant Grove Baptist Church. Rev. Blair was chosen as the alternate for the introductory sermon of the 1859 meeting and would lead the closing prayer of that meeting.

Rev. S.J. Blair had become a pastor of Shepherd Hill Baptist Church before the Civil War, joining J.A. Matthews who was not only primary pastor of Shepherd Hill, but was the first elected moderator of the new Ocoee Baptist Association. In 1866, following the war, Blair had been supply pastor of both the Long Savannah Baptist Church and the Providence Baptist Church in addition to being pastor of Shepherd Hill Baptist Church. He would go on to hold numerous positions with the Ocoee Association including elder and moderator. S.J. Blair was last mentioned in the minutes of the association in 1890 when he was one of three who were "chosen a committee to investigate the soundness of all books placed in hands of [the] Colporteur."[5] The elected Colporteur would be A.L. Stulce.

Salem Baptist Church elected R.H. Jordan as pastor in September 1879 for the ensuing year when W.L. Dale could not accept pastoral care of the Church. R.H. Jordan had been a pastor in the Ocoee Association since 1860 when he was listed as supply pastor for Salem Church. In the minutes of the Ocoee Association for 1866, Jordan is listed as supply pastor for Clear Spring Baptist Church.

A visiting pastor or a member of the clergy would be elected as moderator for the day when the present pastor was absent or an election was held for pastor and/or the current pastor was to be re-elected. A pastor could not be moderator at the meeting in which he was elected, although situations sometimes demanded otherwise. The present pastor would be noted in the minutes as elected moderator for the day at meetings in which elections occurred. At other meetings, he would be referred to as moderator, pastor, or preacher.

It was not unusual for a pastor to resign and be re-elected at the same meeting. Pastors would apparently try to resign and be re-elected for several years in a row, according to the minutes. In October 1875, A.L. Stulce requested that the Church get another pastor but the Church left it until the next meeting. Rev. Stulce would give his resignation as to the pastoral care of the Church in January 1876. As the next order of business at that meeting, he would be elected as pastor for the year. In October of the same year, A.L. Stulce would be elected moderator for the day, and R.T. Howard elected pastor. Rev. Stulce would again be elected moderator for the day in January 1877 when the Church would agree, by motion and second, to give R.T. Howard forty dollars to preach for 12 months and pay it quarterly. At the December meeting, the committee on finance reported $24.25 paid to the pastor and $15.75 still owed.

Church minutes and association records would follow organizational procedures passed along from other churches and associations. Very little published literature was available on parliamentary procedure. Henry Martyn Robert would not publish his Robert's Rules of Order until 1876 which, interestingly, related initially to church business. Robert was an engineering officer in the Army when, without warning, he was asked to preside over a church meeting. Realizing he did not know how to conduct the meeting, he made the attempt anyway, to his embarrassment. He was determined to never attend another meeting until he knew something of parliamentary law. This led to his writing his Rules of Order after finding and studying the few books then available on the subject.[6]

The first mention of deacons in the surviving minutes was in July 1875 when the church elected C.L. Moon and G.W. Rogers to that office. The ordination of Rogers was, by request, postponed indefinitely at the August meeting probably because Rogers and his wife planned to relocate and would be granted letters of dismissal in April 1876. C.L. Moon was ordained as deacon at the August meeting. Ordination of both deacons and preachers was undertaken by the presbytery or officiating clergy. Deacons would be ordained regularly throughout the life of Salem Church and were selected by the church based on qualifications stated in the New Testament.

For preachers on the other hand, God's call to the ministry was the primary qualification. A church member feeling God's call to the ministry would announce his intentions to the church, at which time the church would then release the member from church rolls to be able to preach for two years. After that time, if he was considered dedicated and worthy, he would be ordained. This process is illustrated by the only recorded ordination of a minister at Salem Church during its history—Owen L. Smith in 1911. Smith had been "liberated to exercise himself as a minister of the Gospel" at the September meeting in 1909.

It was common church practice to invite, and be invited by, sister churches to join in communion, church services, and extended meetings. Salem's sister churches principally included the Birchwood, New Union, and Friendship Baptist churches. A prerequisite for communion was conversion, baptism, and church membership. Foot washing was reserved for communion services. A communion season consisted of three or more days of preaching, singing, baptism and foot washing. The practice of foot washing faded at Salem Church sometime in the 1870s. It would not be mentioned in the minutes after May 27, 1876.

Throughout the 1870s, Salem Baptist Church would try, and often succeed, in having a communion season in May. It was sometimes postponed to later months. The church would also have extended meetings in the latter months of the year. Communion seasons were often held over for several days to worship and "commemorate the Lords Death and Suffering."

The church clerk has been the backbone of religious organization since the beginning of the church. In the latter nineteenth century, the clerk took the minutes, kept track of the minutes (or the "book"), and monitored church affairs. Along with keeping the minutes up to date, the clerk was responsible for maintaining the church roll. When a church member was dismissed, granted a letter, excluded, or disciplined by the church, the clerk was expected to make a notation.

The clerk always signed the minutes, as well as the moderator, or pastor, but the clerk did not necessarily write the minutes himself though as a general rule he did. Each clerk would use different terms and phrases. Although the clerk would be chosen from the more educated members of the congregation, he was still prone to spell surnames differently than other clerks and confuse family members of the same surname. It was not unusual for clerks to serve a longer term at the church than the pastors. At Salem Baptist Church, the clerk was often a member of several committees, in addition to his duties as clerk.

In August 1872, at the beginning of the surviving minutes, John Campbell was the clerk of Salem Church. It is not known how long he had been clerk before 1872. John W. Roark would be elected clerk in September. He would resign in December 1874 when John Campbell was again appointed as clerk. Apparently, the terms "appointed" and "elected" were used interchangeably depending on the clerk. Both terms are used to describe similar actions throughout the minutes.

Davis Priddy would be elected as clerk pro tem when John Campbell resigned in November 1875. Priddy would be elected clerk the following month, serving until the next September when he resigned and John Campbell was appointed clerk for the third time. John Campbell's third term as church clerk ended in March 1877 when John W. Roark was elected again upon Campbell's resignation. John and Lucinda Campbell were given letters of recommendation from Salem Baptist Church in September 1877 and neither would be mentioned in the minutes again. John W. Roark would remain as clerk into the 1880s. Assisting Roark in his clerk's duties in 1879 would be Davis Priddy and J.P. Talley.

John Campbell, John W. Roark, Davis Priddy, and J.P. Talley were four of the most involved members in the history of Salem Baptist Church, overshadowed only by Rev. A.L. Stulce. All four were appointed as delegates to the Ocoee Association, John Campbell as an alternate. As clerks they helped run the affairs of the church, often as a member of several committees simultaneously. John W. Roark would be an active member of the church until 1891. His cousins John Lewis Roark and John Mack Roark (J.L.'s son), and his nephew, F.A.B. Roark, would be clerks of Salem Church in later years.

Davis Charles Priddy had been a major purchaser in the Ocoee sale of the former Indian lands, obtaining four grants totaling 160 acres in 1839, and a grant of 80 acres in 1841. Settling first in Meigs County, he gave land for both the Limestone and County Line Baptist Churches. Priddy was on James County's first county court when he was accepted to Salem Baptist Church by letter in July 1873.

After a period of adjustment, Davis Priddy readily accepted any position to which he was elected or appointed by the church. In May 1874, he was appointed to visit New Union and Shepherd Hill Baptist Churches and invite them to assist with a communion season. Davis Priddy would be the last male church member appointed to see a woman of the church in regard to a charge of immoral conduct in August 1875. Priddy would be appointed to the first budget committee of Salem Baptist Church in February 1877 which was formed to arrange collection of the pastor's salary. Davis Priddy would fill every position at Salem Church except pastor. He was an influential member of Salem Church in the 1870s and would serve his church and Lord until his death February 4, 1882.

J.P. (James Pleasant) Talley was first mentioned in the minutes of Salem Baptist Church in May 1876 when a committee was formed to look into finishing the church house, assumably to expand or repair the church building. This was the first mention of any such committee and of any work being planned. It is not known who else was on the committee. Apparently, the work was finished. In March 1877, the Church agreed to assume the debt made by the Building Committee to O.D. Herington and paid the same in full. After helping to form James County, J.P. Talley was justice of the peace for the Second Civil District north of Harrison. He was later postmaster at Thatcher's Landing.[7] J.P. Talley would be elected deacon of Salem Church in November 1877 and ordained with M.H. Conner in January 1878. He would be elected clerk pro tem in March and October of 1879 and would serve Salem Baptist Church in several capacities until his death in 1911.

The 1870s were exciting years of growth for Salem Baptist Church. Meetings became more formal and organized, with committees appointed to raise and handle funds and delegate church business. The decade ended with R.H. Jordan as pastor and John W. Roark once again clerk. The last business by the Church in December 1879 was to appoint messengers to visit the absent members and have them come forward and give a reason for their non-attendance. The appointed messengers were M.H. Conner, J.P. Talley, Joseph Cookston, C.L. Moon, and A.L. Stulce. They were to report at the next meeting. Unfortunately, difficult times lay ahead in the 1880s.

Church Covenant

We, therefore, in order that future generations may know by who our Churchwas constituted and the time it was done. On the Fourth Saturday in May 1835, The Church was constituted by A. Fitzerald and Burk Buckner.

We the Baptist Church of Christ at Salem, having met with the misfortune of having our book and records of the Church all burned up, do now in conference assembled adopt the following Covenant as The Covenant of our Church and agree to live accordingly.

Having been led, as we believe, by the Spirit of God, to receive the Lord Jesus Christ as our Saviour, and on the profession of our faith, having been baptized in the name of our Father and the Son and The Holy Ghost, we do now in the presence of God, angels, and this assembly most solemnly and joyfully enter into Covenant with one unanimous voice in Christ.

We engage therefore by the aid of the Holy Spirit to walk together in Christian love, to strive for the advancement of the church in knowledge, holiness, and comfort. To promote its prosperity and Spirituality. To sustain its worship, ordinances, discipline and doctrine, To contribute cheerfully and regularly to the support of the ministry, the expenses of the church, the relief of the poor and the spread of the gospel. We also engage to maintain family worship and secret devotion, To religiously educate our children, To seek the Salvation of our kindred and acquaintance, To walk cum—spectfully in the world, to be just in our dealings, faithful in our engagements, and exemplary in our deportment. To avoid all tattling, back bitting, and excessive anger, to abstain from sale and use of intoxication drink or beverages and to be zealous in our efforts to advance the Kingdom of our Saviour. We further engage to watch over one another in brotherly love to remember each other in prayer, to aid each other in sickness and distress, to cultivate Christian sympathy in feeling and courtesy in speech, to be slow to take offense, but to be always ready for reconcilation and mindful of the rules of our Saviour to secure it without delay.

We more over engage that when we remove from this place we will as soon as possible unite with some other church where we can carry out the spirit of this covenant and the principles of God's word.

Minutes of Salem Baptist Church
1872–1879

August 24, 1872

the 4th saturday in August, 1872

The church met and after prayer

1 st   *invited visiting brethren to seates*

2nd   *oapened the door*

3rd   *cald fer refferans[1] and took up the case of sisters Nancy Smith and Mary Smith and excluded them for immoral conduct.*

4   *granted Sister Mary Smith a letter of Dismissing*

5   *appointed Messengers to the Association to A.L. Stulce, John W. Roark and M. H. Conner and Silas Witt and W. R. Haney, all tennates*

and then closed   A.L. Stulce Mod

    John Campbell C. Clk   *A. L. Stulce*

September 28, 1872

Fourth saturday in Sept. 1872

The church met and after services proceeded to bussiness

oapend the door for the recption of members & received none.

2nd   *Call for refference. There being reffere the fellowship of the church was called for and on motion there was a charge prefered against Broth Wm. F. McCormack for disorderly conduct, immoral and upon motion the Church declare She can not fellowship* [with] *him.*

3rd   *upon application the Church granted Sister Sarah E. Tally letter of recommendation*

4th   *The Church appointed brother John W. Roark clerk*

Then closed

    J.W. Roark C. Clk   *A.L. Stulce Mod*

October 26, 1872

4th saturday in October 1872

The church met and after preaching oapen the reception

---

[1]   The Church's call for reference is taken to mean a call for any matter referred to the Church as a body.

of members and received Sarah M. Scrovene by letter
2nd   *Call for reffrnce*
3rd   *upon motion the church granted brother John Campbell*
a letter of Recommendation
Then close.
     John W. Roark C. C.lk   *A.L. Stulce Mod*

November 23, 1872

4th Saturday in November 1872
The Church met and after preaching invited visiting
brothery [brethren] *to seats with them made way for the*
reception of members And received none then closed.
     John W. Roark C.C. lk   *A.L. Stulce Mod*

On Sunday received Elizabeth Cross by Experience for Baptism.

December 28, 1872

4th Saturday in Dec. 1872
No meeting
Met on Sabbath Baptised Sister Elizabeth Cross
had preaching then closed
     John W. Roark C.C. lk   *A.L. Stulce Mod*

1873

January 25, 1873

4th Saturday Jan. 1873
The church met and after preaching invited visiting
brothers and sisters to seats with us then made way for the
reception of members rec'd none Then called for referenc was
none The Church then agreed to let the Presbyterians have one
Saturday & Sunday in each successive month on conditions
the conditions being this that they donate or caus to be
donated one fourth of the means to build[2] Furthemore
appointed Brother G. W. Rodgers John Campbell and J.W. Roark

---

2   The amount and purpose of the Presbyterian donation is not at all clear. Most likely the Presbyterian Church was to donate one-fourth of its contributions to Salem Church for maintenance of the Salem Church building.

to covenot and agree with them on the day & the amount to be
raised then closed

        J.W. Roark C.C.   *John S. McCormack*

February 22, 1873

4th Saturday in February 1873
The Church met after preaching made way for the
reception of member recd none The Church then agreed to
have preaching on the 2nd Sunday in each month
then closed

        J. W. Roark C.C.   *A.L. Stulce Mod*

March 22, 1873

4th Saturday in March 1873
The Church met after preaching made way for the reception of
members and received none. Then Closed
Met on Sunday after preaching Made way for the reception of
members received non then closed

        J. W. Roark C.C.   *A.L. Stulce Mod*

Saturday, April 26, 1873

4th Saturday in April 1873
The Church met and after preaching

1   *Made way for the receptions of members and received none*
2   *The Church by application on motion and second agreed*
        to forgive brother Mc. Conner[3] for fighting
3   *The church prefered a Charge against Brother Andrew*
        Ward for immoral conduct and appointed brother John
        S. McCormack to visit him and ask him to come to
        the next meeting and give the Church satisfaction for his
        non attendance. then Closed
        met on Sunday after servis made way for the reception of
        members received sister Rebecca Campbell by experience for
        baptism the[n] Closed

        John W. Roark C.C.   *A. L. Stulce Mod*

---

[3]   Mc Conner, or Mac Conner, was Maximilian C. Conner, son of Maximilian Haney Conner and Martha Palmer Conner.

Saturday, May 24, 1873

4th Saturday May 1873
The Church met after preaching made way for the
reception of members called for refferenc Then stated the
case of brother Andrew Ward the Church agrees to forgive him
then made preparations for a commemoration of the Lords
Supper Then Closed

John W. Roark CC   A.L. Stulce Mod

Sabbath Met and Baptised Sister Rebecca Campbell
after preaching commemorated the Lords Supper
Took up a collection for the Ministry
Then Closed

John W. Roark CC   A.L. Stulce Mod

Saturday, June 28, 1873

4th Saturday in June 1873
The Church met and after preaching
1st *made way for the reception of members*
2 *called for refferenc*
3 *on motion and second the Church agreed to resyn* [rescind] *the*
act of granting John Campbell & Sary E. Talley, letters of
recommendation and restore them.
4 *on application agreed to grant Brother John S. McCormack a*
letter of recommendation
Then Closed

John W. Roark C.C.   A.L. Stulce Mod.

Saturday, July 26, 1873

4th Saturday in July 1873
1st *The Church met and after preaching made way for the*
reception of members and received Brothers Davis Prada⁴ by
letter Aaron Tucker & William E. Tucker by enrollment
Then Closed

J. W. Roark CC   A. L. Stulce Mod.

---

4   This was Davis Priddy whose name was consistently misspelled by the Church Clerk. For the correct spelling, see the minutes for November 27, 1875, when Davis Priddy, as Church Clerk, Pro tem, signed his name.

Saturday, August 23, 1873

4th Saturday August 1873
The Church met and after servis Made way for the
reception of members The Church agreed to send as
messengers to the Association Brothers A.L. Stulce M. H. Conner
John W. Roark and G.W. Rodgers alternate
Then Closed

   John W. Roark CC   *A.L. Stulce*

Saturday, September 27, 1873

4th [Saturday] *in September 1873*
The Church met & after preaching Invited visiting
brothers to seats with [us] *then made way for the reception of*
members and received brother Bird Henry & Charley Moon
& Mollie Moon by enrollment then called for refferenc
then read and excepted [accepted] *the letter to the Ocoee*
association upon motion & second the Church granted
Brother John & Lucinda Campbell letters of recommendation
then dismissed the following named members for constitution
at Birchwood to wit
Maximilian Conner[5] *Margaret Conner James Conner*
Jane Conner M.M. Gross[6] *Latisha Gross John Gass*
Lee Lane Sarah Lane Wm. Curton Mary E Curton
George Campbell Catherine Smith Jacob Baker
Elisabeth Baker John B. Roark Nancy Roark James
Cameron [Senior] *James Cameron* [Junior][7] *Lina*
Dickson[8] *Rosa Gross Duke Kimbro Burton Holman T.J.*
Leonard

---

5   M.C. (Mac) Conner, followed by his wife Margaret. The couple left in the formation of Birchwood Baptist Church. His father, M.H. Conner, remained at Salem Baptist Church.

6   First name is not legible in the minutes. M.M. Gross is listed with Latisha Gross in the 1872–73 Church Rolls.

7   The Church Rolls for 1872–73 lead to the conclusion that this refers to James Cameron Sr. & Jr. Church protocol would list Sr. first.

8   The 1872–73 Church Rolls lists Lina Dixon rather than Lina Dickson as provided in the minutes.

Saturday, October 25, 1873

4th Saturday in October 1873
The Church met and after preaching called for refferenc
then made way for the reception of members recieved
Brother Tomas Elkins George Moon William Short
Evaline Moon & Mary Jane Moon by expieranc [experience]
for Baptism then Closed

      John W. Roark CC   *A.L. Stulce mod*

The Church met on Sunday and after preaching made
way for the reception of members and recieved Wilson
Hays & Nancy Cross by expierence for Baptism
On motion & second the Church Agreed to resyn [rescind]
the [act] *of excluding Henry Killian and grant him letter*
of recommendation further agreed to petition Brother
G. D Oviatt to assist us in a revival at our next meeting
then Closed

      John W. Roark CC   *A.L. Stulce mod*

Saturday, November 22, 1873

4th Saturday in November 1873
the Church met and after preaching
made way for the reception of members and recieved
Elisabeth Newton George Newton
called for referenc
met on Sunday and Baptised Nancy Cross
Continued the meeting From day to day until Sunday
met at the wauters[9] Baptised John C. Smith Ben Talley
Mather McMillion Liza Jane Haney Margaret Jonson
continued until the next Sunday recieved and Baptised
Joseph Roark Abner Smith Roof Rodgers Will Roark
John Haney J.H. Conner Jack Talley David Campbell
Calvin Witt Arnold Mangrum Margaret & James Cross
Hulda Howel & Mary Howel
Recieved by letter
John Campbell Liucinda Campbell
By enrollment

---

[9]   The "wauters" [waters] probably referred to Moon's Landing on the Tennessee River where most baptism services were held.

E. C. McCormack R. T. McCormack & Rebecca Jonson.
Restored
Mary Smith
Recieved by Expierenc for Baptism During the Meeting
~~James Cross~~, Margaret Barns, William Reneau[10] Sarah
Fridle [Friddle] ~~Nancy Howell James Howell~~
Scott Gooden James Monger Phebe Smith ~~David Guinn~~
~~T.J. Guinn James Henry James Denson William~~
~~Jonson Permelia B. Roark Jane McCantie~~ [McCallie][11]
The Church resolved her self into sabbath school to meet
each successive sabbath then Closed

      John W. Roark C.C.   A. L. Stulce mod

P.S.
the Church met at Moons Landing on [the] 1ᵗ sabbath
in November and Baptised Thomas Elkins George Moon
Wm. Short Evaline Moon & Mary Jane Moon
Recieved & Baptised Robert Gooden Marthy Hayes
then Closed

      John W. Roark C.C.   A. L. Stulce mod

Saturday, December 27, 1873

4ᵗʰ Saturday in December 1873
the Church met and after preaching
1ᵗ   made way for the reception of members
2   Called for reference
3   by application the Church for give Brother R. T. McCormack
for using profane language
then Closed

      J. W. Roark C.C.   A.L. Stulce Mod

met on Sabbath & Baptised David Guinn George Newton
James Denson & Elisabeth Newton
after preaching Closed

      J. W. Roark C.C.   A.L. Stulce mod

---

[10]   Spelled "Reno" in the Church Rolls of 1874–75

[11]   The Church Clerk lined through the members so noted, perhaps to indicate the members were not baptized in the Moon's Landing baptismal service. All such members were later baptized and were so noted in the minutes.

1874

January 24, 1874
4ᵗʰ Saturday in January 1874
the [Church] *met and after preaching made way for the reception*
of members rec'd non called for reference & approvel of
the above record second on motion & second the Church
agreed to & did resyn [rescind] *the act on requirement of each*
member paying five cents each successive month as dues on tax
then Closed
        J. W. Roark C.C.   *A.L. Stulce Mod*

Met on Sabbath & Baptised Brother T.J. Guinn James
Henry after preaching Closed
        John W. Roark Clerk   *A.L. Stulce Mod*

Saturday, February 28, 1874
4ᵗʰ Saturday in February 1874
the Church met had preaching But no Conference
then Closed
        John W. Roark Clerk   *A.L. Stulce Mod*

Sunday, February 29, 1874
4ᵗʰ Sunday in February 1874
the Church met Baptised James Howel Betsy Jane McCanlie
[McCallie] *after preaching Closed*
        John W. Roark C.C.   *A.L. Stulce Mod*

Saturday, March 28, 1874
4ᵗʰ Saturday in March 1874
the Church met and after preaching invited visiting Brotheren
& Sisters to seats [with] *us made way for the reception of*
members by motion & second the Church agreed to have a
communion season in April and to have a three days meeting
also to have foot washing on Sunday then Closed
        John W. Roark C.C.   *Rev A. L. Stults Mod*

Sunday, March 29, 1874

4th Sunday in March 1874
Met and Baptised James Cross and ~~Nancy~~ Mary Howell[2] and
after preaching made way for the reception of members and
received Brother Barney Rodgers and Caroline Rodgers by
letter from Mt. Lebanon Blount County Tenn & Martha Carter
by experience By motion and second The Church agreed to
resyn [rescind] the act of having communion in April and have it
[in] June then Closed

       J. W. Roark C.C.   *Rev A.L. Stults mod*

Saturday, April 25, 1874

4th Saturday in April 1874
no meeting
met on Sunday after preaching made way for the reception of
members Rec'd non on application by motion & second the
Church granted Sister S. A. Talley a letter of recommendation
then Closed

       J. W. Roark C.C.   *A.L. Stulce Mod*

Saturday, May 23, 1874

4th Saturday in May 1874
the Church met & after preaching invited visiting Brotheren &
sisters to seats with us made way for the reception of members
then make prepreations [preparations] for communion season at
our next meeting in June agreed to have feet washing
agreed to [invite] sister churches to assist with communion to wit
Birchwood New Union shepard Hill
M. H. Conner to Birchwood Davis Prada [Priddy] to New Union &
Shepherd Hill then Closed

       J.W. Roark CC   *Rev. A. L. Stulce Mod*

Sunday, May 24, 1874

4th sunday in May

---

[12]   It was not uncommon for the clerk to confuse members of the same surname. Mary was baptized and Nancy received for baptism on the same Sunday in November 1873, which would put Nancy in line for baptism here.

the Church met at the wauter Baptised Martha Carter
had preaching then Closed

J.W. Roark CC   Rev A. L. Stulce Mod

Saturday, June 27,1874
4th Saturday in June 1874
the Church met and after preaching made way for the
reception of Members invited visiting Brothers to seats with us
by application agreed to recommend Sarah Scrovene to any
other Church [of the] same faith
& then Closed

J.W. Roark C.C.   A.L. Stulce Mod

Met on Sabbath Baptized Wm. Jonson then commemorated
the Lords Death then Closed

John.W. Roark C.C.   A.L. Stulce

Saturday, July 25, 1874
4th Saturday in July 1874
the Church met & after preaching made way for the reception
of members then Closed

John W. Roark C.C.   A.L. Stulce Mod

Saturday, August 22, 1874
4th Saturday in August 1874
the Church met and after preaching made way for the
reception of members the Church agreed to send as
messengers to the Ocoee Assosiation
Our Brotheren to wit
A.L. Stulce
G.W. Rodgers
W.B. Haney
W.M. Roark
And [a]greed to petition the Assosiation to meet with us
the next meeting
then Closed

John W. Roark   A.L. Stulce Mod

Saturday, September 26, 1874

4ᵗʰ Saturday in Sept 1874
the Church met and after preaching made way for the
reception of members received non then appointed a
committee to investigate the Rumers against J.W. Roark to
witt James Guinn John Campbell Joseph Cookston and G.W.
Rodgers the committee report [ed] *they find him guilty of*
fornnication preferred charge against him agreed to continue
the same until next Meeting then appointed J.A. Roark Clerk
protem the letter to the Association Read and approved of
then agreed [to] *grant Marthy Rains letter of recomendation*
then Closed

        J.A. Roark C. C. pt [pro tem]   *A.L. Stulce Mod*

Saturday, October 24, 1874

4ᵗʰ Saturday in Oct. 1874
the Church met and after preaching made way for the
reception of members rec'd non then Brought up the case of
Brother J.W. Roark by application[13] *the Church Agreed to*
forgive him and restore him to fellowship
by application the Church granted Wm. F. McCormack a
new hearing by motion was continued til next meting
the Church granted Marion Howel wife and Daughter
letters of recommendation then Closed

        J.W. Roark C.C.   *A.L. Stulce Mod*

Saturday, November 28, 1874

Fourth Saturday in November 1874
The church met and after preaching there being but few
members present upon motion the reference was continued
until the next meeting and the meeting continuing from day
to day and opportunity being frequently given for the
reception of members the following persons came forward at
different times and joined the Church to wit Isaac Low
Martha Johnson by experience Susan Smith restored [to
fellowship] *Sarah McCormack by Enrollment Nancy Hany Wm*

---

[13]   In using "by application" the Church apparently meant that the individual acknowledged his or her wrongdoing, asked for forgiveness, and applied for reinstatement into the fellowship of the Church.

Elloy Paralee Gooden Jane Scott Jennie McCormack Mrs
[ ] Scott Newton Haney John Friddel Caroline McCain
William Grimsley by Letter
And upon Saturday Night December the 12ᵗʰ upon motion
the church agreed to hold a church conference upon
Monday the 14ᵗʰ
       A.L. Stulce Mod

Monday, December 14, 1874

Monday morning Dec. the 14ᵗʰ
the Church met according to appointment and after prayr
proceeded to business by appointing Elder R.T. Howard Mod
for the day

1ᵗ   *took up the case of brother Wm. F. McCormack for*
reconsideration which was debated at some length and upon
motion the church agreed to sustain her record of September
1872 and upon the acknowledge [-] ments of Brother Wm. F.
McCormack the church forgave & restored him.

2ⁿᵈ   *Brother J.W. Roark tendered his resignation as clerk*
which was accepted and brother John Campbell was
appointed clerk

3ʳᵈ   *open the door for the reception of members and*
Brother Joseph Roark, Jun.¹⁴ came forward and made an
acknowledgement of his Error & requested the Church to
forgive him and upon motion the church restored him
to fellowship then closed
      John Campbell   *R.T. Howard Mod for the day*

all So Received Elisabeth Rogers by Leter

Saturday, December 26, 1874

4ᵗʰ Saturday in December 1874
the church Met and after preaching Maid way for the
Reception of Members all So the church appointed brothers
George Rogers and Charley Moon to See Brothers Willson Hase

---

14   This was Joseph Roark, son of James P. and Jerusha Blythe Roark. "Junior" was used in reference to him by the community to differentiate him from the elder Joseph Roark, brother to James P. Roark.

[Wilson Hays] *and Robert Gooden and invite them to come to ourNext Meting and give satisfaction to the Church for swaring and Drunkness and then Closed all So Met on Sabbath and Baptised Sister Jiney* [Jennie] *Mccormack and then Closed*

        John Campbell C C lk   *A.L. Stulce Mod*

1875

Saturday, January 23, 1875

4th Saturday in Janarary 1875
The church met and after preaching proceeded to business by opening the door for the reception of members & received Wm. White by Letter

2nd   *Called for the report of committee who were appointed to See brethreren Wilson Hays & Robert Gooden which was received and the Committee discharged*

3rd   *Salem Church Received And there upon the church took up a charge against brother Wilson Hays for immoral conduct*

4th   *and after hearing of the Evidence the Church upon motion declares She can not fellowship* [with] *him*

5th   *upon motion bretheren G.W. Rodgers & C.L. Moon were appointed a committee to see brother Robert Gooden and talk with him & invite him to our next meeting then close*

        John Campbell Cl   *A.L. Stulce Mod*

Saturday, February 27, 1875

4th Saturday in February 1875
Salem Church Met had preaching there beeing but fiew out ther was Now bisnes done

        John Campbell C.Clk   *A.L. Stulce Mod*

Saturday, March 27, 1875

4th Saturday in March 1875
Salem Church Met had preaching there being but fiew out there was nothing done
Met on Sabbath and after preaching Dismist brother Thomas Guin by Leter then Closed

        John Campbell C.C.lk   *A.L. Stulce Mod*

Saturday, April 24, 1875

Salem Church Met and after preaching Proceded to bisnes

1st   *Maid way for the Reception of Members*

2nd   *Red the Records of the January and February and March*
      meeting and received them

3rd   *tuck up the Case of Robert Gooden and after hearing the*
      Report of the Comunity discharged them

4th   *the Church then tuck up a charge against him fer porofanity*
      and Excluded him fer the Same

5th   *the Church agreed to Commune in June and agreed to*
      partition the following Churches to wit Birchwood Newyounion
      [New Union] *shep[h]erd hill and Candayes Creek fer than* [their] *Ministerial*
      and Deacon help and appointedBrother W.L. Grimsby to go to Birchwood and brothers W.F.
      Mcormack and Davis Praday [Priddy] *to go to New younion and Brothers G.W. Rogers*
      and C.L. Moon to go to shepherd hill and Brothers Joseph Cookson William Roark to go to
      Candayes Creek and in
      vite them to come and helpe us and then Closed
                    John Campbell C C lk   *A.L. Stulce Mod*

Saturday, May 22, 1875

4th Saturday in May 1875
the Church Met and after preaching

1st   *invited visiting brothers to seates*

2nd   *Maid way fer the Reception of Members*

3rd   *Red the Record of the April Meeting and Received it*

4th   *by Motion the Church tuck up a charge against brother*
      Thomas Eldridge Colered for profanity and Drunknes and
      Exclded him fer the Same from the fellowship of the Church

5th   *by Motion the Names of the Mebers* [Members]
      was all cald over and then Closed
                    John Campbell C C lk   *A.L. Stulce Mod*

Saturday, June 26, 1875

4th Saturday in June 1875
the church Met and after Preaching

1st   *invited visiting brothers to Seates*

2nd   *Maid way fer the Reception of Members*

3rd   ~~*by Motion and second the Church*~~

3rd   Red the Record of the May Meeting and Received it
4th   by Motion and Second the Church tuck a charg against
       Brother B.L. Talley fer swarin and appointed Brothers G.W.
       Rogers and C.L. Moon to See him and talk with him and
       in vited him to Come and give Satisfaction to the Church
5th   by Motion and Second the Church agreed to Elect too brothers
       fer Deacons and then agreed to postpone it tell Next Meeting
       and then Closed
                John Campbell C C lk   A.L. Stulce Mod

       Met on Sabbath and Baptised Carline Cane [Caroline McCain] and
       Jane Scott and then had preaching and then
       had A Communion Tuck the Lordes Supper Commemorated
       the Lordes deth
       then Closed
                John Campbell C.C.lk   A.L. Stulce Mod

Saturday, July 24, 1875

       4th Saturday in July 1875
       the church Met and after preaching
1t   in vited visiting brothers to Seates
2nd   Maid way fer the Reception of Members
3rd   Red the Record of the June Meeting and Received it
4th   heard the Report of the Commity that was appointed to talk
       with Brother B.L. Talley discharged them
5th   and Excluded him from the fellowship of the Church
6th   Elected Brothers C.L. Moon and G.W. Rogers fer Deacons
7th   Agreed to drop the Names of the following persons from the
       Book to wit Sary Fridle Marg[ar]et Barns Pheby smith
       Scott Gooden Wm Reno William Eldridge [?] John
       Fridal and [M???] Scott fer Not Being Baptised and
       then Closed
       Met on Sabbath and after preaching dismist the following
       Brothers and Sisters David Guin and George Moon and wife
       Eveline Moon By Leter
                John Campbell C C lk   A.L. Stulce Mod

Saturday, August 28, 1875

       4th Saturday in August 1875

the Church Met and after Preaching
1st   in viting visiting brothers to Seates
2nd   Maid way fer the Reception of Members
3rd   by Motion and Second the Church tuck up a charge against
Sister Caldonia Eldridge Hawkins fer profanity and
appointed brother Davis Prada [Priddy] to See her and talk
with her and in vite her to Come and give Satisfaction to the
Church
4th   the Church appointed the following brothers to the Assosiation
to wit Samuel Smith William Roark and Joseph Cookston
delegates to the Assosiation
5th   by Motion and Second granted Sister Molinda Irwin a leter of
Recommendation and and then Closed
N.B.   by Request the Church post pond the ordination of brother G.W.
Rogers indifently [indefinitely]
Met on Sabbath and ordained brother C.L. Moon to the office of
Deacon by the presant presbytery A. L. Stulce and J.J. W. Mathis
and then had preaching and then Closed

        John Campbell C. Clk   A.L. Stulce Mod

Saturday, September 25, 1875

the Church Met and after prar
1st   the [Church] Chose Brother W.F. Mcormack Moderaitor for the
day
2nd   Red the Record of the August Meeting and Received it
3rd   Cald fer the Report of Brother Davis prida [Priddy] that was
appointed to See Caldonia Hawkins and discharge[d] him
4th   by Motion and Second the Church Declares She canot
fellowship [with] her
5th   then Red the Leter to the Assosiation and Received it and then
Closed

        John Campbell C. C lk   W.F. Mcormack Mod

Saturday, October 23, 1875

4th Saturday in October 1875
the Baptist church of Christ at Salem Met and after preaching
1st   Maid way fer the Reception of Members
2nd   invited visiting brothers to Seates
3rd   Red the Record of the September Meeting and Received it

4th   *granted brother William White a leter of Recommendation*

5th   *Brother Stulce Requested the Church to git another pastor ~~and~~*

~~gave them tell~~ but left indefinately untill the Next Meting to

Study on and then Closed

              John Campbell C C lk   *A.L. Stulce Mod*

Saturday, November 27, 1875

Fourth Saturday in Nov. 1875

The church met and after preaching proceeded to business by

opening the door for the reception of members & received none

2nd   *invited visiting bretheren to seat with us*

3rd   *Read the record of the past meeting & corrected it*

4th   *Called for the fellowship of the Church and there upon bro R.T.*

Mccormack Made his acknowledgement for fighting and

requested the church to forgive him which was done upon his

acknowledgement

6[5]th   *the following bretheren & sisters requested letter of*

recommendation to wit Elder Wm. F. Mccormack R.T.

Mccormack Wm Johnson Rebecah Johnson Sally Mccormack

Sarah Mccormack Jeninie Mccormack Eddy Woods

Caroline Johnson Susan Johnson & Martha Johnson

And Upon motion the same were granted

7[6]th   *Brother John Campbell offered his resignation as Clerk of the*

Church which was accepted & Bro Davis Priddy was appointed

to act as clerk protem until there was a clerk elected

8[7]th   *Appointed bretheren Davis Priddy & M.H. Conner a committee*

to atted [attend] the constitution of the church at [Gum?] spring

then closed

            D. Priddy C Ptem   *A.L. Stulce Mod*

Saturday, December 25, 1875

Fourth Saturday in December 1875

Church meet and after preaching proceeded to open the doors

of the church for the reception of Members

Received none

2   *Read the Record of the past Meeting and Received it*

3   *proceed to Elect a Church Clerk and Elected Davis Priddy*

4   *Brother John Campbell asked the Church to give B.J. Webb and*

sarilda [Berrilda] *Kenner*[15] *letters of recommendation and*
the Church agreed to give B.J. Webb a letter and the Clerk
writ the same when cawled on
and it being reported to the Church that Sarelda [Berrilda]
Kenner had join the Methodist church so said and the
Church apointed Brothers John Campbell & Davis Priddy to
see her an[d] *inquire into the facks* [facts] *and report to the*
next meeting
then Closed

   Davis Priddy Ch Clerk   *A.L. Stulce Mod*

1876

Saturday, January 22, 1876

Fourth Saturday in January 1876

1 *Church Meet and after Preaching proceeded to open the*
 Doores of the Church for the reception of Members
 Received none
2 *Read the record of the passed meeting & received it*
3 *the Commity apointed to see Sister Bereldy* [Berrilda] *Kenner*
 Received the report & discharged the committy
4 *Took up the case of Sister Bereldy Kenner and up on motion*
 and second the Church granted her a letter of Recommendation and the clerk write the
 same when cawled on
5 *Brother A.L. Stulce give his resignation as to the Pastoral Ceare*
 of the Church
6 *next proceeded to Elect a moderator for the year 1876 and*
 Brother A.L. Stulce were Elected and then Closed

   Davis Priddy Ch.Cl.   *A.L. Stulce Mod*

Saturday, February 26, 1876

Fourth Saturday in February 1876
Church Meet & after Preaching Proceeded

1 *to Open the Doors of the Church for the reception of Members*
2 *Read the record of the past Meeting & received it*
 and then Closed

   Davis Priddy C.C.   *A.L. Stulce Mod*

---

15 The minutes give the first name of Ms. Kenner as "Sarilda" and "Sarelda" while the Church Rolls refer to her as "Berrilda."

Saturday, March 25, 1876

4 Saturday in March 1876
Church Met after Preaching opened the doors
Of the Church and Then Closed

        Davis Priddy C.C.   *A.L. Stulce Mod*

Saturday, April 22, 1876

4 Saturday April 1876
Church Met after Preaching Opened the doors of The Church &
Then Closed

        Davis Priddy Church C   *A.L. Stulce Mod*

on Sabath after the 4 Saturday the Church granted letters of
dismisial to G.W. Rogers & wife and The Clerk Write When
Cawled on

        Davis Priddy C C   *A.L. Stulce Mod*

Saturday, May 27, 1876

4th Saturday in May 1876
Church Met after Preaching Opened the doores of
the Church

2   *upon the report of Brother Joseph Cookston that he had a*
personal conversation With Brother William Roark and he told
him that he was guilty of fornication and would not come to
the Church Brother Cookston Moved the Church take up a
charg against him the Church Took up a charge against
him and tried his fellowship and excluded him

3   *granted letters to dismiss the following Members when join to*
any other Church of the same faith and order Sister Nancy
Smith & Samuel Smith & wife Rufus Rogers & Wiffe and The
clerk write When cawled then a greed that there next
meeting be a communion Meeting & foot washing

4   *apointed J.P. Tally one of the committy in place of G.W. Rogers*
to super an tend in having the Church house finished
then Closed

        Davis Priddy C C   *A. L. Stulce Mod*

Saturday, June 24, 1876

4 Saturday in June 1876
church Meet and after Preaching Opened The door
of the Church & next cawled for references ther being none
2   *Brother Joseph Cookston reported to the Church that Sister*
Marthy J. Roark had bin playing & dancing the Church
appointed Sister Lucinday Stulce
& then closed

    Davis Priddy C.C.   *A.L. Stulce Mod*

Saturday, July 22, 1876

July 4ᵗʰ Saturday
church Meet and after Preaching Opned the Doors of the
Church Sister Mary J. Scott joine[d] by Letter
2   *next pefered a charge against Marthy J. Roark for Dancing &*
telling a church Member ~~of the church~~ that she did not want
to remain in the church the Church tied [tried] her fellowship
& excluded her & then closed

    Davis Priddy C.C.   *A.L. Stulce Mod*

Saturday, September 23, 1876

4 Saturday in September 1876
the Baptist Church of Christ at Salem Met and after prear Cald
fer Referances then red the Leter to the Association and
Received it and then Brother Davis Priddy offerd his
Resignation as Clerk wich was Received and appointed brother
John Campbell Clerk and then Closed

    John Campbell C.C   *A.L. Stulce Mod*

after the Association the church went continued from day to
day tenn dayes Dunin [during] which time the church dismist
sisters Mry [Mary] Aislinger [Aslinger] and Caty Mangrum Colerd
and Nansy Stulce all by Leter and then brother Stulce gave up
the cear [care] of the Church and then Closed

    John Campbell C Clk   *A.L. Stulce Mod*

Saturday, October 28, 1876

the Baptist Church of Christ at Salem Met and after Prear
proced to bisnes 1ᵗ Chose brother Stulce Moderator fer the day

2nd   *Maid way fer the Reception of Members*

3rd   *went in to an Election fer paster and Elected Brother R.T.*
Howard by reqest of brother Rufus Rodgers and wife the
Church recindes the acts grantin thim Leters and tha [they]
wish to Remain in this Church and then Closed

        John Campbell C. C.lk   *A.L. Stulce Mod fer the day*

Monday, November 13, 1876

November the 13 1876[16]
the Baptist church of Christ at Salem Met and after preaching
Dismist Sister Susan Mathis [Matthews][17] *by Leter and then Closed*

        John Campbell C. C. lk   *R. T. Howard Mod*

1877

Saturday, January 27, 1877

4th Saturday in January 1877
The Baptist Church of Christ at Salem Met had preaching
Dismist till Sabbath Met and after preaching by Motion and
Second Chose Brother A.L. Stulce Moderator fer the day

2nd   *by Motion and Second the Church agreed to give Brother*
R.T. Howard Forty dollars to preach fer her Twelve Months
and pay it quarterly then Closed
R.T. Howard Moderaitor

        A.L. Stulce Mod fer the day   *John Campbell C C lk*

Saturday, February 24, 1877

the baptist Church at Salem Met and after preaching

1t   *Maid way fer the Recption of Members*

2nd   *Red the Records of the October meeting of 1876 and the*
January Meeting of 1877 and Received them then appinted the
following brotherin a commity to witt James A. Roark

---

[16]   With the date written but no day mentioned, it is not known if the clerk was confused as to the date or if the Church actually met on a Monday, which would seem unlikely due to the rarity of the circumstance. The year 1876 was a leap year. Without the extra day in February, the 13th of November would indeed fall on a Sunday.

[17]   Church Rolls for 1874–75 list Susan Mathews rather than Susan Mathis as recorded by the Church Clerk.

W. R. Haney and Davis Priday [Priddy] *a commity to git up the*
Means to pay our pastor and settil with him quarterly

3rd   *by Motion and Second the Church granted Brother Thomas*
Elkins a Leter of Recommendation

John Campbell C. C. lk   R.T. Howard Mod

Saturday, March 24, 1877

4th Saturday in March 1877
the Church Met after preaching

1^t   *Made way for the Reception of Members*
2nd   *read the past record*
3rd   *approved of it with the exeption in the 2nd Claus to insert as*
Collected in Time of quarterly then granted A. Mangrum a
letter of recommendation
4th   *Broth [er] John Campbell resigned his Clerkship*
5th   *Elected Bro John W. Roark to serve as Clerk*
6th   *the Church agreed to assume the debt made by the Building*
Committee to O.D. Herington and paid the same in full
7th   *then Closed by prayer*

J.W. Roark C Clk   R.T. Howard Mod

Saturday, April 28, 1877

4th Saturday in April 1877
The Church met and a[fter] prayer

1^t   *Made way for the reception of members*
2nd   *Read and Received the minnute of the March meeting*
3rd   ~~Received~~ *on motion received an invitation to visit New Union*
Church at her next meeting first Sabbath in May 1877
4th   *on motion agreed that our next meeting be a Sacrimental*
meeting
5th   *on motion agreed to invite Sister Churches to seats with us*
Messengers New Union Bros. Joseph Cookston & John Roark
Birchwood Bro James A. Roark Candys Creek & Gum Spring
Bro A.L. Stulce Shepard Hill Bro John Campbell & W B Haney
then Closed By Prayer

J W Roark CC   R.T. Howard Mod

Saturday, May 26, 1877

the Church met and after preaching by the Moderator

1st   *Made way for the Reception of Members*

2nd   *Read and approved of the minnut of the April meeting*

3rd   *Called for the fellowship of the church found all in harmony*
        then Closed

        J.W. Roark C.C.   *R.T. Howard Mod*

Sunday, May 27, 1877

4th Sunday in May 1877
the Church met and after preaching by Rev A.L. Stulce
commemorated the Lords Death then Closed

Saturday, June 23, 1877

4th Saturday in June 1877
the church met and after preaching by the moderator

1st   *Madway for the Reception of members*

2nd   *Read and approvd the minuts of the May meeting*

3rd   *on motion the Church granted letters of recomendation to*
        Sisters Margaret Jane Cross Nancy Gross and Sister Jennie
        Grimsly

4th   *by request of Bro M.H. Conner the Church continued the*
        application of Bro W.L. Grimsly until next meeting
        then Closed by prayer

        J.W. Roark CC Rev   *R.T. Howard Mod*

Saturday, July 28, 1877

4th Saturday in July 1877
The church met and after preaching by Rev A.L. Stulce

1st   *made way for the reception of members*

2nd   *read and approved the minuts of the June meeting*

3rd   *continued the case of Brother W.L. Grimsly*
        then Closed

        John W. Roark C.C.   *Rev A.L. Stulce mod*

Saturday, August 25, 1877

4th Saturday in August 1877
no meeting

Saturday, September 22, 1877

4th Saturday in Sept 1877

The Church met after preaching by the moderator invited
Visiting Brethern & sisters to Seats

1^t　made way for the reception of members approved the minuts
of the July meeting

2nd　granted Bro W.L. Grimsly a letter of Recommendation

3rd　Granted Sister Mary Jane Campbell Letter of recommendation

4th　Granted Brother John & Sister Lucinda Campbell leters of
recomendation

5　appointed as messengers to the Ocoee Association Bretheren
A L Stulce C L Moon Joseph Cookston Davis Prada [Priddy] & James A. Roark
Then Closed

　　　　J.W. Roark C.C lk　　　　　Rev R.T. Howard mod

Saturday, October 27, 1877

4th Saturday in Oct 1877
the Church met and after preaching made way for the
reception of mem [bers] the church agreed to protract the
meeting the Moderator Being assisted by Brethren A.L. Stulce &
Z.T. Mainas the meeting continued eleven days During which
time the Church received and Baptised Brother James P. Talley
Sister Caroline Talley Sister Emmaline Miller and received
Sister Tennessee Low for Baptism and Sister Nancy Campbell by
experience for Baptism Received Brother A G Irwin by
Enrollment Brother John P. Miller came forward and joined
for enrollment by motion was made a matter of refference
until next Church Meeting granted Bro Isaac Haney Letter of
recomendation then Closed

　　　　John W. Roark C.C.　　　　　Rev R. T. Howard

Saturday, November 24, 1877

4th Saturday in Nov 1877
the Church met after preaching by the mod R. T. Howard
made way for the Reception of mem [bers]

1^t　appointed Rev. A.L. Stulce Clerk protem

2nd　Brougt up the Case Of Brother J.P. Miller and contivued until
the next Church meeting

3rd　by motion against Broth George Newton & James Henry for
using profane Languag and appointed Brethren Joseph
Cookston Isaac Low A.L. Stulce to visit them and request them

to come to the next meeting

4th   *agreed to Elect a Mod nex meeting for the Coming Year*

5th   *upon motion & second elected Brethren James P. Talley*
and M.H. Conner to be ordained as Deacons at our next
meeting then Closed

         A.L. Stulce C.C. pt   *R.T. Howard mod*

Saturday, December 22, 1877

4th Saturday in December 1877

No meeting

Met on Sunday and By motion & second agreed to hav
a Church Session on Monday the 24th of December 1877
Monday Dec 24th 1877 The Church met after prayer by the mod
Invited visiting Brethren to seats Read and approved the
mints of the Oct Nov and December meetings

1t   *Called for the Report of the Com [mittee] who visited Brethren*
James Henry and George Newton The Committee report no
satisfaction given the Church lifted a charge against them for
using profane Language and there upon excluded Them

2nd   *Droped the Case of John P. Miller as unworthy of membership*

3rd   *continued the Ordination of the Deacons until the January*
meeting 1878

4th   *the Committee on finance report $24.25 paid to the pastur*
yet Due fifteen Dollars and seventy five cents respectfully
submied [submitted]

         Joseph Cookston Chair

5th   *went unto and election and elected Brother R.T. Howard to*
Pastor the Church for the Year 1878 then Closed by prayer

         John W. Roark CC   *Rev. R.T. Howard mod*

1878

Saturday, January 26, 1878

4th Saturday in January 1878

the Church met and after preaching by Brother R.T. Howard
the Church elected Brother A.L. Stulce moderator for the day

1t   *made way for the Reception of members*

2nd   *Read and approved of the Record of the Church meeting of*
Monday December the 24th 1877

3rd   the Church agreed to ordain as Deacons on Sunday Brethren
M.H. Conner & J.P. Talley
Then Closed by prayer
       John W. Roark CC   Rev: A.L. Stulce mod
the Church met of Sunday and ordained Brethren M.H. Conner
and J.P. Talley as Deacons

2nd   Granted a letter of Recommendation to Brother A.J. Ward and
his wife Jane then Closed
       J.W. Roark CC   R.T. Howard mod

Saturday, February 23, 1878

4th Saturday in February 1878
The Church Met and aftrer preaching By Rev: R.T. Howard

1st   elected Brother R.T. Howard to Stand as Mod for the day
2nd   invited visiting Brethren and Sisters to Seats
3rd   Made way for the Reception of members
4th   granted letters of recomendation to Brother James A. Roark
and Sister America Roark
Then Closed by prayer
       John W Roark C.C. lk   Rev R.T. Howard Mod

Saturday, March 23, 1878

4th Saturday in March 1878
the Church Met and after preaching Broth W. F. McCormack

1st   elected Rev A.L. Stulce Mod for the day made way for the
reception of members Clerk absent no record Read
by application the Church granted letters of Recommendation
to Sister Jane Alexander and Brother Marion and Sister Hulda
Howel then Closed
       John W. Roark Cclk   Rev A.L. Stulce Mod

The Church Met on Sunday had preaching agreed [to] open
sabbath School next Sabbath then Closed
       J.W. Roark CC   A.L. Stulce Mod

Saturday, April 27, 1878

4th Saturday in April 1878
The Church Met had preaching by Brother A.L. Stulce

1st   Apointed Bro A L Stulce Mod for the day

2nd   invited visiting Bro & Sisters to Seats

3rd   Made way for the reception of members Read and App [approved] past Record

4   by Application on Confession of Drunkness the Church excluded
     Brother Charls Ford

5   agreed to elect a Pastor for the Church and elected Brother S.J.
     Blair

6   agreed to have a communion season fourth Saturday &
     Sunday in May 1878 and agreed to invite the Sister
     Churches verbally
     Then closed
          J W Roark CC   A.L. Stulce Mod

Saturday, May 25, 1878

4th Saturday in May 1878
The Church Met after preaching By Bro I.Z. Kimbro elected Bro
R. T. Howard mod for the Day made way for the reception of
members no reccord present The Church agreed to
Commemorate The Lords Death & suffer [suffering]
Then Closed By prayer
          John W Roark CC   R.T. Howard Mod

Met on Sunday had a Communion Season then Closed
          I.Z. Kimbro
          A.L. Stulce
          R.T. Howard Ministers
          John W Roark CC

Sunday July 14, 1878

Seccond Sunday in July 1878
The Church Met after Preaching by Bro S.J. Blair Made way for
the reception of Members

2nd   Read the Minuts of the March April and May meetings and
     approved them

3d   the Church agreed to change the meeting dayes to the 2nd
     Sunday
     Then Closed
          J W Roark CC   S.J. Blair Mod

Saturday, August 10, 1878

Seccond Saturday in August 1878
No meeting

Saturday, September 14, 1878

Seccond Saturday in Sept 1878
The Church Met after preaching by the moderator SJ Blair
1ᵗ *Made way for the reception of members Read and approved*
past record
2 *Called for the fellowship of* [Church] *found All in Harmony*
3 *Elected as Messengers to the Ocoee Association Brethren A L*
Stulce J.P. Talley Joseph Cookston and C L Moon
4ᵗʰ *Granted Letter of recomendation to Brother William Short*
then Closed
    J.W. Roark CC   *S J Blair Mod*

Met on Sunday had preaching By S.J. Blair Read and approved
the letter to the Ocoee Association granted sister Emaline Miller
letter of recomendation Then Closed
    John W Roark CC   *S J Blair Mod*

Saturday, October 12, 1878

Saturday before the seccond Sunday in October 1878
The Church Met after preaching by the Moderator
1ᵗ *made way for the reception of mem* [members] *and received by*
letter Brother A J Bearns his wife N.E. Bearns[18] *into the fellowship of the Church*
2ⁿᵈ *Read and approvd the Reccord of the September meeting*
then Closed by prayer
    John W Roark CC   *S J Blair Mod*

Met on Sunday had preaching by Brother A.L. Stulce Made
Way for the reception of Members and received by letter into the fellowship of the Church
Brother J.H. Samples his wife Jane Samples and Daughter Mary Allen then Closed
    John W Roark CC   *S J Blair Mod*

Saturday, November 9, 1878

Saturday before the seccond Sunday November 1878
The Church Met after preaching by the moderator Made way

---

[18]   The Church Rolls for 1874–75 list A.J. Barnes and N.E. Barnes.

for the reception of Members Read and approvd the minits of
the October Meeting the [n] *Closed*

   John W Roark CC   *S.J. Blair Mod*

Met on Sunday had preaching by the moderator then Closed

   J W Roark CC   *S J Blair Mod*

Saturday, December 14, 1878

Saturday before the seccond Sunday in December 1878
The Church Met after preaching by the moderator
1^{t} *Made way for the reception of Members*
2nd *Read and approvd the Record of the November meting*
then Closed

   John W Roark CC   *S.J. Blair Mod*

P.S. had preaching on Saturday night and Sunday by the mod
   S.J. Blair Mod

1879

Saturday, January 11, 1879

Saturday before the seccond Sabbath in January 1879
The Church Met after preaching held a conference
1^{t} *Brother Joseph Cookston reported to the Church that Brother*
W.J. Stulce had been guilty of disorderly Conduct
and the Church preferred a charge againz him Brother
Cookston then stated that he had talked to Brother
Stulce and he said it was true and he wanted the Church to
exclude him The Church tried his fellowship ad excluded him
2nd *The Church opened the doors for the reception* [of] *Members and*
James P. Moon joined by giving in an experience of grace
then Closed

   Davis Priddy Clk   *S J Blair Mod*

Met on Sunday Baptised James P. Moon

Saturday, February 8, 1879

Saturday bfore the 2nd sunday in February 1879
the Church Met after preaching by the Moderator

1^t   *Made way for the reception of Members*
2nd   *Read and approved of the Reccord of the Jan Meeting*
        then Closed

              John W Roark C.C.   S J Blair mod

Preaching on sunday by the Mod

Saturday, March 8, 1879

Saturday before the 2nd sunday in March 1879
The Church met & after Preaching by the mod made way for
the Reception of members The clk absent no Reccord Read
then Closed

              J. P. Talley Clk pt   S.J. Blair Mod

Saturday, April 12, 1879

Saturday before the seccond sunday in April 1879
The Church Met Preaching by the mod
1^t   *Made way for the Reception of members and Recd Brother*
        Henry Mcdade by recommendation from New Union Church
2nd   *Read and approvd the Reccord of the February and March*
        meeting
3rd   *the Church Resolvd to have a communion at the May Meeting*
        and extend a general invitation to sister Churches
4th   *granted a Letter of Recomendation [to] sis Sally Sc rovene then*
        Closed

              John W Roark Clk   S.J. Blair Mod

Saturday, May 10, 1879

Saturday before the seccond sunday in May 1879
The Church Met and after Preaching By Rev R.T. Howard
the Mod extended an invitation to Visiting Bretheren & sisters
to take seats with us
1^t   *Made way for the Reception of members*
2nd   *Brother Wm Haney came forward and acknowledged*
        to having been in a difficulty and prayed the Church to
        forgive him by motion and second the Church forgave him
        Then Closed

              J W. Roark CC   S.J. Blair Mod

Saturday, June 14, 1879

Saturday before the seccond Sunday in June 1879
the Church Met after preaching by the Moderator
made way for the reception of Members
2ⁿᵈ *called for the fellowship of the church no record pres*
by Motion continued the Reading of the reccord until next
Meeting agreed to change the Meeting days to the fourth
Sunday the Moderator then anounced that his time was out as
pastor the Church then agreed to have a call cessoion on
Saturday before the 5ᵗʰ Sunday in June 1879 for the purpose of
electing a pastor then Closed

        JWR Clk   *S J Blair Mod*

Sunday, July 27, 1879

4th *Sunday in July 1879*
the Church Met perseuant to adgournment went into an Election
and Called Brother W.L. Dale Then Closed

        John W. Roark CC   *A.L. Stulce Mod"*

Saturday, August 23, 1879

Saturday before the 4ᵗʰ Sunday in August 1879
No meeting

Saturday, September 27, 1879

Saturday before the 4ᵗʰ Sunday in September 1879
1 *The church Met after preaching by Rev R.H. Jordan*
Read and approvd the past Reccord
2 *Being informed that Brother W.L. Dale could not accept the*
Pastorial care of the Church
3 = *by motion the Church agreed to elect a pastor*
4 *went into an election and elected Brother R.H. Jordan*
Pastor for the ensuing year
5 *appointed as messengers to the Ocoee Association Brothers A.L.*
Stulce J.P. Talley W R Haney and J. W. Roark Read and
approvd the letter to the Association Then Closed

        J W Roark CC   *R.H. Jordan Pastor*

Saturday, October 25, 1879

4ᵗʰ Saturday in October 1879

The Church met after preaching by the Moderator Made way for
the reception of members appointed Bro J.P. Talley clk pt
no Reccord present the [n] *Closed*

   J.P. Talley CC[19]   *R.H. Jordan Mod*

Saturday, November 22, 1879

4ᵗʰ Saturday in Nov 1879
the church met after Preaching by the Mod made way for the
Reception of members Read and approvd the Record of the
September and October meetings then Closed

   J W Roark CC   *R.H. Jordan mod*

Met on Sunday Preaching by Broth R.H. Jordan called
Conference granted letter of Recomendation to Bro
Rufus Rodgers and his wife Rebecca Rodgers then Closed

   J W Roark CC   *R H Jordan mod*

December 27, 1879

4ᵗʰ Saturday in December 1879
The Church met after Preaching by Bro W.C. Curton the Church
elected A.L. Stulce mod for the day. Then invited visiting
Brethren to Seats with us Read and app [roved] *the Past Record*
then made way for the reception of members Then considered
the non attendance of the membership agreed to appoint as
Messengers to visit the absent members and have them come
forward and give a reason for their non attendance.
The members appointed wer [e] *Breth* [ren] *M.H. Conner*
J.P. Talley Joseph Cookston C L Moon and A.L. Stulce to report at our next meeting then
Closed

   John W. Roark C.C.   *A.L. Stulce Mod. Pt*

---

19 The October minutes were in the handwriting of Church Clerk John W. Roark. It is possible that J.P. Talley relayed the actions of the Church to J.W. Roark and he wrote the minutes in the book and signed Talley's name as clerk.

Membership Activities of Salem Baptist Church in the Minutes 1872–1879

	1870	1871	1872	1873	1874	1875	1876	1877	1878	1879	Total
Excluded	N/A	N/A	3	0	0	5	2	2	1	1	14
Dismissed	N/A	N/A	1	0	0	4	6	0	0	0	11
Letter of Recommendation	N/A	N/A	2	3	6	14	4	10	9	3	51
Received by Letter	N/A	N/A	1	3	13	1	1	0	5	1	25
Received/ Experience	N/A	N/A	1	32	3	0	0	5	1	0	42
By Enrollment	N/A	N/A	0	8	1	0	0	1	0	0	10
Baptized	N/A	N/A	1	32	9	2	0	3	0	1	48
Restored	N/A	N/A	0	1	3	0	0	0	0	0	4
Dropped from Book	N/A	N/A	0	0	0	8	0	0	0	0	8
Letters rescinded	N/A	N/A	2	0	0	0	2	0	0	0	4

Activities tabulated from the Minutes of Salem Baptist Church.

Letter of Recommendation

A member of a Baptist church who was relocating to another area would request a letter of recommendation from their current church. If he or she were a member in good standing, a letter would be granted and written by the clerk. If the member, after leaving, did not join another church within six months, the recommendation to the fellowship of the new church would be withdrawn.

Chapter Three
Salem Baptist Church
1880–1889

At Salem Baptist Church, the 1880s began with a protracted meeting in January that continued for fifteen days. Assisting Pastor R.H. Jordan with preaching, other pastoral, and moderating duties were R.T. Howard, A.L. Stulce, W.C. Curton, and Brother Baker. Of the group of ministers, Brother Baker was the only one who had not been, or would not be, a Salem Church pastor. He would, however, preach at Salem from time to time. R.H. Jordan was the current pastor.

Ironically, the pastors of the extended meeting made up the officiating clergy of Salem Baptist Church following the Civil War through 1890. Although I.Z. Kimbrough and S.J. Blair, the other two previous pastors of Salem Church, were not assisting with pastoral duties, it is quite within reason to think that they were also at that extended meeting at some time. I.Z. Kimbrough frequently attended meetings and would often preach at Salem. He would be elected pastor again in the latter part of 1883, serving through 1885, and would continue to preach at Salem from time to time. S.J. Blair had been an associational pastor with the Ocoee Association for many years, including his time as pastor of Salem from 1878 to 1879. It was generally the custom in an extended meeting to invite all sister churches and associational representatives.

The only pastor of the 1880s not assisting with pastoral duties at the extended meeting—other than R.C. Collins, who was elected in 1889—was Noah Moon, pastor of Salem Baptist Church from 1882 to 1883 and 1885 to 1886. Rev. Moon was not a stranger to the members of Salem Baptist Church. Noah and his family, along with neighbors, had organized Friendship Baptist Church. He was the first church clerk and his older brother, Jonas Posey Moon, was the first pastor. Noah and his brothers James Harvey and John D. would also take turns as pastor of Friendship Church. The church was often referred to as the "Moon Church."[1] Noah's son, George Posey Moon, married J.P. Talley's daughter, Evaline, in 1869. George P. and Evaline Talley Moon would move to Arkansas in 1875 but would return in 1884 because of George's serious lung problems, returning in time for a reunion with his father before George died on December 8 at the age of thirty-two.[2]

W.C. Curton would be pastor of Salem Church from 1881 to February 1882, when Noah Moon was elected as pastor for the ensuing year. R.T. Howard would be pastor in the latter part of 1883, the year after he retired from his thirty year position as clerk of the Hiwassee Association. He had been pastor in the late 1870s and continued preaching at Salem, being moderator pro-tem at times until he was elected again in June 1883. Rev. Howard would again be pastor of Salem Church in December 1886 and would serve through 1888.

Of particular note in a discussion of Salem Baptist Church pastors in the 1880s is Rev. Thomas B. Frost. Rev. Frost would preach at Salem Church for the first time in March 1882 at the meeting in which Rev. Noah Moon was elected pastor. He would preach again at the July meeting. In August and September, he would not only preach, but be elected moderator for the day. In February 1883, Salem Church "received Brother T.B. Frost by letter Showing that he was in full fellowship in the Sister Church [particular church not mentioned] and that he was an ordained minister of the gospel." On Sunday of the March meeting, Rev. Frost would attend to baptism. He would preach in April on both Saturday and Sunday, in June on Sunday, and be elected as moderator for the meeting in September.

T.B. Frost would next preach at the October meeting of 1885, when, oddly enough, Noah Moon would once again be elected as moderator. Although Thomas Frost would not be mentioned in the minutes again, pastors such as Rev. Frost played a significant part in sustaining churches in East Tennessee in the 1880s. The urge to move west was affecting the young people who would otherwise be pastors in their hometowns rather than starting churches farther west. It would also affect Salem Baptist Church in the latter 1880s and into the last decade of the nineteenth century. The opening of land in Texas and elsewhere made leaving an attractive option to some residents as the farms could no longer support large families.

In 1881, the year that began a decade of "firsts" for Salem Church—the male elders of Salem Church voted to add the words "as sister" to the Rules of Decorum in April. Article 9 of the Rules of Decorum was changed to read "No member of the church shall address another in any other appellation than that of Brother **or as sister**." This would be the first of several advances for the women of the church in the 1880s. Another first for Salem Church would come five months later, in September, when the church by motion agreed to send the following query to the

Ocoee Association: "Is it consistent with the teaching and practice of landmark Baptists to tolerate pulpit affiliation and Sunday School union?"

The first mention of Landmark Baptists in the minutes of Salem Church appearing in 1881 suggests that Salem Church had not severed their Primitive Baptist roots. Ironically, the name one generation would accept as representative of a particular group of people was originally intended to be derogatory by a previous generation. The first derogatory term to be used toward Baptists (most originally derogatory terms toward Baptists were used by other Baptists) was the term "Baptist" itself. It was first used in the 13th century toward those who believe in the biblical legitimacy of baptism by immersion. The term Baptist did, in fact, come from the word baptism, a distinctly biblical term. The term "Anabaptist" (meaning re-baptize) first appeared in 1532 to refer to Baptists who practiced believer's baptism, denounced infant baptism, and re-baptized those who came to them from Catholic and Protestant churches that both practiced infant baptism.

The term "Landmark" began as another patronizing term used to describe those who chose to keep with the teachings of their Anabaptist forefathers. The term came from within the Baptist ranks, originally coming from two scriptures: Proverbs 22:28 and 23:10 ["Remove not the ancient landmark, which thy fathers have set." Prov. 22:28 KJV]. The term was first used by J.M. Pendleton in articles for *The Tennessee Baptist*, edited by J.R. Graves in the early 1850's. These articles later appeared in a pamphlet entitled, *An Old Landmark Re-Set*.

J.M. Pendleton and J.R. Graves disagreed with the Baptist churches who allowed infant baptizing ministers (Pedobaptists) to preach from their pulpits. To Pendleton and Graves this practice disgraced and defiled the true churches of God and therefore needed to be halted immediately. Members of the Southern Baptist Convention, as well as the Pedobaptists, took issue with Graves' and Pendleton's call to banish infant baptizing ministers from the pulpit of Baptist churches and labeled those with similar convictions "Landmarkers," or "Old Landmarkers." The question in the Salem Church minutes as to whether their actions conformed to Landmark Baptist standards suggests that the church agreed with Pendleton and Graves.

Beginning in the 1880s, Salem Church would regularly elect a committee to check the church book (bring it up to date), and call on people for non-attendance. This was not only an attempt to get non-attendees to return to church, but an attempt to find out who had relocated and to keep the church book up to date. Rather than rewrite the church rolls, the most recent roll was appended with notations to the side of the names such as dismissed, excluded, died, and so on. "Dropped from the book," and "written off," referred to those members taken off the rolls for lack of attendance. A more conscientious clerk would put the year in which the action occurred then develop a new and current roll.

A church member would be appointed to assist the clerk in making a report of members not in attendance. The clerk and church member would be required to visit the non-attending members. In November 1883, J.C. Smith (clerk) and J.P. Talley reported that there were eighteen members to be dropped from the church book. However, the church ordered that Eliza Denson and Elizabeth Friddle be retained, but the names of the other sixteen members were to be dropped from the church book with the understanding that if "said members came in the future and gave satisfaction to the church they would still be retained." It is not clear why the two were ordered to be retained; however, the only business in December was that, by motion and second, the church still retained Sister Eliza Denson in the church, she having informed the church that she "has a bad [little] chance to attend church meetings."

In January 1884, the church agreed to have the rules of decorum read every other meeting and to have them enforced. Also in the minutes of that meeting was the first mention of a treasurer when James P. Talley was elected treasurer of Salem Church. The church agreed to take up a collection every Sunday for the incidental expenses of the church. In February, the fellowship of the church was called for "and the church said by her acts that she was in peace." For the remaining life of Salem Baptist Church, the church would periodically call for fellowship to check for any animosity within the church.

In February 1885, the church, by vote, was declared not in fellowship. The matter was repeatedly deferred until April 1886, when the church authorized the clerk, with assistance from J.P. Talley, to rearrange the names of the members of the church in the church book as they thought best. In September, Salem Baptist Church received the report and the committee of two recommended that "said book stand as ever." The minutes do not give a reason for the church not being in fellowship.

According to the minutes, the prayer by Sister Johnson at the July 1887 meeting was the first time prayer was led by a woman at Salem Baptist Church. Similarly, Sister Stivers led the prayer in August 1888. These were signs of change in the Baptist church in general and Salem Baptist Church in particular. The elders were given the responsibility of the care of the church and were exclusively men. Although elders would remain primarily male for years to come, the acceptance of women as prayer leaders did signal a significant change in addition to illustrating the declining years of Salem Church. At the infrequent meetings of the latter part of the decade, it was often reported that there were few members present. With membership declining, and attendance fluctuating, it became necessary for women to fill positions that were formerly reserved for the male members of the church.

Salem Baptist Church was not alone in its struggle to stay active in the Ocoee Baptist Association and up to date in church business. The minutes for September 1887 state that "with brother Cate being present the church agrees to continue the meeting a few days." S.H. Cate was the Ocoee Associational Missionary that year. In his report to the Association, which met shortly after the extended meeting at Salem, Rev. Cate reported:

> "…I find most of the churches in the cold state of religion, and some destitute of pastors, little contigious churches in the country, doing apparently no good. "Brethren, there is cause for great alarm among our Baptist Zion. In the field of labor where I have worked, no young ministers are entering the work in our midst. The old and faithful ministers are leaving us. The harvest is great and the laborers are few."[3]

Rev. R.T. Howard was frequently absent due to illness following his retirement from the Hiwassee Association as clerk and associational minister. During his terms as pastor of Salem Baptist Church, he continually had absences due to health as noted in the minutes. In 1888, Rev. Howard was absent in March, re-elected in May, absent in August and September, and sick in October with R.H. Jordan preaching in his stead. After the "pastor being sick" in October, there were no meetings until April 1889, when R.C. Collins was elected pastor of Salem Church. R.T. Howard would pass to his reward in 1891.

True to their habit of rebounding in the midst of adversity, Salem Church would again attempt to carry on the tradition of Sunday school. The second mention of Sunday school in the minutes of Salem Baptist Church was in June 1889. "[The] Sabbath School had a lesson after which the pastor gave a lecture of 20 minutes on the importance of Sabbath School." Sunday school was not mentioned in the minutes again until several years later, in the mid 1990s. Due to the infrequency of meetings in the later 1880s and early 1890s, holding a Sunday school was, by necessity, apparently even less frequent.

Salem Baptist Church ended the 1880s struggling to pay expenses and keep the church building operational as a place worthy of worshiping the Lord. The congregation would continue to struggle throughout the end of the nineteenth century. But through their faith and pioneering perseverance, the members of Salem Baptist Church would carry on in worship.

Minutes of Salem Baptist Church
1880–1889

Saturday, January 24, 1880

4th Saturday in January

The Church met after Preaching by Brother R.H. Jordan Made way for the reception of members then read and approvd the Record of the December meeting then Recd the Report of Brother M.H. Conner as one of the Commitee by motion continued the Report of the Committee until our next meeting Then heared an acknowledgement from brother W. R. Haney

for leeseing his Room for a dance by motion the Church agreed to forgive him and granted a letter of Recomendation to sister Octavie Harris[20] then Closed

John W. Roark   R.H. Jordan Mod

January Meeting continued Met on Sunday after preaching by Rev R.T. Howard agreed to Protract the Meeting being assisted by R.H. Jordan Pastor Bro R.T. Howard Bro Baker Bro A.L. Stults and Brother W.C. Curton the Meeting Continued 15 days During which time there was added to the Church by letter Brother John Carrell and his wife M.M. Carrell from Church at Union, Bradley County Tenn and sister Jane Sisk from the Church at Friendship, Polk County Tenn Then recd by experience for Baptism Brother James Rusk and his wife Mary J Rusk sis Siller Davis sis Julie Talley and Brother Samuel Stults Then Closed

John W Roark CC   R.H. Jordan Mod

Sunday, February 28, 1880

4th Sunday in Febuwary 1880

The Church met And Baptised Samuil Stulce and Julie Talley then Closed

A.L. Stulce mod Pt

The Church met on the 1st Sunday in March 1880 and Baptized James Rusk and Mary J. Rusk then Closed

John W. Roark Clk   A.L. Stulce Mod P.T.

Sunday, March 27, 1880

4th Sunday in March 1880

the Church met after Preaching by Brther R.H. Jordan

---

20   Possibly Octavia Harris. Listed as Octavy on the 1874–75 Church Rolls.

Made way for the Reception of members
then Closed

   J W Roark C Clk   *R H Jordan Mod*

Saturday, April 24, 1880

4ᵗʰ saturday in April 1880
The Church met after Preaching by the moderator Made way for the Reception of mem-
bers Read and approvd the minuts of the January February and March meeting Recd
the report of the Commitee on the non attendance of the membership And discharged the
Commitee. Appointed Brethren J.P. Talley and M.H. Conner to visit Broth A.G. Irwin and
her [hear] *his reasons for not coming to Church Recd an invitation from the Church at*
Birchwood to commune with them at their meeting on The 3ʳᵈ sunday in May 1880 agreed
to hav a communion season at our meeting in May 1880 and extend a general invitation to
all Churches of the same faith and Order
then Closed by Prayer

   John W Roark C Clk   *R.H. Jordan Mod*

Saturday, May 22, 1880

4ᵗʰ saturday in May 1880
after Preaching by the Moderator Read and approvd the Record of the April meeting by
Request The Church agreed to continue The Report of Brethren M.H. Conner And J.P. Talley
in Broth A.G. Irwin's Case until the June Meeting
Then Closed by Prayer

   John W Roark C Clk   *R.H. Jordan Mod*

4ᵗʰ sunday [in May]
the Church met Preaching by Bro R.T. Howard then the Mod being assisted by Broths R.T.
Howard A.L. Stulce Held a communion Season in Commemoration of Our Lords Death and
Sufferings then Closed

   John W Roark C.C.   *R.H. Jordan Mod*

Saturday, June 26, 1880

4ᵗʰ saturday in June 1880
The Church met after Preaching by the moderator no record Present The church on her-
ing [hearing] *the rumor That Brother Henry Mcdade had been using Profane language*
appointed Brethren C.L. Moon ~~and M H Conner~~ to visit him and see as to the truth of the
report and Report to the nex [next] *meeting then Closed*

   R.H. Jordan Mod

Saturday, July 24, 1880

4th Saturday in July 1880

The Church met after Preaching by the moderator Invited visiting Brethren to take seats with us called for the Case of Brother Mcdade The Committee not present by Motion the Church agreed to continue the report until next meeting in Cores [Chorus]
Then Closed with Prayer by Brother R.T. Howard

John W Roark   R.H. Jordan Mod

Saturday, August 28, 1880

4th Saturday in August 1880

the Church met after Preaching by Brother James Corvin.

The Pastor being absent by motion the the Church Elected Brother Corvin mod for the day then made way for the reception of members and recd by expierence for Baptism Bro William Parette and his wife Amanda Marian Mop and
Sarah A Moon Then Heard the report of the Committee in
the case of Bro Henry Mcdade then discharged the Committee
the Church then lifted a charge v.s. Henry Mcdade and Excluded him for Immorrel Conduct then Closed

John W. Roark C.C.   James Corvin mod

4th Sunday in August— 1880

the Church met at Moons Landing and Baptised Brother William Parett and his wife Amanda Marian Mop and
Sarah A. Moon Then Closed

C.L. Moon Clerk Pt   W. C. Curton Mod P.t.

Saturday, September 25, 1880

4th Saturday in September 1880

the Church met and after Preaching by Brother A.L. Stults
by motion the Church elected bro A.L. Stulce Moderator for the day then read and approvd the minits of the June July and August 1880 Meetings called for the fellowship of the Church
by Motion lifted a Charge v.s. brother William E. Tucker for Immorrel Conduct and Excluded him Then Charged Brother
Mathew Mcmillian of Immorrel Conduct and Contemful of Church and Excluded him then then appointed as Messengers to the Ocoee Association Brethren A.L. Stults. J.P. Talley C.L. Moon and James P. Moon then read and approvd the Letter [to] the Association it having been anouncd that Bother R H Jordans time was up as pastor the Church then by motion appointed Brother A.G. Irwin to hold the Election then went into an Election by

Ballot and Elected Brother R.H. Jordan Pastor for the coming year and appointed a commit-
tee of brother W.R Haney and John W Roark to inform Broth Jordan
of his Election and report the amount he had recievd for his
last years servis as Pastor of the Church and report the next Meeting in cores [chorus]
then Closed

       John W Roark. C.C.   *A L Stulce Mod Pt*

Saturday, October 23, 1880

4ᵗʰ Saturday in Oct 1880
No Meeting

Met on Sunday had Preaching by Bro R.H. Jordan
granted a recomendation to Sister Betty J. Malone
Then Closed

       John W Roark C.C.   *R.H. Jordan Mod*

4ᵗʰ Saturday in November 1880
no Meeting

4ᵗʰ Saturday in December 1880
no Meeting

1881

4ᵗʰ Saturday in January 1881
No Meeting

Saturday, February 26, 1881

4ᵗʰ Saturday in Feb 1881
the Church Met after Preaching by Broth W.C. Curton
the Church went in to an Election by Ballot and Elected
Bro W. C. Curton Pastor for the Ensuing year
Then Closed by Prayer

       John w Roark CC   *W. C. Curton Mod*

Saturday, March 26, 1881

4ᵗʰ Saturday in March 1881

the Church met after Preaching by the Moderator granted letters of recomendation [to] bro
A.L. Stulce Sister Lucinda Stulce and Bro Sameul Stulce granted letters of recomendation to
Bro J.L. Carrell and sister Millie m. Carrell
th [then] Closed by Prayer

J.P. Talley Clk Pt   W C Curton Mod

Met on Sunday had preaching by Broth W.C. Curton called conference and granted sister
Marthy [Martha] Hayes a Letter of recomendation the [then] Closed by Prayer

John W Roark CC   W C Curton Mod

Saturday, April 23, 1881

4th Saturday in April 1881
the Church met after Preaching by the moderator made way for the reception of members
Read and approvd the minutes
of the Feb & March Meetings Read the Rules of Decorum and
in the 9th Item agreed to insert the words (As Sister) agreed to have a communion at our
next meeting and the Church resolve its self in to a commitee of the Whole and Extend an
invitation to Sister Churches
then Closed by Prayer

J.W. Roark C.C.   W C Curton Mod

Saturday, May 28, 1881

4th Saturday in May 1881
The Church met after Preaching by the moderator
1t   Made way for the reception of members
2nd   read and approvd the minuts of the April meeting Recd an
invitation to meet with Birchwood & Union Hill Churches on
the 3rd Saturday in June next agreed to accept and comply with Granted letters of recomendation to Bro Herald Hayes and wife Nancy Hayes then Closed by Prayer

John W Roark C Clk   W.C. Curton Mod

Saturday, June 25, 1881

4th Saturday in June 1881
The Church Meet After Preaching by the mod W. C. Curton
Made way for the reception of members no Clerk Present
Postponed the reading of the minute
then Closed by Prayer

John W Roark C.C.   W. C. Curton Mod

Saturday, July 23, 1881

4ᵗʰ Saturday in July 1881
the Church Met no Moderator Pres Prayer and Preaching
by Bro Noah moon then Closed
John W Roark C.C.

Saturday, August 27, 1881

4ᵗʰ Saturday in August 1881
The Church met after Preaching by the Moderator
1   *Made way for the reception of members*
2   *the Reccord not Presant agreed to postpone the reading*
of the minutes until next meeting
3   *Appointed messengers to the Ocoee Association Agreed to*
send Bro J.P. Talley A.G. Irwin and Isaac Lowe as Messengers
then Closed by Prayer
John W Roark C.C.   *W.C. Curton Mod*

Saturday, September 24, 1881

4ᵗʰ Saturday in September 1881
The Church met after Preaching by brother A.L. Stults
made way for the reception of members Read and approved of
the Records of the May June July and August meetings
by motion agreed to send the following queary to the association = Is it concistant with the
teaching and Practice
of land mark Baptist to tolerate Pulpit affilliation and Sabbath School union [?] *= then*
Closed by Prayer
John W Roark C.C.   *W. C. Curton Mod*

Met on Sunday after preaching by Bro A.L. Sulce [Stulce]
Elected Bro A.L. Stulce mod for the day Read and approvd of
the Letter to the Ocoee Association then Closed by Prayer
John W Roark C.C.   *A.L. Stulce mod*

Saturday, October 22, 1881

4ᵗʰ Saturday in October 1881
The Church met after Preaching by the moderator W. C. Curton
made way for the Reception of members and Recd by letter
Bro J.L. Carrell & sister M M Carrell
2   *Read and approvd the minutes of the September meeting*

3   *granted letter of recomendation to Sister Clem* [Clementine] *Ford agreed to Protrac the meeting the meeting continued until Friday and Recieved by letter Sister Sarah Hatfield Recieved by Expierance for Baptism Sister Judy Baker and Bro Linch Hatfield then Closed by Prayer*

        J W Roark C C   *R. T. Howard mod Pt*

[No record of Church meeting in November 1881]

Saturday, December 24, 1881

4 Saturday in December 1881
the church met and preaching by the Modiator but there Was
no buisness transacted more than J.C. Smith Was appointed
Clerk protem

        J.C. Smith C.C protem   *W C Curton*

1882

[No record of Church meeting in January 1882]

Saturday, February 25, 1882

4 Saturday in Feb 1882 the Church met preaching By
Rev R. T. Howard by Motion & Second J.L. Roark was appointed Clerk protem and there
was no business transacted

        J L Roark Clerk   *W C Curtin Mod*

Saturday, March 25, 1882

4th Forth Saturday in March 1882 the Church met and ther
was preaching By Rev Frost then maid way for the reseptoin of
members
Second J.L. Roark was appointed Clerk pro [tem] *then the Church proseed to Busness and*
Elected Brother Noah Moon Modiator for the insuing year
Then Closed

        Bro Frost Mod   *J.L. Roark CC*

Saturday, April 22, 1882

4 Saturday in April 1882 the church met on the Sabbath
after preaching by the Mod
1.   *by motion and secon J.C. Smith was appointed Clerk protem*

2.   *by motion and second it was ordered that the Clerk Issue a letter of recomendation to brother R.C. Smith When calld on*

3.   *the church agreed to hold there communion meeting on the Sabbath after the 4 Saturday in May folering then closed*

      J.C. Smith C Clerk pro   *Noah Moon Mod*

Saturday, May 27, 1882

4 Saturday in May 1882

the Church met after preaching by the modiator

1.   *Maid way for the reseptions of member*

2.   *Called for minut of last meeting but there was non red*

3.   *J.C. Smith was appointed protem Clerk in absant of the Clerk*

4   *By motion and Second it was ordered that the Clerk Isue letters of Recomendation to Brother William parett and Wifie* [Amanda] *When called on Then Closed by Prayer*

      J.C. Smith C. Clerk   *Noah Moon mod*

5.   *the Church met on the Sabbath and after preaching by the Modiator on account of the inclemency of the wether the comunion meeting was postponed untill the 4 Saturday and Sabbath in June then Closed*

      J.C. Smith CC protem   *Noah Moon Mod*

Saturday, June 24, 1882

4. Saturday in June 1882

the Church met preaching by Brother Frost

1   *mad way for the reseption of members and received by letter Sister Carline Johnson*

2   *received Sister Jane Ward She having had a letter of recommendation from this Church and States that her letter*

is lost and the Church Exstens the rite hand of fellow Ship to the Sister there Being minyets of Dec. 1881 4ᵗʰ Saturday in Feb 1882 & 4ᵗʰ Saturday in March the church ordered that the clerk make a minet of the Same Which ws dun on page 55

next red and approvd the minet of the April and meeting then prayer by the Mod and closed to meet at 11 o clock a.m. the day followi ng

      J.C. Smith C C   *Noah Moon Mod*

Second day proseedings met according preaching By Rev R.T. Howard then an Exortation by the modiator on invitation to visiting Bro next commemorated the Lords Supper then Colsed

      J.C. Smith C. C.   *Noah Moon Mod*

Saturday, July 22, 1882

Fourth Saturday in July 1882

the Church met after preaching by Rev Thomas Frost an exortation By The modiator

1 *invited visiting brethern to Seats*

2 *made way for the Reseption of members*

3 *Red and approved the minyet of our June meeting*

4 *by motion and Second received the Resignation of brother John W. Roark as church Clerk*

5th *by motion and Second J.C. Smith Was Ellectied church Clark*

then preyer by Rev. R.T. Howard Then closed

6 *met on Sunday and had preaching by the modiator*

Then closed

        J. C. Smith C.C.   *Noah Moon Mod*

Saturday, August 26, 1882

Fourth Saturday in August 1882

the church met and after preaching By Brother Thomas Frost

1ft *by motion & Second Brother Frost was Elected Modiator for the day*

2nd *maid way for the reseption of members*

3 *red and approved the minut of our July meeting*

4th *by motion and second the Church appointed the follering brethern as deliget* [delegate] *to the association to Witt*

Brothers J.P. Talley James Russ James Moon and C.L. Moon

Then closed to meet at cannel lite [candlelight] *& after preaching maid way for the reseption of members & received by ExSperence for baptisam Bro George Eldridge Then Closed*

Then on Sunday at 10 o Clock a.m. Met at the waters Edge and

Baptised brother George Eldridge then retired to the house and there was preaching by brother Thomas Frost and preyed

then closed

        J.C. Smith C C   *Thomas Frost Mod protem*

Saturday, September 23, 1882

4th Saturday in Sept 1882

the Church met after Preaching by Bro Thomas Frost

the Church Elected Bro Frost mod for the day and also to administer Baptism to such candidats as might present them Selves made way for the reception of members and recievd by Expierence for Baptism Bro Thomas A. Roark Charles A. Smith Thomas Talley Reese Bare and Sister Margaret J. Roark

Read and approved the Letter to Ocoee association and appointed as a Commitee Bros J. W. Roark and J.L. Roark to assist the Clerk in making a statistical Report of the Church and agreed to show in this Reccord that Bro Silas Witt and his wife Jane witt J.H. Sample his wife Jane Samples and daughter Mary Allen wer dismissed by letter and to futher Show That the members Baptised at this meeting Show in this Statistical Report
Then Closed by Prayer

   J.C. Smith C C   *Thomas Frost Mod*

Met on Sunday at the wauter and Babtised Bro Thomas A. Roark C.A. Smith Reese Bare & Sister Margaret J. Roark and maid way for the ReSeption of members at the waters and received and Baptised the following brothers and Sisters to wit
Franlin [Franklin] *Johnson William Johnson Amanda Bare Elisebett Simes Lodemia Webb Martha J. Webb Nancy Samples*
Jerusha Samples Hanner Johnson Angeline Johnson Jerusha Roark and received by letter Sister Jane Alxander & Sister Sarah E. Barnett then retired to the House and had preaching by Rev. Zackariar Kimbrough
Then Closed by prayer to meet at canel liting [candlelight"ing"]

   J.C. Smith C Clerk   *Thomas Frost Mod*

met according to appointment and preaching by Thomas Frost
maid way for the reseption of members and received by Exsperncs [Experience] *for baptism Sister Pheba* [Phoebe] *Smith Sister Mary R. bell Smith and Sister Sidney Johnson then closed to met at the waters at 10 o clock a.m.*
and met at the waters and Baptised the above sisters adminestered by Bro. Thomas Frost and the meeting continued as conducted by Thomas Frost and there was preaching at cannel light by Bro Frost after preaching maid way for the reSeption member and received By ExSperence for batisum
John Baker and Thomas Haney
then closed to meet at The waters at Ten o clock and met at the water and Baptised Bro John Baker and bro Thomas Haney
Then after preaching the meeting Brok up

   J. C. Smith C.C. Broth   *Thomas Frost Mod*

Sunday, October 15, 1882

Second Sunday in Oct 1882
A Speshel meeting at the waters and maid way for the reSeption of members and recieved by ExSpernse for baptisum Bro Daniel Roark and bro Daniel Roark Bro Lynch Hatfield and

Bro Thomas Talley was baptised by Rev. R.T. Howard
then retired to the House and there was preaching by
         rev R.T. Howard then Closed

Saturday, November 25, 1882

4ᵗʰ Saturday in November 1882
the church met after preaching by the modiator maid way for the reseption of members
then called for minyett of last meeting but the minyet of our last meeting was not red as
bro J.W. Roark was appointed Clerk protem he had ~~never~~ not returned his minyett then
red and approved of our September meeting next called for any buisness that should be
attended to but there was nothing brought before the Church then had prayer and closed to
meet Sunday at 11 o clock Am 1882
Second Day Met persusant to agournment preaching by the
modiator and an Exertation by rev R.T. Howard
then after prayer Closed
         J. C. Smith C.C.   Noah Moon Mod

Saturday, December 23, 1882

4ᵗʰ Saturday in December 1882
the church met after preaching by the Modiator
1ᵗ   *maid way for the reseption of Member*
2ⁿᵈ   *called for the minyett of our last meeting which was red and approved*
3ʳᵈ   *granted letters of Recommendation to bro. C.L. Moon and his wife Sister Mary Jane Moon*
       and bro Franklin Johnson and ordered the clerk to write them when called on letters
       Issued
       to C.L. Moon & wife and bro Johnson then after prayer closed to meet on the Sabbath at 11
       o clock a.m.
       met and had preaching by the modiator
       then Closed
         J.C. Smith C. Clerk   Noah Moon Mod

1883

Saturday, January 27, 1883

4ᵗʰ Saturday in Jan. 1883
the Church met and after preaching by the modiator
1ᵗ   *maid way for the reseption of members*
2ⁿᵈ   *called for the minuet of our last meeting which was red and approved then closed*
         J.C. Smith C.C.   Noah Moon Mod

Saturday, February 24, 1883

4th Saturday in Feb 1883
the church met and after preaching by the modiator

1st *maid way for the reseption of members and received Bro T.B. Frost by letter Showing that he was in full fellow* [fellowship]
in the Sister Church and that he was an ordained minister of the gospel

2nd *called for minuet of our last meeting which was red and apporoved then after preyer Closed*

         J.C. Smith CC   *Noah Moon Mod*

Saturday, March 24, 1883

4th Saturday in March 1883
the church met and after preaching by Rev R.T. Howard

1st *invited visiting brethren to Seats with us*

2nd *Maid way for the reseption of members and recevied by Ex.Spearnc for Baptism Sister Irena J. Carrel*

3rd *called for minuet of our last meeting which was read and approved*

4th *granted a letter of recommendation to Sister Parlee Gooden and order the Clerk to write when called on which was done*
then afte prayer Closed to meet at the waters the day following
at 10 o clock a.m. met at the water according to appointment
and Baptised Sister Irena Carrel administerd by Rev T.B. Frost
and the Modiator not present Closed

         J.C. Smith C Clerk   *Noah Moon Mod*

Saturday, April 28, 1883

4th Saturday in April 1883
the church met and after preaching by Bro. T.B. Frost an
Exertation by the Modiator

1   *invited visiting Brethren to Seats with us*

2nd *Maid way for the Reseption of members and recevied. By inrolement Sister Sarah Frost*

3rd *called for minuet of our last meeting which was Red and approved*

4th *granted letters of recommendation to Bro. A.G. Irwin and Bro. Marion Moss* [Church Clerk] *to write when called on which was don*

5   *The Church agreed to hold there communion meeting fourth Saturday and Sabbath in May 1883 then after prayer Closed to meet at 11 o clock A.m. the day fallowing met according to appointment and there was preaching by rev. T.B. Frost an Exertation by the modiator*

then Closed

        J.C. Smith C.C.   Noah Moon Mod

Saturday, May 26, 1883

4th Saturday in May 1883
the church met and there was So few of the members out there was sining [Singing] *and*
preyer by the modiator and Closed
And met on the Sabbath and there was preaching by the Mod.
& others and the Lords Suppur was administered
then Closed

        J.C. Smith C.C.   Noah Moon Mod

Saturday, June 23, 1883

4th Saturday in June 1883
the Church met and after preaching By rev R.T. Howard
proseed to Buisness By Electing bro R.T. Howard Mod for the day

1st   *invited viseting Brethren to Seats with us*
2nd   *maid way for the reseption of members*
3rd   *proseeded to Elect a modiator for the insewing year and by Ballot Bro R.T. Howard was*
        Ellected By a Majorty of the members present
4th   *The Church granted letters of recommendation to Bro Benjamin F. Talley and Bro A.J.*
        Talley and ordered the Clerk to write when called on which was done then Closed to meet
        the day following at 11 o clock a.m.
        Met according to appointment and there was preaching by bro
        T.B. Frost and then Closed

        J.C. Smith CC   R.T. Howard Mod pro

[No record of Church meetings in July and August 1883]

Saturday, September 22, 1883

4th Saturday in Sept 1883
the church met but there was no preaching and after sining
[signing] *a him* [hymn] *and preyer by brother T.B. Frost Mod for the day*

1st   *maid way for the Reseption of members*
2nd   *Red and approved of the minuet of our last meeting then appointed a Delagats to the*
        Association to wit bro John Roark J.W. Roark W.R. Haney & Thomas Talley
3rd   *proseed to Ellect a Modiator for the in sewing year and Brother I.Z. Kimbrough was Elected*
        By a margorty of the members present then after preyer closed to meet the Day following
        at 11 o clock a.m. met according to appointment. There was preaching by Brother I.Z.

Kimbrough as he had Bin notified that he had Bin Ellected pastor of this church he notified us that he would take charge of the church

then after Reeding the letter to the Ocoee Association Closed

   J.C. Smith C. C.   T.B. Frost Mod pro

Saturday, October 27, 1883

4ʰ Saturday in Oct 1883

the church met and after preaching By the Modiator

1ᵗ   *invited visiting Brethren to Seats with us*

2ⁿᵈ   *red and approved of the minuet of our last meeting*

3ʳᵈ   *By motion of Second it was orded that a committie Bee appointed to assist the Clark*
[Clerk] *in making out a Report of the members that was not in attendanc with the
Church and could not attend and said commitee to report to our next meeting the 4ʰ
Saturday in Nov. the committie consisted of Brother J.P. Talley then closed to meet The
day following at 11 o clock am met according to appointment on Sunday and afer Singing
and preyer maid way for the reSeption of members and received Bro. S.M. Cooley By letter
of recommendation and Sister Elisabeth Priddy By ExSperanc for Baptisum after which an
InSterresting Serment was preached By the Modiator*

then Closed

   J.C. Smith C Clerk   I.Z. Kimbrough Modiator

Saturday, November 24, 1883

4ʰ Saturday in Nov 1883

the Church met and after preaching By the Modiator

1ᵗ   *invited visiting Brethren to Seats with us*

2ⁿᵈ   *red and approved of the minuet of our last meeting*

3ʳᵈ   *called for the report of the committe and the committie Reported 18 members to Be Droped
from the church Book But*

the Church ordered that Eliza Densen [Denson] *and Elisebeth Friddle would Still Be
retained But ordered the names of the following members To Be droped from the church
Book with the unders Standing that if said member came in the fewtsr* [future] *and gave
Satisfaction to the church that they would Still Bee Retained*

to witt M.A. Campbell

D L Campbell	Martha Carter
Marjeria Carrel	James Denson
Siller Davis	James Howel
Mary Howel	Jane Harden
A.A. McCallie	Clementine Martin
James Monger	Margit [Margaret] Pickens

Mahala Smith   Hetty Tucker

Calvin B Witt

4th   the church ordered letters of Recommendation to Be granted to the following Brothers and-
Sisters to witt Joseph Roark Elisebeth Roark Jerusha Roark J.L Carrel Clementine Stulce
Phronia Monger Manervia Blair then Closed to meet at the waters Edge on Sunday at 9 o
clock A.m. Seconde days proseeding Met at the waters according to appointment and maid
way for the ReSeption of members and received By inrolement Sister Eliza Priddy and By
ExSperanc for Baptisum Brother William Priddy and Brother William Priddy and Sister
Elisebeth Priddy was Baptised By Brother I.Z. Kimbrough after which retired to the House
and there was preaching By the Modiator

          J.C. Smith CC   I.Z. Kimbrough Mod

Saturday, December 22, 1883

4th Saturday in December 1883

Salem church met and after preaching By the Modiator

1st   invited visiting Brethren To Seats

2nd   By motion and Second the church Still Retains Sister Eliza Denson in the Church She having informed the Church that She has a Bad chance to attend church meetings
and there Being But few members present Closed

          J.C. Smith CC   I.Z. Kimbrough Mod

1884

Saturday, January 26, 1884

4th Saturday in Jan 1884

the Church met after preaching by the mod I.Z. Kimbrough

Sec   called for the reccord of the past meeting the Clerk being absent by motion appointed Bro
J.W. Roark Clrk protem

By motion and Second the church agreed to have the rules
of decarum [decorum] read Every other meeting and have them Enforced by Motion and
Second the Church Elect Bro James P. Tally [Talley] Treasurr of the church the church
agreed to take up a Collection Every Sunday forthe Incidental Expences of the Church
Granted a letter of recommendation to Sister Emily Millard
then closed by Preyer

          J W Roark C.C.   I.Z. Kimbrough Mod

Saturday, February 23, 1884

4 Saturday in Feb 1884

Salem church met and after preaching By the Modiator

1ˢᵗ	*invited visiting Brethren to Seats with us*
2ⁿᵈ	*called for minyet of our last meeting But the minyet was not red as the clerk was not pres-ent at the last meeting and the Clerk pro. Had not returned the minyet*
3ʳᵈ	*the minyet of Dec. 1883 was red and approved*
4ᵗʰ	*called for the fellowship of the Church and the church siad* [said] *By her acts that She was in pease* [peace]
5ᵗʰ	*By Request of the Modiator there was no preaching on Sunday and as there was but few members present Closed*

J.C. Smith C.C.   *I.Z. Kimbrough Mod*

Saturday, March 22, 1884

4ᵗʰ Saturday in March 1884

First	*Salem Church met after preaching by the Moderator invited visiting members to Seats with us.*
Sec	*Called for the reading of the minute of the previous meeting which was read and approved*
3d	*by request of Brother J.C. Smith He and Daughter was granted letters of recommendation.*
4ᵗʰ	*by motion and Sec Brother S.M. Cooley was Electeded Church Clerk*
5ᵗʰ	*Then Closed to meet Sunday at 11 oclock*
	Sec day Preaching by the Moderator at the hour appointed made way for the Reception of members and received none Closed

S.M. Cooley Ch Cl   *I.Z. Kimbrough Mod*

Saturday, April 26, 1884

4ᵗʰ Saturday in April 1884

Salem Church met after Preaching by the Moderator

First	*Invited visiting members to Seats with us*
Sec	*Defered making way for members untill toMorrow and Called for the reading of the Previous meeting which was read and recived*
3d	*Also the Minute of the January meeting was read and approved*
	Fourth The Church resolved to have a communion meeting next meeting and appointed Brother James Russ [Rusk][21] *to invite Friendship Church and Brother Haney Conner to invite Birchwood Church to Commune with us*
5ᵗʰ	*Received and invitation by Brother McConner* [Mack Conner] *Inviting Our Church to Commune with the Birchwood Church 3d Sunday in 84*[22] *Which was recived Closed by Prayer*

---

[21] The Church Rolls of '76–'82 list James Rusk, not Russ. Russ could not be found in 1880 Census.

[22] The date of the invitation is not at all clear.

Sabbath Meeting Preaching at 11A.M. by the Moderator made way for the reception of members and recived none Closed

      S.M. Cooley Ch Cl   *I.Z. Kimbrough Mod*

Saturday, May 24, 1884

Fourth Sat in May 1884

Salem Ch met after Preaching by the Mod

First   *invited visiting members to seats with us*

Sec   *Called for the reading of the Previous meeting which was read and approved.*

3d   *By motion and Sec a Charge was lifted against Bro George Eldridge for Immoral Conduct. And Brothers James P. Tally* [Talley] *James Russ* [Rusk] *was appointed to make known Said Charge to Said Bro Eldridge and to report to the Church at our next meeting The Deacons reporting ready for the Communion to morrow and Closed Said meeting by Prayer Sabbath Meeting Preaching by Mod 1100 AM giving Intermition of about 15 minets Called to gether by singing after which we Eat the Pasover and Sang a hymn and Closed*

      S.M. Cooley C C   *I.Z. Kimbrough Mod*

Saturday, June 28, 1884

Fourth Sat in June 1884

Salem Church met meeting opened by Prayer Preaching by the moderator.

First   *Called for the Reading of the minute of the Previous meeting which* [was read] *and approved*

Sec   *Called for the report of the Commity that was appointed to make known the Charge to Bro Eldridge So they did So and Brother Eldridge being Present Acknowledge being guilty Saying He Was Sorrow and wanted to be forgiven of the Church and the church forgive him on his Acknowledgement and Closed by Prayer*

        S.M. Cooley Ch Cl   *I.Z. Kimbrough Mod*

Sunday Meeting No business Except Preaching by the mod

Saturday, July 26, 1884

Fourth Saturday in July 1884

Salem Church met meeting Opned by Prayer Preaching by the Moderator

First   ~~Called~~ *Defered making way for members untill To morrow*

Sec   *Called for the Reading of the minute of the Previous meeting the Clerk not being Present or the minute it was lend over untell the Next meeting and Bro James Russ* [Rusk] *appointed Cl Protem*

No Other Business done Closed

      S.M. Cooley Ch Cl   *I.Z. Kymbrough* [Kimbrough] *Mod*

Sunday Meeting Preaching by the Mod made way for members and Received none

Saturday, August 23, 1884

Fourth Saturday in Aug. 1884
Salem Church met Preaching by the Mod
Firs   *Defered making way for members untill to morrow*
Sec   *Called for the minute of the last meeting which was Read and approved No other Business*
         of the Church done Closed
               S.M. Cooley Ch Cl   *I.Z. Kimbrough Mod*

Saturday, September 27, 1884

Fourth Saturday in Sep 1884
(First)   *Called for the Reading of the minute of the Past meeting and*
           the Cl not being Present it was defered untell the next meeting
(Sec)   *Bro James Russ* [Rusk] *apponted Clerk for day*
(Third)   *the Church Elected Rev I.Z. Kimbrough as her moderator for the next insuing year*
(Fourth)   *Iaac* [Isaac] *Lowe was granted a leter of Dismission*
(5ᵗʰ)   *The Church Resolved to Represent in the Ocoee association and to Send as her deligates Bros*
           vis J.P. Tally [Talley] *J.L. stults* [Stulce] *Closed*
               S.M. Cooley Ch Clk   *I.Z. Kmibrough* [Kimbrough] *Mod*

Sabbath Meeting Preaching by the mod

Saturday, October 25, 1884

Fourth Saturday in Oct 1884
Salem Church did not have any Preaching Saturday or Sabbath or do any Church Business

Saturday, November 22, 1884

Fourth Saturday in Nov 1884
Salem Church met meeting opned by Prayer Preaching by the moderator then proceeded to
business of the day
First   *invited viset members to Seats with us and Called for the Reading of the minute of the last*
         meeting Which was Read and approved no Other Busines done Closed
         Sabath meeting Preaching by the Mod
               S M Cooley Ch Cl   *I.Z. Kimbrogh* [Kimbrough] *Mod*

Saturday, December 27, 1884

Fourth Saturday in Dec 1884

Salem Church met meeting opned by Prayer Preaching by the Mod

First   *Defered making way for members untell to morrow and Call for the Reading of the minute*
of the last meeting Which was read and approved and Closed
Sabbath Meeting Preaching by the Mod and Closed

        S M Cooley Ch Cl   *I.Z. Kimbrough Mod*

1885

Saturday, January 24, 1885

Fourth Saturday in Jan 1885
The Weather being very unfavorable and our Mod not being Present there was no Preaching
either on Saturday or Sunday or any Church Business done

        S M Cooley Ch Cl   *I.Z. Kimbrough Mod*

Saturday March 28, 1885[23]

Fourth Sat in March 1885
Salem Church met Preaching by Rev Noah Moon

(1)   *The Church appointed Bro Moon as Mod for the day and Called for the Reading of the min-*
ute of the last meeting Which was Read and approvd

(2)   *The Reference to Fellowship was defered till Next meeting and Bro James Russ* [Rusk]
and Wife was granted letters of dismission and Closed
Sabbat Meeting Preaching by Rev Noah Moon And Closed

        S.M. Cooley Ch Cl   *Noah Moon Mod*

Saturday, February 28, 1885

Fourth Sat in Feb. 85
Salem Church met meeting opened by Prayer Preaching by the Mod

(1ᵗ)   *Called for the Reading of the minut Previous meeting which was Read and Recived*

(2)   *defered making way for members untell to morrow.*

(3d)   *A motian made Whether the Church was in fellowship and by vote declared not to be in*
fellowship but defered the matter untell Next meeting and Closed
Sabbath Meeting Preaching by the Mod and Closed

        S.M. Cooley Ch Cl   *I.Z. Kimbrough Mod*

---

[23]   There are duplicate entries for February and March with March written first. They
are left as they were. With at least two different handwriting styles, it is quite possible they were mistakenly entered twice by two people interpreting the meeting
differently.

Saturday, February 28, 1885

Fourth Saturday in Feb 1885
Salem Church met Preaching by the Moderator

(1)   *Invited viset members to Seats with us & Called for the minute of the Previous meeting*
Which Was Read and approved
No Other Business done and Closed
Sabbath Meeting Preaching by the Mod and Closed

   S.M. Cooley Ch Cl   *I.Z. Kimbrough Mod*

Saturday, March 28, 1885

Fourth Saturday in Mar 1885
Salem Church Met and the Mod not being Presen there was no Business done on Saturday
or Sunday

   S.M. Cooly Ch. Cl.

Saturday, April 25, 1885

Fourth Saturday in Apr 1885
Salem church met the Moder not being presnt Rev Noah Moon was Elected Mod Protem.
Preaching by Rev Moon and Proceeded to the Business of the church

(1)   *Resolved to hold a Cummuniam meeting fourth Sunday in May 1885 and to invite Sister*
Churches viz Frendship & Birchwood Bro J.P. Tally [Talley] *to invite Frendship and Bro*
Lonard Stults [Leonard Stulce] *to in vite Brichwood* [Birchwood] *and Closed*
Sabbath Meeting Preaching by Rev Noah Moon and Lettered off A J Barns & wife Closed

   S.M. Cooley Ch Cl   *Noah Moon Mod Pro*

Saturday, May 23, 1885

Fourth Sat in May 1885
Salem Church met Preaching by the Mod
Called for the Reading of the minute of the Past meeting and the Cl [Clerk] *and the min-*
ute was not Present and it was defered untill the next meeting No oher [other] *business*
done and Closed
Sabbath Meeting Preaching by the mod at the hour apponted then dismiss for fifteen min-
utes and was Called to gether by singing and theneat the Remembering Supper of Our
master and sang and went out

   S M Cooley Ch Cl   *I Z Kimbrough Mod*

Saturday, June 27, 1885

Fourth Sat in June 1885

Salem Church Met and the Mod not being Present there was not any Preaching done Either
on Saturday or Sunday
or Church business

Saturday, July 25, 1885

Fourth Saturday in July 1885
Salem Church met Preaching by the Mod

(1)   *Invited visetng members to Seats with us*
(2)   *Called for the reading of the Minute of the Past Meeting which was Read and approved no*
other Business done
Sabbath Meeting Preaching by the Mod and Closed
            S.M. Cooley Ch Cl   *I.Z. Kimbrough Mod*

Saturday, August 22, 1885

Fourth Saturday in Aug. 1885
Salem Church did not meet or have any church business the Association meeting with
Friend [ship] *church at the same tim*
            S.M. Cooley Ch Cl   *I Z Kimb* [r]*ough Mod*

Saturday, September 26, 1885

Fourth Saturday in Sept 1885
Salem Church Met Preaching by Rev Noah Moon after Preaching

(1)   *by Aclimation Rev Moon was appointed Mod for the day*
(2)   *by motion and sec the Church held and Election Which Resulted in the Electing of Noah*
Moon as our pasture [pastor] *for the insueng year*
No other Bu [Business] *done and Closed*
Sabbath Meeting Preaching by the Mod
            S.M. Cooley Ch Cl   *Noah Moon Mod*

Saturday, October 24, 1885

Fourth Saturday in Oct 1885
Salem Church met after Prayer Preaching by Rev Thos [Thomas] *Frost by motion and Sec*
Bro Moon Acceped as moderator
the Cl being Absent by motion and sec appointed J.L. Roark
protem Cl Then made way for the Receptun of Members
Recveid Jacab [Jacob] *Bare J Mc Roark* [24] *& Martha Roark by Experance & Baptism then*
Bro Moon Exciped [accepted] *the Care of the Church & after prayer by the Mod adjorned*

---

[24]   John Mack Roark, son of John Lewis Roark and Victoria Conner Roark.

to 11 O clock Sabbath met and baptised Jacob Bare J Mc Roark & Martha Roark then
Preaching by the Mod & Prayer by Bro John Smith then Closed

J.L. Roark pro Cl   Noah Moon Mod

Saturday, November 28, 1885

Fourth Saturday Nov 1885
Salem Church met Preaching by Mod

(1) *Invited visiting Members to Seats With us*
(2) *Called for the minute of the last Meeting Which Was Read*
     and Recived also the Minute of the Oct meeting Which Was Read and Recived
3d   *Made way to Recived mem* [bers]
4ᵗʰ *Resolved to dispence With the Past referencs at the Dec Meeting*
     and Closed by Prayer
     saba [Sabbath] *Meeting Preaching by the Mod*

S M Cooley Ch Cl   Noah Moon Mod

Saturday, December 26, 1885

Fourth Saturday in Dec 1885
Salem Church Met Preaching by the Mod and Proceeded to Business Invited visit members
to seats with us and Called for the minute of the last meeting Which was Read & Recived
and the Reference laid over to the next meeting and Closed
till 11 oclock on Sunday When there was Preaching
by the Mod and Closed

SM Cooley Ch Cl   Noah Moon Mod

1886

Saturday, January 23, 1886

Fourth Saturday in Jan 1886
Salem Church met opned by Prayer Preaching by the Mod

(1)   *Made Way to Rcive members and Recived nun*
(Sec) *Called for the Reading of the minute of the Pas meeting*
      Which was Read and Recived no other Business done and Closed
      Sabbath Meeting Preaching by the Mod & Closed

S.M. Cooley Ch Cl   Noah Moon Mod

Saturday, February 27, 1886

Fourth Saturday in Feb 1886

salem Churn [Church] *met Preaching by the Mod & then being a very few members Presant ther was no business done and Closed Sabbath Meeting Preaching by the Mod & Closed*

      S.M. Cooley Ch Cl   *Noah Moon Mod*

Saturday, March 27, 1886

Fourth Saturday in Mar 1886

salem Church met Preaching by the Pastor firs invited viset members to Seats with us and Called for the Reading of the Minite of the past meeting which was read and recivd and Closed

Sabbath Meeting Fourth Sabbath in Mar 1886

(1)   *Preaching by R.T. Howard*

(2)   *The church was Called to order and restored Mathew McMillion & granted him a letter of dismission and Closed*

      S.M. Cooley Ch Cl   *Noah Moon Mod*

Saturday, April 24, 1886

Fourth Saturday in Apr 1886

salem Church met Preaching by the Mod.

(1)   *made way to recive members and recivd nun*

(2)   *Called for the reading of the minute of the past meeting which was read and recived*

(3)   *A Charge was lifted against Mary Jane Scott for luidness and also to try her fellowship with the Church and by unanimas voice of the Church was Excluded*

(4)   *A Charge was brought against Bro G W Eldridge for immoral Conduct and also to try his fellowship and by vote of the Church was Excluded*

(5)   *by motion & Sec the Church Authorized the Cl with the assistance of Bro J.P. Tally* [Talley] *to Rearange the names of the member of the Church on the Church Book as they thought best*

(6ᵗʰ) *By motion and Sec the Church Said The* [y] *Would have a Communion Season fourth Sabbath of May 1886 and would invite Friendship and Birchwood with their deacon and and ministerial and to Commune with us*

(7ᵗʰ) *by motion and Sec we Recevd and Excepted* [Accepted] *an invitation to the Communion Season with the George Town Church Sec Sabbath in May 1886 and Closed*

      S M Cooley Ch Cl   *Noah Moon Mod*

Sabbath meeting Preaching by the Mod

Saturday, May 22, 1886

Fourth Saturday in May 1886

Salem Church met Preaching by the Mod

(1ˢᵗ) *Called for the Reading of the minute of the Past meeting which was Read Recived no other Business done Closed*

Sabbath meeting Preaching by Rev R.T. Howard after preaching the Church was Called to gether by Singing and

Eat thePasover in Remembrance of our lord and Savor [Savior] *Jesus Christ and ended Singing a Hymn and went out or Closed*

      S M Cooley Ch Cl   *Rev Noah Moon Mod*

Saturday, June 26, 1886

Fourth Saturday in June 1886

Salem Church met Preaching by the Mod

(1) *Invited vist members to Seats with us and Call for the minute of the Past meeting which was Read and Recived*

(Sec) *Made way to Recive members and Recive nun and Closed*

Sabbath meeting Preaching by the Mod and Closed

      S.M. Cooley Ch Cl   *Noah Moon Mod*

Saturday, July 24, 1886

Fourth Sat in July 1886

Salem Church met Preaching by The Mod

(1) *Made way to recive members and recived nun*

(Sec) *Call for the reading of the last meeting and the Cl not being Present the Reading of the minute was land over untell next meeting no other Bu* [Business] *done Closed by Prayer*

Sabbath meeting Preaching by the Mod and Closed

      S.M. Cooley Ch Cl   *Noah Moon Mod*

Saturday, August 28, 1886

Fourth Sat in Aug 1886

No meeting Either on Saturday or Sunday on the account of Our Mod being gone to the Ocoee Association

Saturday, September 25, 1886

Fourth Saturday in Sept 1886

Salem Church met Preaching by the Mod

(1) *made way to recive members and recived nun*

(2) *Called for the reading of the minute of the last meeting and there was no minute or meeting and the Minute of the July meeting was read and recivd*

(3)   The Church to represent in Ocoee Association which meets the last Thursday in Sep. 1886
and to Send as our mesenger
viz Bro John W Roark SM Cooley Lenard stults [Leonard Stulce]

(4)   The Church ricived the report of the Commity that was appointed to rearange the names of
the Church and Said
Committy recommends that said Book Stand as ever
no Other Business done and Closed by Prayer
Sunday meeting Preaching by the Mod and Closed
        S.M. Cooley Ch Cl   Noah Moon Mod

Saturday, October 23, 1886

4ᵗʰ Saturday in Oc [t] 1886
Salem church met preaching by the Modrator then made
way for reception of members then call for the the minnet of the last meeting and the clerk
being absent by motion & Second appointed J L Roark clerk protem for the Day then omitted the buisness untill Sabbath then prary [prayer] by modrator then closed til candle
lighting
        J.L. Roark protem Cl   Noah Moon Modrater

Saturday, December 25, 1886

4 Satur Dec 1886
Salem church met there being no minister the church poseeded [proceeded] to Elect a
pastor for the insuning [ensuing] year
and broher [brother] R T Howard was Elected then closed
L J Hatley Cerk [Clerk] protem JC Smith moderator for the Day

1887

Saturday, January 22, 1887

4 Saturay January 1887
Salem church met after preaching by the modrator Set for buisness
1ᵗ   one motion & Second L.H. Stulce was apointed Clerk all so request him to see bro S M Cooley
and get the church Book
2ⁿᵈ   on motion the church grants Sister Liza Jane Welch a Leter of recomendation then Closed
        L.H. Stulce C C protem   R.T. Howard modrator

Saturday, February 26, 1887

4 Saturay Feb 1887 no buisness Done

Saturday, March 26, 1887

4 Saturday March 1887

Salem church met and after preaching by themodrator proseeded to buisness

1 *made way for the reseption of members*

2 *read the minit of the January meating and approvd the same*

3rd *brother S.M. Cooley tendered his resignation as church Clerk which the church accepted*

5th (4th) *then Went in to an election of A.C.C.* [a Church Clerk] *and L.H. Stulce was elected*

6th (5th) *J.L. Roark was elected assistant Clerk*

7th (6th) *one motion and Second the church grants brother Marion Howell a leter of recomendation*

then closed to meet Sabath

met persuant to agurnmant preaching by the modrator

then closed By prar

        L.H. Stulce C.C.   *R.T. Howrd Modrator*

Saturday, April 23, 1887

4 1887 fourth Saturday In aprile

Salem church and after preaching by the Modrator

call for the minuet of the March meeting read and approv the same the church then

agrees to hold a communion meeting at our next regular meeting by motion and Second

Brothers S.M. Cooley & L.H. Stulce was appointed to Confer with Brother Talley in regard

to the communion one motion & second the church grants Brother Calvin Witt A Letar of

reconindation ten [then] *closed to meet Sunday met Sunday at 11 oclock preaching by the*

modrator then closed by prayer

        L.H. Stulce C.C.   *R.T. Howrd Modrator*

Saturday, May 28, 1887

1887 Saturday beefore the fourth Sunday in May

Salem met after preaching by the modrator in vited visitin brethering and Sisters to Seets

with us called for the minet of the April meeting red and approvd the same mad way for

the reception of members recivd none then closed to meet Saboath

met Sunday preaching by the modrator then commemorated

the lords Deth and Suffering then closed

        L.H. Stulce C.C.   *R.T. Howrd Mod*

Saturday, June 25, 1887

1887 June there was no meeting

Saturday, July 23, 1887

1887 4 Saturday in July

Salem church met preaching by the modrator
then called for the minute of the last meeting and the clerk beeing absent recivd minute for
the June meeting then made way for the reception of members & recevd none then prayre by
Sister Johnson & closed until 11 oclock on Sabaath

       J.L. Roark as sisten clk   *R.T. Howrd Mod*

Saturday, August 27, 1887

1887 Aug no meeting

Saturday, September 24, 1887

Sept 1887 fourth Saturday
Salem church met the modrator not beeing present was no buisness done met on the
Sabaath folowing preaching by the modrator after whitch the church appointed following
brethering J.P. Talley Jacob Bair L.H. Stulce to represent her in the association by motion the
church grants Sister Sarah Barnet a leter of recommendation brother Gate beeing present
the church agrees at continue the meeting a fiew days
then closed to met 71/2 oclock

       L.H. Stulce C.C.   *R.T. Howrd Mod*

Saturday, October 22, 1887

4 Saturday Oct 1887
Salem church did not meet met the Sabaath folowing preaching by the Modrator then
closed

       L.H. Stulce C.C.   *R.T. Howrd Mod*

Saturday, November 26, 1887

fourth Saturday Nov 1887
Salem church met preaching Modrator there beeing but
fiew members present ther was no buissness done
met on the Sabaath folowing preaching by the Modrator
then closed by praire

       L.H. Stulce C.C.   *R.T. Howrd Mod*

Saturday, December 24, 1887

4th Saturday Dec 1887
Salem church met the Modrator beeing absent there was
no bisiness Done met on the Saboath folowing but had
no preaching the modrator beeing absent

       L.H. Stulce CC   *R.T. Howrd Mod*

1888

Saturday, January 28, 1888

4th Saturday in Jan 1888

There was no preaching at Salem the church [?] to meet next on the Saboath folowing
preaching by the Moderator then Closed

      L.H. Stulce C.C.   *R.T. Howard Mod*

Saturday, February 25, 1888

Fourth Saturday in Feb 1888

Ther was no preaching at Salem the Church [?] to come to gether the Modrator beeing
present met the Sabath folowing preaching by the modrator then Closed by prarr

      L.H. Stulce C C   *R.T. Howard Mod*

Saturday, March 24, 1888

Fourth Saturday in March 1888

Salem Church met the pastor beeing absent prair was offerd
by brother M.H. Conner then closed

      L.H. Stulce CC   *R.T. Howard Mod*

Saturday, April 28, 1888

Saturday before the 4th Sunday in apr 1888

Salem church met the pastor read the 18th Psalm then mad some verry appropreate remarks
after whitch prier [prayer] was offerd by brother M.H. Conner then called for the minuet
of the past meeting whitch was read and approvd it then beeing agreed that the church
elect a pastor at her next meeting one motion the clerk & J.L. Roark was appointed as a
commita to Setel with the pastor for his past years servis the same bretherin was appointed
to see the members of the church in regard [to] a pastor then closed to meet on the Saboath
folowing
met at ½ past 3 oclock preaching by the modrator then closed

      L.H. Stulce C. Clerk   *R.T. Howrd Modrator*

Saturday, May 26, 1888

4th Saturday in May 88

Salem church met the modrator beeing absent by motion and second Bro M.H. Conner was
appointed Modrator for the day, then singin & prayer then proceded to business and elected
Bro R.T. Howard pastor for the ensuing year then closed until 10 oclock Sunday

      L.H. Stulce CC   *M.H. Conner Modrator*

Church met Sabbath preaching by the modrator then intermision 10 or 15 minets then administered the Sacrement and granted Bro James P. Moon and S.M. Cooley leters of rec-ommendation then accpted invitation of the Georgetown church to meet with them the 2nd sunday
then closed

      J.L. Rark [Roark] *assistant clk*[25]   *R.T. Howard Modrator*

Saturday, June 23, 1888

Fourth Saturday in June 1888
Salem church met preaching by the Modrator read minets of the April and May meetings approvd the same then closed to meet the following Saboath

      L.H. Stulce CC   *R.T. Howrd* [Howard] *Mod*

Saturday, July 28, 1888

Fourth Saturday in July 1888
Salem church met preaching by brother Felzer ther beeing
but fiew members present was no buisness Done
met the Saboath following preaching by the modrator the
church then granted Sister Sarah Webb a leter of Dismission
then closed

      L.H. Stulce CC   *R.T. Howrd* [Howard] *Mod*

Saturday, August 25, 1888

Fourth Saturday in Aug 1888
Salem church met the modrator beeing absent
prare was offered by Sister Stivers then closed

      L.H. Stulce CC   *R.T. Howard Mod*

Saturday, September 22, 1888

Fourth Saturday in Sept 1888
Salem church met preaching by the Modrator then red the minets of the 3 past meeting approvd the same by mossion [motion] *and Second the church appointed Delegats to reprisent her in the Association L.H. Stulce W.R. Haney John Haney Tomas* [Thomas] *Roark appointed to carry the leter and contribution it was then agreed not to hav meeting Sunday*

      L.H. Stulce CC   *R.T. Howard Mod*

---

[25]   J.L. Roark was the first assistant clerk mentioned in the minutes. Salem Church would continue to elect assistant clerks into the twentieth century.

Saturday, October 27, 1888

Fourth Saturday in Oct 1888
ther was no preaching at Salem church the pastor beeing
sick preaching the Saboath following by Brother Jordan
the church then granted Sisters Sarah Moon and Sarah C
Moon Leters of recomendation then closed
         L.H. Stulce CC   *R.T. Howrd Modrator*

[No record of meetings in November or December, 1888.][26]

1889

[No record of meetings in January, February, or March of 1889.]

Saturday, April 27, 1889

Fourth Saturday Aprile 1889
Salem church met [not] *having modrator by motion & second elected bro Cookson*
[Cookston] *modrator for the Day the modrator appointed Bro Tomas* [Thomas] *Roark*
to hold the Election for to Elect a pastor for the insewing year and Brother Colins [Collins]
was Elected with the understanding that the church wold pay him $20 for his servis then
closed
        J.L. Roark assist Clk   *Joseph Cookson* [Cookston] *Mod*

Saturday, May 25, 1889

Fourth Saturday in May 1889
Salem church met preaching by the pastor then read the minuet of the Aprile meeting
then closed to meet on the Saboath fowling met preaching [by] *the pastor then closed*
        L.H. Stulce CC   *R.C. Collins pastor*

Saturday, June 22, 1889

Fourth Saturday June 1889
the church met preaching by pastor then made way for the
reception of members recivd none by motion and second it was agreed to over hall the
church book so as to larn acteul

---

26   The bottom 75% of Page 94 of the Salem ledger book was left vacant ostensibly in anticipation of the minutes being added later. Page 95 of the ledger book begins with the fourth Saturday in April 1889.

membership the clerk and assistant was appointed a committa to Do the same by motion
and second it was agreed to change owr meeting Days from the fourth to the second
Saturday by motion and second the church agreed to hav communion at our next meeting
then closed

met the Day following at 10 oclock the Saboath School had

a lesson after whitch the pastor gav a lecture of 20 minets one [on] the importance of
Saboath School then preach a vrry interesting Sermon made way for the reseption of members and recivd non then closed

        L.H. Stulce CC   R C Collins pastor

Saturday, July 13, 1889

Second Saturday in July 1889

Salem church met preaching by the pastor then made way for the reception of Members
recivd none then read the Minuet of the June meeting approvd the same after whitch the
rules of Decorum was read then closed by Prair

met the Day folowing preaching by the pastor

then 10 Minuets intermision call to gether by singin

then commemorated the Lords Supper then closed

        L.H. Stulce CC   R.C. Collins pastor

Saturday, August 10, 1889

2nd Saturday in Aug.

the church met preaching by the pastor there beeing but fiew presint it was anounce we
wold hav church conference the day folowing then closed

met Saboath morning at 10 oclock preaching by the pastor then made way for the recption
of members rec'd none

then read the minet of the past meeting approvd the same

then closed

        L.H. Stulce CC   R.C. Collins pastor

Saturday, September 14, 1889

Saturday before the 2nd Sunday in Sept 1889

the church [met] preaching by the pastor then made way for the recption of members
recivd none read the minet of the past meeting by Motion it was agreed that wee represent
in the Association Bothers Joseph Cookson [Cookston] J.L. Roark

L.H. Stulce was appointed to carry the Leter and contribution it was agreed not to hav
meeting sunday following then closed

        L.H. Stulce CC   R.C. Collins pastor

Saturday, October 12, 1889

Second Saturday in Oct 1889

the church met preaching by the pastor then made way for the reception of members recivd
Sister Harett [Harriet] *Roark Lenora Stulce Clementine Stulce Stacy Stulce A.L. Stulce* [27]
as candats for Baptism then read minet of the past meeting then closed to meet at nite
        L.H. Stulce CC   *R.C. Collins pastor*

met at 7 oclock preaching by the pastor made way for the recption of members Then closed
to meet Sunday at 10 oclock
met Sunday preaching by Brother Jordan
then closed to attend to the ordnance of Baptism
        R.C. Collins pastor

Saturday, November 16, 1889

Third Saturday in Nov 1889
no preaching at Salem

Saturday, December 21, 1889

Third Saturday in Dec 1889
the church met preaching by the pastor then made way for
the reception of members then read minet of the Oct meeting by Motion and Second the
church agrees to recind the act [of]
exclusion of W.M. Roark and restore him to all the privlidg of the church by Motion the
church grants Sister Eliza Denson a Leter of recomendation then closed to meet one [on]
the Saboath folowing met according to appointment preaching by Brother Smith then
closed
        L.H. Stulce CC   *R.C. Collins pastor*

---

[27]   It is possible that the clerk meant A.S. Stulce, who was appointed Clerk in August 1892. A.L. Stulce would have been baptized before being ordained.

Membership Activities of Salem Baptist Church in the Minutes 1880–1889

	1880	1881	1882	1883	1884	1885	1886	1887	1888	1889	Total
Excluded	3	0	0	0	0	0	2	0	0	0	5
Dismissed	0	0	5	0	1	4	1	0	0	0	11
Letter of Recommendation	2	9	7	12	3	0	0	4	4	1	42
Received by Letter	3	3	4	2	0	0	0	0	0	0	12
Received/ Experience	9	2	23	4	0	3	0	0	0	0	41
Enrollment	0	0	0	2	0	0	0	0	0	0	2
Baptized	8	0	24	2	0	3	0	0	0	0	37
Restored	0	0	0	0	0	0	1	0	0	0	1
Dropped from the book	0	0	0	16	0	0	0	0	0	0	16
Letters rescinded	0	0	1	0	0	0	0	0	0	0	1
Exclusion rescinded	0	0	0	0	0	0	0	0	0	1	1
Candidates for Baptism	0	0	0	0	0	0	0	0	0	5	5

Activities tabulated from the Minutes of Salem Baptist Church.

Letter of Dismissal

A member of a Baptist church relocating to a different area would ask for a "letter," and, if granted, the letter was written by the clerk. Although it seems that a letter of dismissal and a letter of recommendation both served the same purpose, it is not clear why one was used in a situation rather than the other. This fragment was found in the Salem Church archives.

Chapter Four
Salem Baptist Church
1890–1899

Pastors at Salem Baptist Church were elected for the associational year, which was September to September, the month of the Ocoee Association's annual meeting. However, it was not out of the ordinary for a pastor to be elected at other times of the year, should the current pastor resign, or be incapable of attending to the responsibilities of pastor. According to the minutes, if a pastor was elected in a month other than September, he was elected for the remainder of the associational year, and often continued as pastor through December, or even into the next year, regardless of whether Salem Church sent delegates to the association's meeting that year.

When the church did not meet for an significant period, due to harvest time, bad weather, or illness, the next meeting gave a sense of trying to carry on, firm in their faith, despite adversity or circumstances. The most common months with no meetings in the 1890s were January through April. East Tennessee recorded record snowfall in the winters of 1892–1895. Before the time of modern medicine, illnesses were hard to contain and could easily affect an entire area.

R.C. Collins was pastor of Salem Church from May 1889 through February 1890. There were no meetings from March to June of 1890. At the July meeting, Rev. Collins served as moderator pro tem when J.H. Gass was elected pastor of Salem Baptist Church. Rev. Gass was returning to the fold after 17 years, having been one of the 24 members sent to form Birchwood Baptist Church in 1873. J.H. Gass would be re-elected and would remain pastor through October 1892 and would return to preach in November 1893.

The year of 1892 was another rough year for Salem Baptist Church, with no meeting in January, preaching only in February and March, and no meetings through July. J.B. Trotter was the guest preacher at the September meeting and was elected pastor at the November meeting. It is not known whether Salem Church requested him to visit and preach or whether he was on his pastoral rounds and happened to preach at Salem when the church was in need of a pastor.

Pastors in the 1800s were known to travel from church to church (called "circuit riders"), ministering to current churches or beginning new churches where none yet existed. With generally four weeks in a month, and churches only having services one weekend per month, it was possible for a minister to be pastor of four churches simultaneously. Many Baptist pastors in the south felt themselves duty bound to keep moving to new destinations to which they felt called.

Like Salem, other churches were struggling in the face of changing times and continual movement toward increasing urban areas and the west. The Ocoee Association's Executive Committee report for 1897 states the following:

> "Your committee finds more churches without pastors at the present time than at any other time within our knowledge. The churches are becoming cold, and in many places our cause is rapidly declining. There are places within our bounds, in good communities, where there is no Baptist preaching."
>
> We therefore, recommend that it be made the duty of the Executive Committee to solicit contributions from all the churches to pay a reasonable salary to a missionary to hold meetings in these places for the purpose of leading the churches to a higher state of Christian living and duty, and that this committee have charge of the work; also that they keep a missionary in the field as much of the time as possible."[1]

J.B. Trotter would be re-elected twice, being pastor of Salem Baptist Church from November 1892 to September 1895. He would return to preach at Salem in September 1896, be elected pastor in December 1897, and be elected again in December 1908. In October 1893, Salem Church had preaching by B.N. Brooks. Reverend B. Newton Brooks was an associational pastor preaching to support Sunday Schools. In November he was elected Secretary and Treasurer of the Sunday School and Colportage Board of the Ocoee Association. In March 1894, Salem Church contributed $1.03 for State Sunday School work. The receipt in the minutes was signed by B.N. Brooks.

Salem Baptist Church made another effort to organize a consistent Sunday school as the Ocoee Association continued with a Sunday school drive, helping to organize Sunday schools in Salem and Birchwood, among others, in 1894. Rev. Brooks would preach at Salem again in May 1895. In September of that year he was elected pastor. In December Brother Allen was elected pastor because "Brother Brooks never came to our assistance." It is quite possible that Rev. Brooks was busy with associational duties.

The election of D.J. Alexander as treasurer in 1893 was another advancement for women at Salem Baptist Church. She would also be the first woman elected and ordained as a deacon in May 1895. It is not clear from the minutes if the attitudes of the church were becoming more liberal or if the lack of attending male members made electing a woman a necessity. Sister Alexander would be elected to various committees at Salem throughout the 1890s.

Salem Baptist Church read the Rules of Decorum and the Church Covenant at the December, 1893 meeting, as they did periodically throughout the life of the church. The reading of the two documents was to reinforce the principles, ideals, and beliefs put forth in the documents. It was usually followed by a call to check on the conduct of the members of the church, or preceded a series of actions by the church whose aim was to do good works. In 1894, Salem Church made a concentrated attempt to start a Sunday school, began observing the Lords Supper at meetings again, and had an extended meeting in October in a failed attempt to add new members.

J.P. Talley, who had been a regular delegate to the Ocoee Association meetings from 1878 to 1894, was also appointed delegate to the Fifth Sunday meeting.in April 1894. The Fifth Sunday meetings of the Ocoee Association began in 1883 when the resolutions stated that:

> "Sunday Schools are not for the children only, but for every church member to work, either as a teacher, or pupil. Every school organized should be a part of the church work, and is included in all things commanded by Christ, and to be observed by the church. We further recommend that the pastors urge this duty in all our churches."

It was also resolved at the Fifth Sunday organizational meeting that there would be a series of meetings for the investigation of the scriptures on Sunday schools and the doctrinal issues of the age. A committee was appointed to divide the Association into districts. The result was that the territory represented by the Association was divided into four districts. Each of the four Fifth Sunday meetings each year would be at a church in a different district. The focus of Fifth Sunday meetings when they began was on Sunday schools. The emphasis varied between missions and Sunday schools over the next twelve years. At the Association meeting in1895, it was resolved that the Fifth Sunday meetings be called "Young People and Sunday School Meetings." The Baptist Young People's Union (BYPU) of each church received a request to send a delegate along with delegates from the Sunday school, the congregation, and the pastor.[2] But in the Ocoee Association Executive Committee report for 1897, the only report of the

5th Sunday meetings was that "[the] meeting at Antioch was one of great spiritual power," with a report of the money collected for missions.

In the meeting for May 1894, Salem Church agreed to have children's day. Emphasis on a "children's day" illustrates the growing awareness that the growth of the church was through the children and continuing concern for the welfare of the children and growth of the church. Children would attend church when their parents could not. A children's day would be an all day affair with activities, study, and worship.

Rev. Allen was elected pastor at the first December meeting in 1895 when B.N. Brooks was considered negligent. At the second meeting in December Rev. Allen tendered his resignation. John Carrell was elected moderator for an indefinite time. Carrell was the only non-ordained member elected in the minutes as moderator.

In January 1896 the church authorized the moderator to write Brother Curtain to come and attend to the ordinance of Baptism at the next regular meeting. The only apparent reason for the church to ask an ordained preacher to attend to baptism at a meeting that was not extended would be because John Carrell was not ordained. If that is the case, Carrell was also the only non-ordained preacher at Salem Church. Since a preacher would need to preach for two years before being ordained, any responsible, dedicated church member could preach. Baptism would require an ordained minister. According to the minutes, it was very rare for the church to ask a preacher to come simply to attend to baptism. John Carrell was preacher for the service at which Brother Curtain attended to baptism.

A.L. Stulce was moderator pro tem in July 1896 when William Grimsby was elected pastor for the remainder of the associational year. Not meeting in August, Salem Church met in September and asked for the report of the committee appointed at the July meeting to overhaul the Church book. There is no record of the committee's appointment in the July minutes. The September meeting was extended for several days and nights, with sixteen people coming forward to join the church as candidates for baptism.

At the October meeting, the committee appointed to see delinquent members reported that they had seen some of the members. The church gave the members another meeting to give satisfaction to the church. It is interesting to note that the church must have come to the conclusion that a male committee was insufficient in meeting with a female member. From that October meeting through the end of the existing minutes, the church would always appoint a "Sister," or "committee of Sisters," to see female members who were rumored to not be living right or were not attending church.

There "being but few out," there was only preaching at Salem Baptist Church at the January and February meetings of 1897. There was no meeting in March. In April, the church took up the cases of five male members and excluded them for immoral conduct. At the May meeting the church observed the Lord's Supper. There were no meetings from August to November. In December, J.B. Trotter was elected pastor for an indefinite time.

There were only two meetings in 1898—one in January and one in April. J.C. Eldridge was elected treasurer in April. Likewise, there were only two meetings in 1899. In January, Salem Baptist Church elected S.J. Stulce assistant clerk. In March, the "pastor being elected for an indefinite time," the church agreed to call a pastor at the next meeting in April. There would not be another meeting in 1899.

Minutes of Salem Baptist Church
1890–1899

Saturday, January 18, 1890
Third Saturday in Jan 1890
the church met preaching by the pastor there beeing but fiew present no buisness done
preaching the Saboath following
         L.H. Stulce CC   *R.C. Collins pastor*

Saturday, February 15, 1890
Third Saturday Feb 1890
The church met preaching by the pastor then made way for the recption of members
then read minet of the Dec and Jan meetings then closed
met one [on] *saboath folowing*
preaching by the pastor then closed
         L.H. Stulce CC   *R.C. Collins pastor*

[No record of meetings March thru June 1890]

Saturday, July 5, 1890
First Saturday July 1890
the church met [preaching] *by bro* [Collins] *the church* [then elected Bro. Collins Mod]28 *protem the church then elected brother Gess* [Gass] *as pastor for indefinite time then cosed to meet the next day*
Met Saboath preaching by the pastor then closed
         L.H. Stulce CC   *J.H. Gess* [Gass] *pastor*

Saturday, July 19, 1890
3rd Saturday in July 1890
the church met preaching by the pastor
then read the minet of the past meeting approvd the same
by motion the church grants Sister Nancy Blair a leter of
recommendation then closed [to] *meet the saboath folowing*

---

28   Although J.H. Gass was listed as pastor for the meeting, it was not usual for a pastor to preside as moderator for the meeting in which he was elected. It was the common practice for the outgoing pastor to act as moderator at the meeting.

met Saboath preaching by the pastor then closed by prair
by bro Howard

    L.H. Stulce CC   *J.H. Gess* [Gass] *pastor*

Saturday, August 16, 1890

3rd Saturday August 1890
the church met preaching by the pastor then read minet of
the past meeting made way for the reception [of] *members*
then closed by praire
met Saboath folowing preaching by the pastor then closed

    L.H. Stulce CC   *J.H. Gess* [Gass] *Mod*

[No record of church meeting in September 1890.]

Saturday, October 18, 1890

third Saturday Oct 1890
the church met preaching by thepastor then made way for the reseption of members then
read then [the] *minet of the*
August meeting approved the same then closed
met Saboath preaching by the pastor then closed

    L.H. Stulce CC   *J.H. Gess* [Gass] *pas*

Saturday, November 15, 1890

third Saturday Nov 1890
the Church met preaching by the pastor the read minet of the past meeting then Closed
Closed to meet Saboath morning
met preaching by the pastor then closed to meet at night

    L.H. Stulce C.C.   *J.H. Gess* [Gass] *pas*

Saturday, December 20, 1890

third Saturday Dec 1890
the Church met preaching by the pastor then read minet
past meeting approved the same
then closed to meet at candle light for preaching
met Saboath preaching by the pastor
then cosed

    L.H. Stulce C.C.   *J.H. Gess* [Gass] *pas*

1891

Saturday, January 17, 1891

Third Saturday January 1891
Salem church met preaching by the pastor read minets
of the past meeting approved the same then closed by prare
met Sabboath preaching by the pastor then closed

        L.H. Stulce CC   *J.H. Gess* [Gass] *pastor*

Saturday, February 21, 1891

Third Saturday Feb 1891
no meeting

Saturday, March 21, 1891

Third Saturday March 1891
the church met Saboath preaching by the pastor then closed

        L.H. Stulce CC   *J.H. Gess* [Gass] *pastor*

Saturday, April 18, 1891

Third Saturday Aprile 1891
Salem church [met] *preaching by pas* [pastor] *read the minet of*
the January meeting approvd the same then closed
met Saboath morning preaching by the pastor then closed

        L.H. Stulce CC   *J.H. Gess* [Gass] *pastor*

Saturday, May 16, 1891

3rd Saturday in May 1891
Salem church met preaching by the past [pastor] *then made way for the reception of*
members by motion and Second the church agrees to hold a communion at her next meet-
ing then closed to Sabboath met Saboath preaching by the pastor closed

        L.H. Stulce CC   *J.H. Gess* [Gass] *pastor*

Saturday, June 20, 1891

Third Saturday in June 1891
the church met preaching by the pastor clerk beeing absent
no further buisness then closed

        J.L. Roark assist Clk   *J.H. Gess* [Gass] *pastor*

met Saboath preaching by the pas [pastor] *after intermision*
ten minets they hell [held] *a communion then closed*

   L.H. Stulce C.C.   *J.H. Gess pastor*

Saturday, July 18, 1891

Third Saturday July 1891
Salem church met preaching by the pastor then read the
minets of the May and June meetings then closed to meet
Saboath
met according to appointment preaching by the pastor
then closed

   L.H. Stulce CC   *J.H. Gess* [Gass] *pastor*

Saturday, August 15, 1891

Third Saturday in Aug 1891
Salem church met preaching by the pastor then read the
minet of the past meeting ther beeing but fiew present [no]
bisness Done then closed to meet Saboath
met Saboath morning preaching by pastor then closed

   L.H. Stulce CC   *J.H. Gess* [Gass] *pastor*

Saturday, September 19, 1891

3rd Saturday in September 1891
Salem Church met and had preaching by the moderator,
after which the church was called in Session for Business

1t   *Made way for the reception of members*
2nd   *Invited visiting Bre.* [Brethren] *To seats*
3rd   *Called for the Reading of the minute of the preceeding meeting which was read and*
    approved
4th   *Moderators time being out, the church by Motion agreed and held an Election for Moderator*
    to Serve for next assotiational
    year, which resulted in the re election of J.H. Gass
5th   *The Bro Clerk offered his resignation which was received and C.A. Smith was Elected Clerk*
6th   *The Church agreed to represent in their Association and appointed Bro Thos. Roark D.B.*
    Roark and C.A. Smith as her Delagates with one dollar contribution then closed till night
    the Church met [at] *Night Preaching By the Modderater*
    then Closed till Sabbath morning
    met Sabbath Preaching by the Modderater The meeting
    continued from Day to Day for Nine Days and oppertunity

Being frequently Given for the Reception of members the follow
Persons Came forward at Differt Times & joined the Church
to wit Sister Salley Irwin and Sister Juda Roark[29] by Experiance for Babtism
Then Closed to meat The Third Satturday in September

C.A. Smith CC   *J.H. Gass Moderator*

Saturday, October 17, 1891

3rd Satturday in Oct 1891
The Baptist Church of Christ at Salem Met had Preaching by the Modderater after Which
the Church was called in Session for Business

1st   *Made way for the Reception of Members and Recived Non*
2nd   *Ivited visiting Brothers to Seats*
3rd   *Called for The Reading of The minute of The Preseeding Meeting Which was Red And*
      Approved
4th   *the Church by Motion and Second agreed on the Next meeting to have the Church Covinant*
      and the Rules of Decarum Red then Closed Till Night Met at Night Preaching by the
      Moderator Then Closed to Meat at the Watters Edge on Sabbath Morning to attend to The
      Ordinances of Baptism Met Sabbath and Baptised Sistrs Salley Irwin and Juda Roark Then
      after Preaching By The Madderater
      The Church was Dismissed [until] *3 Satturday in November*

C.A. Smith CC   *J.H. Gass Pastor*

Saturday, November 21, 1891

Third Satturday in November 1891
No Meeting
Met Sabbath Had Preaching by the Paster
then Closed to meat the third Saturday in Dec

C.A. Smith CC   *J.H. Gass Pastor*

Saturday, December 19, 1891

Third Saturday in Dec 1891
the Baptist Church of Christ at Salem met had Preaching by the Pastor after which the
Church was Called in Session
made way for Reception of members and recieved none
and then Closed to meet Sabath
met Sunday morning
Preaching by the mod and then Closed by Prayer

C.A. Smith CC   *J.H. Gass*

---

[29]   This is Julia Roark, daughter of John W. Roark.

1892

Saturday, January 6, 1892
Third Saturday in January 1892
and Sunday no Preaching at Salem

Saturday, February 20, 1892
Third Saturday in Feb 1892
We the Baptist Church met Preaching by the pastor
Then Closed by prayer
        C.A. Smith CC   *J.H. Gass Mod*

Saturday, March 19, 1892
3rd Saturday in March 1892
No meeting at Salem
Met Sunday Preaching by the pastor then Closed by Preyr
        C.A. Smith CC   *J.H. Gass Mod*

[No church meeting recorded April through July, 1892.]

Saturday, August 20, 1892
Third Saturday in August 1892
Salem Church met preaching by the Pastor thare being but
Few present No buisness was Done
met Sabath morning Preaching by the pastor
then the Church Was Called in Session
Brother C.A. Smith having tendered his Clerk Ship by motion of the Church A.S. Stulce was apointed Clerk The Church
agred to Represent in the Assosiation and the fowling Brething
was aponited [appointed]. *To wit W.M. Roark J.P. Talley was apointed by motion and Second the Church granted Sister Mosouri* [Misouri] *Aslinger a leter of Recommendation*
and then closed
        A.S. Stulce CC   *J.H. Gass Pastor*

Saturday, September 17, 1892
Third Saturday in September 1892
Salem Church met Preaching by the Pastor then made way

for members and recivd Brother B.F. Baker as a Candidate for Baptism then Called for the
Report of last meeting was Red and aproved the same then Closed to meet Sabath
Met Sunday morning Preaching by Rev J.B. Trotter
and Closed With Prayer by Brother Millard

        A.S. Stulce CC   *J.H. Gass Pastor*

Saturday, October 15, 1892

Third Saturday in October 1892
the Baptist Church of Christ at Salem met Preaching by the pastor after Which The Church
Proceed to buisness made way for Reception of members and Recived the fowling Brething
[Brethren] *to wit Wesley Millard by Leter and Jonney* [Johnny] *Cross*
as a Candidate for Baptism then Closed to meet at ten o Clock Sunday met acording to
apoint ment Preaching by the Pastor then Closed to meet at 3 p.m. at the waters Edge to
attend to the ordinance of Baptism
met and after atending to the Same Closed

        A.S. Stulce CC   *J.H. Gass Mod*

Saturday, November 19, 1892

Third Saturdy in November 1892
No Meeting at Salem
the Church met Sunday morning and Proceed to Elect a Pastor for the yer 1893 and By
motion and Second Brother Thomas Campbell Was Elected Moderator for the Day And
Then the Church Elected Brother J.B. Trotter as Pastor for the yer 92 [93]
and Then Closed

        A.S. Stulce CC   *Thomas Campbell Mderator pro tem*

Saturday, December 17, 1892

3ʳᵈ Saturdy in Dec 1892
No meeting at Salem
met Sunday morning the Pastor beeing absent Brother David Hubbard Preached a very
interesting sermont and then Closed

1893

Saturday, January 21, 1893

3ʳᵈ Saturday in Jan 1893
No meeting a t Salem
Sunday No meeting at Salem

Saturday, February 18, 1893

3ʳᵈ Saturday in Feb 1893
No meeting at Salem
Sundy no meeting

Saturday, March 11, 1893

2ⁿᵈ Saturday in March 1893
No meeting at Salem
Sundy no meeting

Saturday, April 15, 1893

Third Saturday in April 1893
No meeting at Salem and Sundy no meetin

Saturday, May 20, 1893

Third Saturday in May 1893
Salem Church met Preaching by the Pastor There beeing But few out no Buisness Was done
after prayer By Brother Millard Closed met Sunday morning Preaching by The Pastor
after Which The Church agred to hold thir Communion meeting The next fowling meeting
and Then Closed
        A.S. Stulce CC   *J.B. Trotter Mod*

Saturday, June 17, 1893

Third Saturday in June 1893
We The Baptist Church of Christ at Salem met in Regular Session Preaching by the modera-
tor

2 *Called for The minit of last meeting Red and aprovd The same Thare Being no futher bus-*
ness Closed to meet Sunday at
10 ½ o clock met acardin to ap [appointment] *Preaching by The Maderator After a*
bout 10 minits intermission was given
Called to gether by singin & administerd the Lords Super and
sang a him [hymn] *and Closed*
        A.S. Stulce CC   *J.B. Trotter Mod*

Saturday, July 15, 1893

Third Saturday in July 1893
1 *We The Baptist Church of Christ at Salem met Preaching by The Moderator*
2 *Called for The minit of last meeting Read and aproved The same Thare beeing no further*
buisness Closed to meet Sunday

at 10 ½ o clock met accardin to apoint ment
Preaching by The Pastor and Closed by Prayer
                A.L. Stulce CC   J.B. Trotter Maderator

[No Church meeting recorded for August, 1893.]

Saturday, September 16, 1893
3rd Saturday in September 1893
Salem Church met Preaching by The moderator in absent of The Clerk J.P. Talley Was
apointed Clerk Pro [tem] Thare beeing but few out no buisness was done Closed to meet at
night Met at night Preaching by The Pastor Then made way for Reception of members and
Recived non The Pastors time beeing out it was thought best to wate tell The next Monday
and Closed to meet Sunday at 10 ½ met Sunday and Bro Jorden [Jordan] Preached Bro
[M.H.] Conners and wifes furenal Thare were meeting Sunday night and Monday
The Church met to Elect Her Pastor and Reelected J.B. Trotter for the next assosiational yer
The meetin Continued for Several Days The Privliges of The Church were frequently given
and The foweling persons came forward at difernt times and joind as Candi [Candidates]
for Baptism to Wit Sister Molley Rains haty [Hattey Rains][30] Lydda Smith Sarah L.
Stulce Adda Talley Marthey Smith and Brother arch Smith S.J. Stulce Willam Erwin
[Irwin] and Samuel davis by Letter and Marthey Dartey[31] Came fward and Said she
had lost her letter This Church had given her some time a go The Clerk was autherized to
enRoll her name on the Book
On Wensday Sep the 27 met at The waters Edge to attend to The ordinance of Baptism
after atending to the Same met at The Church and had Preaching by The Pastor Servis at
night and
opend The doors of The Church and Recived D.J. Elixander [Alexander] and Thursday
night Sister Ema Reins [Emma Rains] as Candidates for Baptism and A Journd
                A.S. Stulce CC   J.B. Trotter Mod

Saturday, October 21, 1893
3rd Saturday in October 1893
Salem Church met in Regular Sesion Preaching by B.N. Brooks
after Which The Church was called in Sesion made way for rection [reception] of members and recived non
3   Called for The mint of last meeting was Red and aproved

---

[30]   The Church Rolls list Molley Rains and Hattey Rains (both alternately ending
with an "ie") although it is not clear if Hattey is meant to be included here.
[31]   Listed in the Church Rolls as both Martha Darty and Marthey Darhartey.

4   *agred to open The doors of The Church at Pleasant grove School hose* [house] *Saturday night if Thought proper agred to not have meeting Sunday Then Closed to meet Sunday at J.L. Roark's Landing at 10 ½ to atend to The ordinance of Baptism*

met acording to apoint ment and Baptised Sister Ema Rans [Emma Rains] *Matie Cross & D.J. Elixander* [Alexander] *and T.J. Cross joind at The water and was Baptised Then Closed*

A.L. Stulce CC   J.B. Trotter Mederator

Saturday, November 18, 1893

The 3ʳᵈ Saturday in November 1893
Salem Church met Preaching by The md [moderator]
Then made way for Reception of members and Rcvd Sister Mamie Smith Ema Thomas and Bro Charley Pendergrass
Called for The mint of last meeting was Red and aprovd
Then Elected D.J. Elixander [Alexander] *treasury Then Closed to meet Saturday night met had Preaching by The md* [moderator] *Then opend The Doors of The Church and Recvd Sister S.E. Allison For Baptism Then ajornd to meet Sunday at 10 ½*
Met Preaching by J.H. Gass folowed by J.B. Trotter Then ajournd to meet at The pm at The waters to atend to The ordinance of Baptism met and Baptised Sister S.E. Allison Ema Thomas Mamie Smith and Bro Charley Pendergrass and Then ajournd

A.S. Stulce Church Clk   J.B. Trotter md [moderator]

Saturday, December 16, 1893

The 3ʳᵈ Saturday in December 1893
Salem Church met in Regular Sesion had Preaching by The moderator Then made way for Reception of members and Rcved non Then Called for The minit of last meeting Was red and Aproved The Same and Then Red The Rules of Decorum and The Church Covenant and There being no futher buissness ajornd to meet Saturday night Met acordin to apoint-ment had Preaching by The moderator and extended The Priveliges of the Church Then Closed by Prayer to meet Sunday at E11 oclock met Sunday morning had Preaching by The Pastor
Then Closed by Prayer

A.L. Stulce Clerk   J.B. Trotter Moder

1894

Saturday, January 20, 1894

Salem Church met in Regular Sesion January The 20ᵗʰ 1894

had *Preaching by The md* [moderator] *Then made way for Reception of mems* [members] *and Recivd non Then Red and aproved The minit of last meeting Thare beeing no futher buisness aJornd to meet at night Met had Preaching by The mder Then a Journd by Pryer to meet January 21ᵗ Met Sunday morning Preaching by The moderator and a Journd by Prayer*

   A.S. Stulce CC   *J.B. Trotter moder*

Saturday, February 17, 1894

Salem Church met in Sesion Feb The 17ᵗʰ 1894

had Preaching by The Pastor Then The Church Was Called in Sesion After in viting visiting Brethern and Sisters To Seats made Way for Reception of members and Recvd non Then Called For minit of last meeting was Red and aproved Thare beeing mo futher buisness Closed to meet at night met acording to apoint ment Preaching by The Md Then a Journd by Prayer to meet March [February] *The 18ᵗʰ*

met Sunday had Preaching by the moderator Then a Journd by Prayer

   A.L. Stulce CC   *J.B. Trotter md*

Saturday, March 17, 1894

Third Saturday in March 1894

Salem Baptist Church met Had Preaching by Rv. Thos McCanless after Which The moderator Called The Church in Sesion made way For Reception of members and Recvd non Red and aprovd The minit of last meeting Thare Beeing no futher buisness a Jornd to meet at night met at Candle light

had Preaching by the moderator Then a Journd

met Sunday at Eleven A.M. Had Preaching by Rev. Thos McCanless Then a Journd by Preyer

   A.S. Stulce CC   *J.B. Trotter md*

Contribute in March $1.03 for State Sunday School Work

Recvd of Salem Bap Church $1.03 for State Sunday School Work

March 18ᵗʰ 1894 B.N. Brooks Sec & Tres [of Sunday School and Colportage Board][32]

---

[32] B.N. Brooks was elected to the Sunday School and Colportage Board of the Ocoee Association at the Association's Executive Committee meeting on November 13, 1893.

Saturday, April 21, 1894

Third Saturday in April 1894

Salem Baptist Church met in Regular Sesion had Preaching by the moderator Then made way for Reception of members and Recvd non Then Called for The minit of last meeting Was Red and aproved Then apointed J.P. Talley as a delegate to The 5ᵗʰ Sunday meeting Then a Journd With Preyr by Brother McCanless to meet at Candle light met had Preaching by The Pastor and a Journd to meet Sunday at Eleven

met had preaching by Brother McCanless and a Journd With Preyr

          A.L. Stulce CC   J.B. Trotter moder

Saturday, May 19, 1894

Third Saturday in May 1894

Salem Church met had preaching by the Mod

there being but few out red ad approved the minit of last

meeting and ajourned to meet Sunday at 11 oclock

met Sunday morning acording to appointment

had preaching By the Mod.r. then made way for reception of members and recived none by motion of the Church a gred to dis pense with Preaching at our next meeting on Sunday morning and have children's day at 11 o clock

and ajourned with Prayer.

          A.L. Stulce C.C.   J.B. Trotter Mod

Saturday, June 16, 1894

Salem Baptist Church met in Regular Sesion June 16ᵗʰ 1894 had Preaching by the moder then Called for Minit of last meeting Red and aproved the Same Then made way for recption of mem and Recvd non Then by motion of the Church agred to hold thir Commune [Communion] meeting June 17ᵗʰ at 3 o clock in the eavning by motion of the Church apointed J.P. Talley Wm Roark J.L. Roark D.J. Alixander and L.H. Stulce as a Comitie to See all the members of Salem Church to See how much Each member thought they ought to pay to the pastor Salrey

then Bro D.B. Roark made a Request of the Church he Said that after Joining this Church that he be Came DisSatisfied and thought he had no Religin and after goin on that way a While he Profess and Joind a nother Church and his request was granted to Erase his name from the Book and a Journd With Preyr to meet June The 17 at 3 met Sunday Eavning had Preaching by Rev Wm Cheek after a bot 10 mints intermision Was given Was Called to gether by singing and eat the lords Super and a Journd

          A.L. Stulce CC   J.B. Trotter Mod

Saturday, July 21, 1894

Third Saturday in July 1894

The Baptist Church of Christ at Salem met in Regular Sesion had Preaching by the Pastor then made way for Reception of members & Recvd non then Called for minit of last meeting

Red and aproved the Same and a journd to meet Saturday night had Preaching Saturday night By the pastor and A journd to meet Sunday

Met Sunday morning at 10 o Clock had Preaching By the maderater and A Jourd With preyer

A.S. Stulce CC   J.B. Trotter md

Saturday, August 18, 1894

Third Saturday in August 1894

Salem Church met had Preaching by the mader

Made way for Reception of members and Recvd Brother Frank Allison as a condidate for Baptism The Clerk Beeing absent

L.H. Stulce was apointed Clerk Pro [tem] *By motion and Second the Church agred to Represent in the Assosiation and the folloing mesegers was apointed J.L. Roark L.H. Stulce J.P. Talley no other buisness and With Prey to meet Sunday at 10 ½ o Clock at the watters edge to at tend to the ordinance of Baptism met and Baptised Bro Frank Allison and Repaird to the Church and had Preaching by A.L. Stulce*

and a Journd With Preyr

L.H. Stulce Pt [Pro tem]   J.B. Trotter moder

Saturday, September 15, 1894

Third Saturday in Septem 1894

Salem Church met had Preaching by the Pastor after Which the Church was Called in Sesion made way for Reception of members and Recvd non Called for minit of last meeting Red and aproved the Same & The pastors time beeing out by motion and Second a gred to hold an Election For the purpos of electing a Pastor for the next yer then went in to an election and J.B. Trotter Was elected for the next yer

No other buis ness a Journd there Was Preaching Saturday night as usual and a Journd to meet Sunday morning

met at 11 o ck Sunday morning had Preaching by the Pastor

and a Journd With Preyr

A.L. Stulce C clerk   J.B. Trotter moderator

Saturday, October 20, 1894

Third Saturday in Octo 1894

Salem Church met had Preaching by Rev. S.H. Johnston after Which the mod Called the Church in Sesion made way for Recption of members and Recvd non Called for minit of last meeting Red and aproved the Same then granted a letter of Dismision to Bro Wesley Millard Thare beeing no futher buisness a Journd to meet Saturday night Thare was Preaching Saturday night as usual a Journd to meet Sunday

Met Sunday had Preaching by Rev S.H. Johnston

the meeting Continued For Sevarl Days and nights and the Doors of the Church was opend frequently but Recvd no adition

  A.S. Stulce Cclerk   J.B. Trotter moder

Saturday, November 17, 1894

Third Saturday in November 94

had no meeting

met Saturday had Preaching by the Pastor thare beeing but Few out no buisness was Done a Journd to meet Sunday

met according to apointment had Preaching by the Pastor and aJournd With Prayr thare Was letters of Recommendating granted to Sister Nancy Haney and Bro John Haney at October meeting and Was not fild away in Octo minit

  A.S. Stulce Cclerk   J.B. Trotter moder

Saturday, December 15, 1894

The Third Saturday in December 1894

Salem Baptist Church met had Preaching by the Pastor

then made way for Reception of members and Recvd Sister Salley Cross By letter Red and aprovd minit of November meeting thare beeing no futher buisnes a Journd Thare was meeting Satur night as usual and a Journd to meet Sunday

met Sunday morning at eleven clk had Preaching by the Pastor and a Journd With Preyr

  A.L. Stulce Clerk   J.B. Trotter moder

1895

Saturday, January 19, 1895

Third Saturday in January had No meeting

Saturday, February 16, 1895

Third Saturday in February had No meeting

Saturday, March 16, 1895

Third Saturday March 1895
Salem Church met Preaching by the mod then made Way for Reception of members and
Recvd non Then Red and aproved minit of Dec meeting thare beeing no futher buis ness a
Journd to meet Saturday nig [night] *there was Preaching Saturday night as usual and a*
Journd to meet Sunday morning met at 11 clk
had Preaching by the mod and a Journd With Preyr
    A.L. Stulce Clerk   *J.B. Trotter mod*

Saturday, April 20, 1895

Third Saturday in Aprl 1895
the Baptist Church of Christ at Salem met had Preaching by the Pastor and then made
way for Recption of members and Recvd non Called For minit of last meeting Red and
aprovd the Same thare beeing no futher Buisness A Journd to meet Saturday night there
Was Preaching Saturday night as usual By the moder and aJourned to meet Sunday at 11
o clock
met Sunday morning had Preaching by the moder
after Preaching the Church aGreed to hold thier Communeing meeting the next Regular
meeting in May and then aJourned to meet the Third Saturday in May
    A.L. Stulce clerk   *J.B. Trotter moder*

Saturday, May 18, 1895

Third Saturday in May 1895
the Baptist Church of Christ at Salem met had Preach by the mod mde way for Reception
of member and Recvd non
Called for minit of last meeting Red and aproved the Same
by motion and Sec Elected Brother T.J. Cross D.J. Alixander [Alexander] *and A.L. Stulce*
as Decans of Salem Church then a Journd to meet Saturday night met Saturday night Had
Preaching by Bro Brooks and a Journed to meet Sunday
met Sunday at 10 ½ clock and after Ordaining the Deacans
Elected on Saturday had Preaching by Bro Brooks and
ad minsterd the lords Supper and a Journd
    A.L. Stulce Cclerk   *J.B. Trotter mod*

Saturday, June 15, 1895

Third Saturday in June 1895
Salem Baptist Church met had Preaching by Bro W.W. Cheek after Which the moderator
Called the Church in Sesion Made way for Reception of members and Recvd non Called

for minit of last meeting Red and aproved the Same thare beeing no futher buis [ness] *a
Journd to meet Saturday night met had Preaching by moder and a Journd With Preyr until
Sunday morning met had Preaching by the moderator and a Journd With Preyr*

    A.L. Stulce Clerk   *J.B. Trotter moder*

Saturday, July 20, 1895
*Third Saturday in July 1895
Salem Baptist Church met had Preaching by the moder
then made Way for Recption of members and Recvd non
Called for minit of last meeting Red and aproved the Same
thare Beeing no futher buiss* [ness] *A Journd till Sunday
met Sunday at Eleven o clock had Preaching by the mod and
a Journd With Pryr*

    A.S. Stulce Clerk   *J.B. Trotter mod*

Saturday, August 17, 1895
*3ʳᵈ Saturday in August 1895
Salem Baptist Church met had Preaching By the moder
made way for Reception of members and Recvd non Called for minit of last meeting Red
and aprovd the Same then a Journd With Preyr till Sunday met Sunday had Preaching by
mod and a Journd With Benediction by moder*

    A.S. Stulce CC   *J.B. Trotter mod*

Saturday, September 21, 1895
*3ʳᵈ Saturday in September 1895
the Baptist Church met in Salem*

2 *Had Preaching by the mod made Way for Reception of members and Recvd non*

3 *Called for minit of last meeting Red and approved the Same*

4 *Apointed J.L. Roark and L.H. Stulce as Delegates to the Assosiation*

5 *Bro Trotter then Notified The Church that his time Was out. By motion and Sc the Church
Went in to an Electio For the Purpos
of Electing A Pastor For the next yer then Cast Ballot For Pastor and Rev B.N. Brooks Was
Elected Pastor for the next yr
there beeing No Futher Buisness A Journd untell night*

6 *Met Saturday night had Preach By the mod then A Journd tell Sunday*

7 *Met Sunday at eleven clock Had Preaching by Rev A.S. Stulce
A Journd With Preyr By mod*

    A.L. Stulce CC   *J.B. Trotter mod*

There Was no meeting From September untell Dec the church
met in Sesion Dec 15ᵗʰ 1895 Had Preaching By Bro Allen By motion and Sec Bro Allen Was
Elected maderator For the Day the Church Having Called Bro Brooks in September He never
came to our assistance the church then Cast Ballot for Pastor and Elected Bro Allen was
Elected Pastor For the Rest of the yr
thare beeing no Futher Buisness A Journd

      A.L. Stulce clerk   *Rev. Allen mod*

Saturday, December 21, 1895

Dec 21ᵗ '95
the Church met in Sesion had preaching by Bro John Carrall [John Carrell] *the mod*
then Called the Church in Sesion opened the Door of the church & Recvd as Candidates
for Baptism Brerethen W.T. Heaten [Heaton] *J.P. Davis and Sisters Carey Dartey Matie*
Davis and Sister Lias Henry³³ then Bro Allen Said He Wanted to tender his Resignation as
Pastor By motion and Sec the Church aceped his Resignation and Elected John Carrell mod
For an indefinite time and then a Journd

      A.L. Stulce clerk   *John Carell mod*

1896

Saturday, January 18, 1896

Third Saturday in Jan 1896
Salem Church met had Preaching by the moderator Thare beeing but Few out no Buiss
[ness] *was Done then A Journd*
tell Sunday at Eleven met acording to apointment had Preaching by mod by motion & Sc
the Church authorised the mod to Write Bro Curtain to Come & at tend to the Ordinance
of Baptism at our next Regular meeting then a Journd

      A.S. Stulce CC   *John Carall mod*

Saturday, February 15, 1896

3ʳᵈ Saturday in Feb 1896
Salem Baptist Church met in Sesion had Preaching by the mod thare was no buisness
Done a Journd tell night met at Candle light Preaching by the moder and A Journd with
Benediction by Bro Curtain met Sunday at 10 clk at the Waters edg to at tend to the ordi-
nance of Baptism and Bro Curtain Baptised Brethern W.M. [W.T.] *Heaton James Davis*
and Sisters Matie Davis and Lisebeth Henry then Repaird to the Church and Had

---

33   Elizabeth or Lisabeth Henry according to the Church Rolls and the February 1896
minutes.

Preaching by William Curtain [Curton] *and A Journd*
              A.L. Stulce Clerk   *John Carall mod*

thar was no meeting From February tell July the 18ᵗʰ

Saturday, July 18, 1896
[Third Saturday in July 1896]
*the Church met July the 18ᵗʰ and A.L. Stulce was Elected mod for the Day and by motion
and Sec The Church agred to hold an election for the Purpos of Election a Pastor for the
Remainder of the assosiational yr the Church then Cast Balat* [Ballot] *for Pastor and Bro
Grimsby was Elected by a unanimasly vote Then A Journed*
              A.L. Stulce Moder Protem

Thare Was no meeting in Aug 1896

September 12, 1896
The Sec Saturday in Sept 1896
Salem Church met in Sesion had Preaching by moder

2   *heard the Report of the Comite that was apointed at our July meeting to or haul The
      Church Book they Reported that Some of The Breth had been living immorly and also a
      Sister. By motion and Sec the Church Ricvd the Commite*

3   *apointed a commite of 3 namely J.L. Roark J.P. Talley and W.M. Roark to Go and See the
      Persons and invit Them to our
      next meeting*

4   *The Church a gred to Represent in the Assosiation and the foweling Brethern was apointed
      to Bare our letter D.J. Alixander T.J. Cross and A.L. Stulce*

5   *thare beeing no futher buisness A Journd tell night met at Candle lite had Preaching by Bro
      Heaton*

6   *A Journd*

7   *met Sunday had Preaching by J.B. Trotter The meeting Continued For Seaverl Days and
      nights and the foweling Persons Came Forward at Diferent times and Joind the Church as
      Candidates for Baptism Namely Sister Nancey Priddy Besey* [Bessie] *Irwin Carie Darty
      Liley McClanhan Adda Smith Eller Smith Minie Lowe Jenie Friddle Margret Smith
      Alcey Talley and Brother J.N. Smith C.S. Richey J.W. Talley
      Dike Eldridge and Marthey Runians by letter and Nancy Smith by enRollment Then
      met Sunday morning September 27 at 10 at The Waters edge to atend to the Ordinance of
      Baptism and Baptised Margret Smith
      Eller Smith
      Adda Smith*

Alcie Talley
J.W. Talley
Jan Smith
then Repard to the Church and had Preaching by Bro Grimsby
and A Journd

      A.L. Stulce CC   *William Grimsby Mod*

Saturday, October 10, 1896

Sec Saturday in Octo 1896
Salem Baptist Church met in Sesion Preaching by S.H. Helton
in Absens of the Pastor Bro Helton was Elected moderator for the Day then maid way for
Reception of members recvd non Called for minit of Sep meeting Red and aproved the same
then Called for Report of commite that was apointed to Go and See the Persons Who had
been Reported to the Church
they said they had Seen some of them and they ask to give them
a nother meeting and thier Request was granted Bro Mack Rark [Roark] *came and*
ask the church to forgive him and She done so then Relievd the comite of going to see
Sister Salley Erwin [Irwin] *and apointed Sister Vick* [Victoria] *Roark to go and See her*
then a journd tell night met Saturday night had Preaching by Bro Helton then a Journd
to meet Sunday morning at the waters edg to atend to the ordinance of Baptism Met
acording to apointmet and baptised Bro Dike Eldridge Sisters Bessey Erwin [Irwin] *Liley*
McClahanane [McClanahan] *then Repaird to the Church and had Preaching by bro*
Helton and a Journd

      A.L. Stulce clerk   *S.H. Helton Mod Protem*

Saturday, November 14, 1896

Sec Saturday in Novem 1896
Salem Church met in Sesion had Preaching by mod
made way for Reception of members and Recvd non Red
and aproved minit of last meeting Called for Report of commite that was to go and see the
bros and Sisters Sister Vick [Victoria] *Roark said She had Sen Sister Irwin and said she*
was sorry She had done rong and wanted the Church to forgive her by motion and Sc the
Church forgave her gave the male comite a nother month then A Journd tell night met
Saturday night Preaching by the moderator and A Journd tell Sunday
met Sunday had Preaching by the Pastor and a Journd

      A.L. Stulce clerk   *William Grimsly Mod*

Saturday, December 12, 1896

Sec Saturday in Dec 1896

Preaching by The moderator then made way for Reception of members & recvd non the Clerk beeing absent by motion and Secd J.L. Roark was apointed clerk protem Then gave the Commite a nother month to See The Brothers and Sisters thare beeing no futher buisness a Journd With preyr by Brother Helton met Saturday night had Preaching by S.H. Helton and a Journd With Preyr to meet Sunday met Sunday had Preaching by the Pastor and Closed

A.L. Sutlce [Stulce] cc   *Wm Grimsly moderator*

1897

Saturday, January 9, 1897

Second Saturday in Jan 1897
Salem Baptist Church met in Sesion had Preaching by the moder thare beeing but few out no buisness was done
met Sunday at eleven o clock had Preaching by the moder and then Closed

A.L. Stulce ch clerk   W.B. [W.R.] Grimsly mod

Saturday, February 13, 1897

Secnd Saturday in February 1897
Salem Baptist Church met in Ses had Preaching by the moderator then maid way for Reception of members and recvd non thare beeing no futher buisness closed to meet Sunday met acording to apointment had preaching by the moderator and a Journd With Preyr

A.L. Stulce ch clerk   W.R. Grimsly moderator

Saturday, April 10, 1897

Scnd Saturday in April 1897
Salem Baptist Church met in Sesion had Preaching by the Pastor then maid way for recption of members and recvd non

2   *taken up the cases of John Baker Jacob Bare Rease [Bare] Thos Talley Frank Allison and Excluded them for immoral conduck*

4(3)   *then brought charges a gainst Brother Dike Eldridge and Sister Bessie Erwin [Irwin] who had been reported to the church to have been living immoraley & apointed Bro Wm Roark A.L. Stulce to go and See Bro Eldridge and Sister D.J. Alixander and*
Vick [Victoria] Roark to go and See Bessey Erwin [Irwin] and in vite them to our next meeting thare beeing no futher buisness a Journd tell night met Saturday night Preaching by the moderator a Journd to meet Sunday met Sunday
at 11 eleven had preaching by the moderator and Journd With Preyr

A.L. Stulce c clerk   W. R. Grimsly moderator

Saturday, May 8, 1897

2nd   Saturday in May 1897

Salem Baptist Church met in sesion had preaching by the moderator

2   made way for reception of members and recved non

3   Called for minit of Aprl meeting red and aproved the same

4   Gave the Commite a nother month to see Bro Eldridge

5   taken up the case of Bessie Erwin [Irwin] and excluded her for immoral conduct thare
was meeting as usual Saturday night

met Sunday at 11 Preaching by the moderator and a Journd

      A.L. Stulce c clerk   W.R. Grimsly Mod

Saturday, June 12, 1897

2nd Saturday in June 1897

the Baptist Church at Salem met in Sesion preaching by the
moderator

2   maid way for recption of members and recvd non

3   Called for minit of last meeting red and aproved the Same

4   Gave the commite a nother month to See bro Eldridge in[?]

5   Thare beeing no futher buisness a Journd tell night

Met Saturday night had preaching by the moderator and a Journd to meet Sunday met
Sunday at eleven o clock had preaching by Rev. Phelps   then gave a bout 10 minits
intermision and administerd the lords supper and Closed

      A.L. Stulce c clerk   W.R. Grimsly moder

Saturday, July 10, 1897

2nd Saturday in July 1897

Salem Baptist Church met in Sesion had preaching by the moder then maid way for reception of members and recvd non then heard the report of The Comite they had Seen Bro Dike
Eldridge and he said he was sorey he had done wrong and wanted the church to forgive
him By motion and Sec the church forgave him Thare beeing no futher buisness closed

Met Sunday had preaching by the pastor the pastors time beeing out next meeting he asked
the church to give him the remains of his time. by motion and 2nd the church give him the
remainder of his time and a Journd

      A.L. Stulce c Clerk   W.R. Grimsley Mod

thare was no meeting from Sec Saturday in July untell December The 18

Saturday, December 18, 1897
[Third Saturday in December 1897]

1 *The Church met in Sesion Dec 18ᵗʰ 1897 had preaching by J.B. Trotter*

2 *Elected J.B. Trotter mod protem then made way for Reception of members and recvd Bro John Eldridge as candidate for Baptism thare beeing no futher buisness a Journd the meeting continued untill Dec 20ᵗʰ 97 met Dec The 20 and went into an election and elected J.B. Trotter moder for an indefinite time then Repard to the waters edge to atend to the ordnance and Baptised Johney Eldrige and Then closed*

       A.L. Stulce c clerk   *J.B. Trotter moderator*

1898

Saturday, January 8, 1898

Jan 8ᵗʰ Salem Baptist met in regular Sesion preaching by the moderator then maid way for reception of members red and aproved minit of Dec meeting then granted Bro William Eldridge a letter showing he was once a member of this Church Then beeing no futher buisness a Journd met Saturday with Preaching by the pastor then closed to meet Sunday met acording to apointment preaching by moder
Then closed

       A.L. Stulce clerk   *J.B. Trotter moder*

[No record of Church meeting in February and March, 1898][34]

Saturday, April 9, 1898

Salem Baptist Church met in Reglur Sesion Aprl 9ᵗʰ 1898
had preaching by the moder made way for reception of members an recvd non then Elected Bro J.C. Eldridge Treasurer of the church then a Journd to meet at night
met had preaching by the moder and closed to meet Sunday at eleven o clock met Sunday had preaching by the pastor
and closed

       A.L. Stulce clerk   *J.B. Trotter Mod*

[No record of Church meetings from May through December, 1898][35]

---

[34]   A page of the Salem Church log was left blank, with the apparent intention to complete it later.

[35]   The majority of page left blank, it is assumed that the clerk planned to get back to it.

1899

Saturday, January 14, 1899

Saturday before the 2ⁿᵈ Sunday in Jan. 1899

Salem Baptist Church met in cission, had preaching by The Moderator, and made way for reception of members.

The clerk being absent, S.J. Stulce was elected ass't clerk, and adjourned to meet Saturday night.

Met, had preaching by the Mod'r and adjourned to meet Sunday.

Met Sunday had preaching by The Pastor and adjourned.

S.J. Stulce ass't C.C.   J.B. Trotter, Mod'r

[No record of Church meeting in February, 1899]

Saturday, March 11, 1899

Salem Baptist Church met Saturday March 11, '99

had preaching by the Mod'r and made way for reception of members The election of the present pastor being on record

as being elected for an indefinite time, the church by a unanimious vote agreed to call a pastor at the next regular meeting time Saturday before the 2ⁿᵈ Sunday in Apr. No other business coming before the Church, it adjourned to meet Saturday night. Met Sat. night had preaching by the Mod'r.

and adjourned to meet Sunday. Met according to appointment, had preaching by the Moderator, and adjourned.

S.J. Stulce, ass't. CC.   J.B. Trotter Mod

[No record of Church meetings from April through December, 1899.]

Membership Activities of Salem Baptist Church in the Minutes 1890–1899

	1890	1891	1892	1893	1894	1895	1896	1897	1898	1899	Total
Excluded	0	0	0	0	0	0	0	6	0	0	6
Dismissed	0	0	0	0	1	0	0	0	0	0	1
Letter of Recommendation	1	0	1	0	2	0	0	0	0	0	4
Received by Letter	0	0	1	10	1	0	15	0	0	0	27
Received/ Experience	0	2	0	0	0	0	0	0	0	0	2
Enrollment	0	0	0	0	0	0	0	0	0	0	0
Baptized	0	2	3	19	1	0	13	1	0	0	39
Restored	0	0	0	0	0	0	0	0	0	0	0
Dropped from the book	0	0	0	0	0	0	0	0	0	0	0
Letters rescinded	0	0	0	0	0	0	0	0	0	0	0
Exclusion rescinded	0	0	0	0	0	0	0	0	0	0	0
Candidates for Baptism	0	0	2	5	1	5	1	1	0	0	15

Activities tabulated from the Minutes of Salem Baptist Church.

PROGRAM:

SATURDAY.

9:00 a. m.   Devotional Exercise   G. J. Lewis.
9:30 a. m.   Duties of Superintendent. F. J Hoge
10:00 a. m. Does God require a minister to attend Sunday School when convenient Rev. D. W. Padgett.
10:30 a. m. Sermon. T. E. Rowlands.
1:30 p. m.   Can we interest both old and young in Sunday School? If so, how? Rev. Lewis Carter.
2:00 p. m.   Mission work in Sunday School. R. T. Rutherford.
2:30 p. m.   Will God hold parents responsible for not taking their children to Sunday School? S. J. Stulce.
4:00 p. m.   Report of Sunday Schools.
7:00 p. m.   Sermon. Rev. N. Blevins.

PROGRAM:

SUNDAY

9:30 a. m.   Sunday School Rally.
10:00 a. m. What relation does the Sunday School bear to the church? Rev. D. H. Wood.
10:30 a. m. Duty of parents in training their children at home. Mrs. J. G. Campbell.
11:00 a. m. Sermon. D. W. Padgett.
2:00 p. m.   What would be the result if money spent for fines in James county be used for Sunday School purposes? Esq. J. H. Smith.
2:30 p. m.   Is any community what God would have it be without a Sunday school? J. E. Conner.
3:00 p. m.   What Christian people accomplish when properly united. C. G. Cross and C. E. McClanahan.

By order of Executive Board,
        S. J. STULCE, Sec'y.

Sunday School Program for September 26–27, 1903
The James County Sunday School Institute met with Salem Church on the last weekend of September 1903. Although Sunday schools are seldom mentioned in the minutes of Salem Baptist Church, evidence such as this Sunday school program suggests that Sunday schools were not always recorded in the minutes. As the program above illustrates, Sunday schools were often all day affairs involving numerous preachers and the entire congregation of Salem Baptist Church.

Chapter Five
Salem Baptist Church
1900–1909

The new century began at Salem Baptist Church the same way the preceding century concluded, with J.B. Trotter as pastor and only two meetings in January and March for the entire year. Although the church had agreed in March 1899 to elect a new pastor in April, there were no other meetings in 1899. There was no mention of the church planning to elect a new pastor in the minutes of the two meetings the church had in 1900.

The first order of business in the twentieth century was to prefer charges against a member and withdraw fellowship from him on his own confession. No church business was transacted at the March meeting. There would be preaching by John Gross on Sunday. Brother Gross would preach at Salem again in February 1903. He would also preach and be moderator for the day for the re-election of T.J. Hoge in September of that year.

Salem Baptist Church would not meet at all in 1901 and only met in December in 1902. At that December meeting, J.C. Smith would act as moderator pro tem and S.J. Stulce would be elected clerk pro tem. T.J. Hoge was elected pastor and J.M. Roark was elected permanent clerk. The use of the term "permanent" is unclear. J.M. Roark was re-elected in September 1903. F.A.B. Roark was elected in September 1904, serving as clerk until 1911 when J.M. Roark would again be elected clerk and treasurer.

In February 1903, the Church would hold a protracted meeting for two weeks and receive seventeen for Baptism. The names of those received were not listed. Only five members were baptized on May 3rd at the meeting set aside as a day of baptism. No other members were listed as baptized in 1903.

Despite the lack of meetings for the past five years, Salem Church in 1903 demonstrated a concerted effort to conduct business as usual and a renewed attempt to have an effective, solidified church in full fellowship. For the first time in nine years the church would have all twelve meetings during the year. In April, a committee was appointed to look after the conduct of the members. At the meeting held the week after the day of baptism in May, the church appointed six committees: Committee on Home Mission—Joe Roark, Wilkie Eldridge, Rosa Wrinkle; Committee on Sunday School—Otis Cross, J.L. Roark, Jeff Cross; Committee on Foreign Mission—Jeff Stulce, Laura Roark, Grace Stulce; Ocoee Missions— Mack Roark, John Davis, Ellen Stulce; Orphan's Home—Jack Eldridge, Lillie Roark, Freeland Defriese: State Missions— Berry Roark*, Sammie Smith, Mamie Smith, Burk Roark.

In June, the church was reported not in fellowship. A committee was appointed to settle some hardness between two members. A committee was appointed to see another member and report at the next meeting. On Sunday, Salem Baptist Church administered the Lord's Supper. The church then extended the hand of church fellowship to Brother Burk Roark. Burk Roark had been appointed to the State Missions Committee in May. The only business of Salem Church at the July 1903 meeting, after preaching and approval of the previous minutes, was to consider again the moral conduct of the members.

At the August meeting of Salem Baptist Church, following devotional exercises and the reading of the minutes, the church appointed a committee consisting of T.J. Hoge, Joe Roark, Jack Eldridge and J.M. Roark to write a letter of sympathy to Friendship Church and give it to the clerk. On Sunday they read and approved the letter. The Friendship meeting house had burned to the ground in 1902. The church had resumed its meetings at the local schoolhouse, as the congregation had from the beginning of the church in 1854 until the church building was erected in1857. Having had their own church building burn while Friendship Church was originally building its meeting house, the congregation at Salem was sympathetic to their sister church's plight.

T.J. Hoge was re-elected pastor in September 1903. He would tender his resignation in December, yet he would remain pastor of Salem Baptist Church until September 1904. Rev. Tomie Lewis would preach in December and be moderator of the day at the second Saturday meeting in January. Sister Lillie Roark became the first woman to be appointed as a delegate to the Ocoee Association from Salem Church in September 1903. She would be appointed as an alternate delegate in 1904, when Ellen Stulce would be appointed one of the delegates.

In December 1903 the Church, on motion and second, changed the meeting from the second Saturday of the month to the fourth Saturday. In January, Salem Church would meet on both the second and fourth Saturdays. Jeff Stulce, Berry (F.A.B.) Roark, and J.M. Roark were ordained as deacons at the second Saturday

---

*   F.A.B. Roark, as he was known to the community.

meeting in January, having been elected in December. Jack Eldridge was elected deacon as well in December 1903, but was not ordained with the others. At the fourth Saturday meeting, the deacons were requested to collect what was left on the pastor's salary from the year before. A committee of Burk Roark, Berry Roark, J.P. Talley and Johnnie Cross had been appointed in October to take collection for the pastor. It is not clear what happened to the committee. Throughout the remaining years of Salem Baptist Church as recorded in the existing minutes, the Deacons (later the Board of Deacons) would increasingly be given the decision-making power of the Church.

The only business done from February through June 1904 was the receiving of, and extending the hand of fellowship to, Sister S.E. Allison, and a communion service in June. There were no meetings in July and August. In September, L.E. Rowland was elected pastor. Salem Baptist Church appointed delegates to the Ocoee Association and also appointed alternates. It was the first, and only, time recorded in the minutes when the Church appointed alternate delegates to the association.

Salem Church met the fourth Sunday in September 1904 after a general review of the Sunday school. Oddly, the Church minutes rarely mentioned Sunday school, although there seemed to periodically be a renewed effort in the minutes to maintain a Sunday school. Evidence of Sunday school outside of the minutes indicates that Sunday schools were not always recorded in the minutes. Sunday school would not be mentioned in the minutes again until March 1907.

Salem Baptist Church held no meetings in 1905 until June when the "former effort of entertaining the Ocoee Association was withdrawn." Whether the church was contemplating offering to host an associational meeting or a Fifth Sunday meeting is not known. Salem Baptist Church had been host for the Ocoee Association meeting in 1869 and 1876. There is no mention of the two meetings in the Salem Church minutes, and the Ocoee Minutes do not specifically refer to Salem Baptist Church.

J.E. Eldridge was elected treasurer at the June meeting, at which Salem Church would revert back to meeting on the second Saturday of the month. The pastor's salary was taken into consideration. Salem Baptist Church agreed to pay L.E. Rowland thirty-six dollars a year. The clerk was directed to see the members and ask how much each would pay.

The average annual salary paid to preachers outside the big cities of the United States in 1911 was $573. H.D. Huffaker, of the Ocoee Association, also reported that the average salary in the association in 1910 was $457. After excluding the six churches of the Ocoee Association paying $1000 or more to their pastor, the average dropped to $177 per church. The average salary paid by all association churches in 1900 had been $252, illustrating an increase in pastor's salaries during the decade.[1] Smaller churches such as Salem operated with the ongoing pressure of the inability to pay their pastors the salary they deserved.

At the August 1905 meeting of Salem Church an effort was made toward repairing the meeting house. The matter was put before the church and without further investigation the members agreed to repair the meeting house. There would be no further mention of repairing the church house until April 1909 when a committee would be appointed to make repairs. During the discussions throughout 1909, the church would be faced with the choice of whether to repair the meeting house or build a new one. If repairs were made in 1905, the repairs could have possibly deteriorated or further wear and decay had done damage to the house. It is also possible that work was never done in 1905 for one reason or another.

S.J. Stulce and F.A.B. Roark were appointed in September as delegates to the Ocoee Baptist Association and the church made a collection of one dollar for the minutes of the association. The two delegates were also appointed as committeemen for the general benevolence funds for the ensuing year. A collection was made for the orphan's house and totaled 38 cents. After re-electing L.E. Rowland as pastor, the church adjourned.

With no business or services in October, the church adjourned to meet the second Saturday in November when the congregation called for the report of the treasurer and appointed more members to the mission committee. There was no further church business transacted in November. Salem Baptist Church again called for the report of the treasurer and appointed more members to the mission committee at the December meeting. Missions would not be mentioned again, nor a collection taken for missions, until August of 1908.

In February 1906, a committee of John Cross, Berry (F.A.B.)Roark, Mamie Smith, and Ellen Stulce was appointed to investigate the members charged with dancing or non-attendance. The clerk was appointed to communicate with the non-attendees. The report of the committee was called for in March and J.L. Roark, A.L. Stulce, and Nannie Allison were added to the committee to talk to the named members and investigate the dancing charges. At the May meeting of Salem Baptist Church, the church read and approved the previous minutes after which the committee on the conduct of members reported that their business had been left unattended. By motion and second the charges against the members for dancing or any other act was withdrawn on their statement given to the Church or its representatives. On Sunday of the February meeting, the only business was to switch the church meetings from the second Saturday to the first Saturday of each month, changing the church's pattern of switching from the second to the fourth Saturday.

The minutes report that S.J. Stulce gave his resignation, which the church granted, in March. The only known position that S.J. Stulce had been elected to, and from which he had not been released, was assistant church clerk. J.M. Roark, and later F.A.B. Roark, had been meticulous, as well as dedicated, in carrying out their duties as church clerk, making an assistant clerk unnecessary. S.J. Stulce had not acted as clerk for several years. Stulce was not mentioned again in the minutes of Salem Baptist Church until December 1914, when he was granted a letter of dismissal in full fellowship.

In August, there being no business on Saturday, the church was adjourned to meet Sunday. On Sunday, after preaching by the pastor, the church adjourned following prayer and song. This is the first evidence in the minutes of singing at Salem Baptist Church although singing was a powerful and critical element of the church.After the August meeting, the church would not meet again until February 1907. Rev. Robert Phelpps would become pastor at that meeting. Rev. Phelpps would not be officially elected until August of 1908. L.E. Rowland would return as pastor in 1911 and remain pastor until 1916, the year following the end of the surviving minutes.

Under the leadership of Rev. Phelpps, the church launched another concentrated effort to maintain a church worthy of worship of the Lord. Eleven people were baptized in February and eight in May. The only new members in 1907 known in the minutes to join the church would be one woman in May not specified by name and the six people baptized in October "which were added to the Church." Following the baptism in May, Salem Baptist Church observed the Lord's Supper.

Rev. Phelpps began his pastoral duties in February with a sermon on Saturday from Exodus 14–15. Rev Phelpps was apparently a forceful Baptist preacher. The clerk, unlike previous years, not only recorded the scripture for the sermon on numerous occasions, but would note that the pastor preached an interesting or excellent sermon. Reading Exodus 14 and 15 in the King James Version, one can hear Rev. Phelpp's voice echo off the walls of the small church building, his voice rising as he read and told of the Children of Israel's flight from Egypt. The small congregation sits spellbound in reverent awe, hearing this vibrant preacher relay the story of the parting of the sea. The sermon was so effective that eleven members were baptized. After baptism the congregation met at the church. The pastor spoke on the origin of the church. Whether he spoke of the origin of the original church or of Salem Church, it was a fitting end to a weekend of worship.

In March, after an "interesting sermon," there was no business coming before the church. On Sunday there was a lecture on Sunday school work, after which the pastor presided. A collection was made on the pastor's salary. April of 1907 brought a reading of the church covenant and the rules of decorum. Rev. Phelpps would preach another excellent sermon in May. When the invitation was extended, a woman came forward to give her statement and confession of accepting Christ as her Savior and was extended the hand of fellowship. The name of the woman was not mentioned. After a collection of $1.30 was made on the pastor's salary, the pastor called for all contemplating baptism to make it known, and they adjourned to meet Sunday at the water's edge.

At the water's edge, the eight people having made their intentions known the day before came forward to be baptized. The minutes do not state whether the woman coming forward on Saturday was one of the eight baptized on Sunday. The congregation met back at the church where there was preaching by the pastor then a fifteen minute intermission. Following the intermission, the church met and conducted the Lord's Supper.

When Salem Baptist Church met in June 1907, the church was called to order by song and prayer. Sunday school was held on Sunday. After Sunday school, the pastor gave a lecture on Sunday school work. The only business done in July was to elect J.A. Shropshire treasurer of the church. No business was done at the first of two August meetings.

The church met again on the last day of August. Owen Smith, Floyd Smith, J.W. Roark, and Berry (F.A.B.) Roark were elected delegates to the Ocoee Baptist Association. However, the only business at the September meeting was again to elect delegates. The same four delegates were elected. October brought the baptism of six people who were added to the church. The names were not listed in the minutes. There was no business done at the November meeting and no meeting in December.

The church would not meet again until June 1908, with Rev. E. Edwards presiding and Sister Phoebe Cannon granted a letter of dismissal. After not meeting in July, the church met in August and elected Rev. Phelpps pastor at the first meeting noted in the minutes in which the clerk was elected moderator for the day and signed as both moderator and clerk. A committee consisting of Will Stulce, Martha Ellen Allison, Owen Smith and Nettie Smith was organized for the work of missions. The only business done at Salem Baptist Church for the rest of the year was the enrollment of Jennie Eldridge by letter as a member in full fellowship at the second August meeting, the granting of a letter of dismissal to Mattie Darharty in November, and the election of J.B. Trotter as pastor for

1909 in December. There was no business done in September, and no meeting in October.

Salem Baptist Church began 1909 by deciding at the January meeting to come to some conclusion as to the pastor's salary. At the February meeting, as was usual when the church would consider a call for funds, a treasurer, J.M. Roark, was elected. No mention was made of a decision on the pastor's salary. The first collection made for the pastor's salary would be in August. There was no meeting in March. Rhoda J. Hixon was granted a letter of dismissal in April.

The only other business done in April was to appoint John Cross, J.M. Roark, and Owen Smith as a committee to repair the church building. The committee did not report until June, when J.M. Roark would state that the committee would be ready to report at the next meeting on July 10. Their decision was to call a meeting on Saturday, July 17, requesting that all members possible be present. There was no record of the meeting on the 17th, and in August the committee requested more time.

When the August meeting was extended, the church had a conference during which they decided to build a new house of worship. A soliciting committee was appointed which included Berry (F.A.B.) Roark, Will Stulce, Jess Hindman, Jim Allison, Floyd Smith, Laura Moon, Sallie Cross, Jennie Stulce, Ether Eldridge, and Nettie Smith. The committee on repairing the church house reported in September that the committee had failed to meet. On Sunday after preaching, more members were added to the building committee and the church decided to begin work. There is no indication in the minutes as to whether the committee on repairing the church building and the soliciting committee were combined into a single building committee. Yet it is entirely possible that the small congregation as a whole became involved in building the new church house.

As the church wrestled with the decision between repairing or rebuilding the meeting house, they were also concerned with the conduct of the members. At the August meeting, a committee was appointed to look after the conduct of the members. The church also authorized the clerk to write all non-attending members to attend meetings or ask for their letter. It was usual for Salem Baptist Church, when funds were needed, to authorize the clerk to write all non-attending members.

Not only was this an attempt, in conjunction with looking after the conduct of its members, to strengthen the fellowship of the church, but it was also to get all members to attend meetings and services. The end result was to have as many members present as possible when it was time to take up a collection. In 1909, Salem Baptist Church contributed $3.25 to missions, $1.00 to the orphans, and an undisclosed amount for the pastor's salary.

On the final Sunday night of the extended meeting in August, the revival closed with twenty-two additions to the church. Ten of the new members were baptized on August 15, and thirteen on August 20, the last day of the revival. This was by far the most members to join the church at an extended meeting in decades. The minutes of the August 20 meeting mention that twelve members were baptized. However, when the minutes later listed the members who were baptized, thirteen names were listed.

At the September meeting, while the church was concerned with having enough members on the building committee, Bro. Owen Smith was liberated to exercise himself as a minister of the Gospel. The clerk was authorized to write a recommendation showing that he had been liberated by the church. After serving his two year ministerial apprenticeship, Bro. Owen Smith would, in 1911, become the first pastor known to have been ordained at Salem Baptist Church.

In October, by motion and second the church accepted the apportionment of the Ocoee Association and agreed to raise the amount and more if they could. At the September meeting of the Ocoee Association, the Special Committee on Apportionment for Benevolent Causes set up a budget for how much the association would contribute to various causes, committees, and functions. The apportionment committee had divided the budgeted amounts into what should be required of each church in the association. Although it is not certain how the committee arrived at the amounts for each church, it was common practice for the association to keep track of how much its churches paid their pastors and it is probable that they used those totals to compute the percentage each church should contribute. The apportionment amount for Salem Church was twenty dollars. Following the apportionment list in the minutes of the Ocoee Association, it was stated by the apportionment committee that they "would urge that a subscription be circulated in each church and that a collection on the same be taken and forwarded at least once each quarter.[2]

Salem Baptist Church met on Saturday, October 9 at the Conner Cemetery to clean the graveyard. They had services and dinner at the cemetery and then proceeded to work on the graves. After accepting the apportionment of the association on Saturday night they adjourned to meet Sunday. Doing so, they took up a collection of $1.35 for missions. In November, it being the month set apart by the State Board of Missions to contribute to the orphans, the church made a collection of one dollar.

In December, the church held an election by ballot and re-elected J.B. Trotter as pastor. Following the election, they agreed to meet at the Salem school building on Saturday night. After meeting at the school house on Saturday night, the congregation agreed to meet back at the old church house Sunday morning if the weather would permit. With the deteriorating condition of the church house, the congregation had decided to build a new building at the August meeting. Yet in September, the committee on repairing the church house reported that the committee had failed to meet. It would seem there were two committees—one to repair the present building and one to see to the building of the new church building. Apparently the current structure was in such a condition that holding services there during inclement weather was inadvisable. On Sunday, the weather was bad and the church failed to assemble.

Letter to the Ocoee Association

State of Tennessee }
James County } We the Baptist Church of Christ at Salem
to the Ministers & Messengers composing the Ocoee Association
greeting when convened with <u>Cookston Creek Church Polk County Tenn.</u>

Dear Brethren we send as Messengers Our beloved Brethren—
A.L. Stulce G. W. Rodgers W.B. Haney and W.M. Roark whom
we pray you receive to be with you in all of your Godly Conversation.

Our statistics are as follows

Ordained Ministers	1
Licentiate	0
Recieved by Baptism	41
" " by letter	4
" " by Enrollment	3
Dismissed by Letter	3
Restored	2
Deceased	2
total	166
Meeting dayes	4 Saturday
Post office	Birchwood

The 1874 letter to the Ocoee Association from Salem Baptist Church. Churches in the Ocoee Association were required to submit a letter to the Association with the delegates to the Association's yearly meeting.

Minutes of Salem Baptist Church
1900–1909

Saturday, January 13, 1900

Saturday before the 2ⁿᵈ Sun in Jan. 1900

Salem Baptist Church met. Had preaching by Mod'r, adopted previous minites, and then by motion and second The Church agreed to prefer charges against, and also to withdraw fellowship from Bro Wm Irwin on his own confession of immoral conduct. There coming nothing else before the body adjourned to meet Sunday.

Met Sunday had preaching by mod'r, and adjourned

     S.J. Stulce asst CC   *Rev J.B. Trotter Mod'r*

[No record of Church meeting for February, 1900.]

Saturday, March 10, 1900

Saturday before the 2ⁿᵈ Sunday in March 1900

Salem Baptist Church met, had preaching by Mod'r, adopted previous minute, and made way for reception of members. No other business coming before the body adjourned to meet Sat. Night. Met Sat. Night had preaching by Mod'r, and adjourned to meet Sunday.

Met Sunday had preaching by Bro John Gross, and adjourned

     S.J. Stulce ass't CC   *Rev. J.B. Trotter Mod'r*

[No record of Church meetings April through December, 1900]

1901

[No record of any Church meetings at Salem Church in 1901.]

1902

[No record of Church meetings at Salem from January through November, 1902]

Sunday Dec, 14, 1902

Salem Church met in conference and elected Bro J.C. Smith Mod'r protem and S.J. Stulce clerk protem. Then went into an election to elect a pastor and clerk. Bro. T.J. Hoge was elected Pastor by a unanimous vote, and Bro. J.M. Roark permanent clerk, and adjourned.

     S.J. Stulce clerk protem   *J.C. Smith Mod'r*

1903

Saturday, January 10, 1903

Saturday Before the 2ⁿᵈ Sunday in January 1903
Salem Baptist Church met. Thir being but few present had no preaching met Saturday
Knight preaching by the pastor and Closed to meet Sunday at 10: 30 A.M.
Met Sunday had Preaching by the Pastor. then Closed.

      J.M. Roark C Clerk   *T.J. Hoge Mod'r*

Saturday, February 28, 1903

Saturday February 28ᵗʰ 1903
Salem Baptist Church met Preaching by the pastor
their being but few present did not transact any Church Business. Then Closed to meet
Sunday at 10: 30 A.M.
Met Sunday Preaching by Rev John Gross. it being the time for our protracted meating the
meating was continued for two weeks during This meating the Church Rec'd 17 members
for Baptism

      J.M. Roark Clerk   *T.J. Hoge Pastor*

Sunday, March 8, 1903

Sunday February [March]³⁶ *the 8ᵗʰ 1903*
Salem Church met had preaching by the Pastor
Saturday being a bad day had no Preaching.
The Church desided to have a series of meatings to begin
the 4ᵗʰ Sat in Febry [March]. *Then Closed.*

      J.M. Roark Clerk   *T.J. Hoge Mod*

Saturday, April 11, 1903

Saturday before the Second Sunday in April
Salem Church met. Preaching by the modr— The Clerk being absent Bro John Roark was
elected Clerk Pro [tem] *Their was a comittie appointed to look after the conduct of the*
members the committie was Bro Jeff Stulce Berrie [F.A.B.] *Roark & Bro Burk Roark. then*
Closed to meat Sunday to tend to the ordinance of Baptisam at 10 oclock Met Sunday at the
waters Edge and Baptised Bro John Davis Bro Odos [Otis] *Cross and Sister Grace Stulce &*

---

36   It is assumed that March is meant since it follows a meeting on the fourth Saturday
    in February. The possibility that the reports were switched is further confused by
    the fact that both February and March had the second Sunday on the 8ᵗʰ of the
    month and fourth Saturday on the 28th.

Elen [Ellen] *Stulce. Then met at the Church for preaching. Preaching by the mod'r and then extended the hand of Church fellow Ship to those that were Baptised*
Then Closed

      J.M. Roark Clerk   *T.J. Hoge Mod'r*

Saturday, May 3, 1903

Salem Church met sunday may the 3rd at the watter to attend to the ordinance of Baptisam and Baptised Bro Fredey Defris [Freelen DeFriese] *and Sister Laura Roark Lillie Roark Wilkie Eldridge & Sister Rosie Wrinkle after which met at the Church Preaching by the Modr and extended the hand of Church fellow ship to those that were Baptised*
Then Closed

      J.M. Roark Clerk   *T.J. Hoge Mod*

Sunday, May 10, 1903

Salem Church met Sunday May the 10th Preaching By the Modr Then mad way for Reception of membrs and recd none. Red and Approved the previous minuets. Their was Six commiatties appointed.
First on Home Mission Joe Roark Wilkie Eldridge Rosa Wrinkle
Second on Sunday School Odos [Otis] *Cross J.L. Roark Jeff Cross*
3rd   *committie on Foreign mission Jeff Stulce Laura Roark and Grace Stulce*
4th   *Ocoee Missions Mack Roark John Davis Ellen Stulce*
5th   *Orphants Home Jack Eldridge Lillie Roark Freeland Defriese.*
6th   *State missions Berry* [F.A.B.] *Roark Sammie Smith Mamie Smith Burk Roark motion and Second that the Rules of Decorum be Red at our next regular meating and that we have a roll coll and Comunion the next meating Then Closed*

      J.M. Roark Clerk   *T.J. Hoge Modr*

Saturday, June 13, 1903

Salem Church Met the Second Saturday in June
Preaching by the Pastor. Red and approved the minuet of the previous Meating. The Church was ask whether it was in Fellow Ship or not. And was reported not in Fellow Ship. Their was a commitie appointed to Settle Some hardness Between Sister Eliza Priddy and Sister Victoria Roark Report of commitie on the living of members. the Comittie Reported Bro Charly Pendergrass and Bro Keys and Bro Dike Eldridge not living Right and Sister Lillie McClanahan. committie appointed to See Sister McClanahan J.P. Talley Sister Roark and Sister Stulce. Bro Bill Talley Reported not liveing Right. the committie was to See Bro Talley and report next meeting
No other Buisiness. Then Closed to meet Saturday Knight.
Met Saturday Knight Preaching by the Pastor

Then closed to meet Sunday at 10:30
Met Sunday Preaching by the past or and adminstered the Lords Supper then extended the
hand of Church fellow ship to Bro Burk Roark then Closed

      J.M. Roark CC   *T.J. Hoge Pastor*

Saturday, July 11, 1903

Salem Church Met the Second Saturday in July Preaching by the Pastor then minuets of the
prvious meating was Red and approved Report of committie on Sister Lillie McClanahan
Report that She was not fit to belong to the Church
on Motion and Second the Church withdrew Fellow Ship From her. on motion and Second
Bro Charley Pendergrass was granted another monthe to make his acknolage ments.
Committie to See Sister Eliza Priddy Bro Hoge Bro J.P. Taley [Talley] *and Sister Alison*
[Allison] *no other Buisness The Church Closed to meet Sunday at 11 O Clock*
Met Sunday Preaching By the Pastor then Closed.

      J.M. Roark C.Clerk   *T.J. Hoge Modr*

Saturday, August 8, 1903

Salem Aug 8ᵗʰ 1903 [Second Saturday]
The Church met for business at Eleven Oclock the Pastor presiding. After devotional exer-
cises the minutes of the Previous meeting were red and approved.
Bro Charley Pendergrass's case was laid over till Sunday.
The committie to See Sister Eliza Priddy was granted another month. Committie to See Bro
Bill Talley was releiced and another appointed consisting of Bro J.P.Talley L.H. Stulce
and Bro Jack Eldridge. By motion and Second Their was a committie appointed to wright
out our Sympathy to Sister Friend Ship Church and Send to the clerk committie Bro Hoge
Joe Roark Bro Jack Eldridge and J.M. Roark. The Church invited Bro Rolen [Rowland] *to*
help hold our Protracted meeting
to begin at our next Regular meeting.
No other Buisness adjourned to meet Saturday Knight.
Met Saturday Knight Preaching by the Pastor then Closed to meet Sunday. Met Sunday
Preaching by the Modr. the Church was Called in Session Red and approved our Sympathy
to Sister Friend Ship Church.
No other Buisness then Closed.

      J.M. Roark Clerk   *T.J. Hoge Modr*

Saturday, September 12, 1903

Salem Sept. 12 1903
The Church met for buisiness at Eleven Oclock. The Pastor presiding. after devotional exer-
cises the minnets of the previous meating were red and approved. Bro Charley Pendergrass

was granted an other month to make his acknolledge ments. the committie to See Sister
Priddy was granted an other month. Bro Bill Talley was granted an
other month to mke his acknolledge ments to the Church. It being the time to Elect a pastor. Bro J.P. Talley was Elected Modr for the Day and J.M. Roark Clerk. Then went into an
Election to Elect a pastor for the insewing year. Bro Hoge was Elected by a unanimous vote.
No other business then Closed to meet Saturday Knight Met Saturday Knight Preaching by
Bro Rolen [Rowland]. Met Sunday Preaching Bro John Gross. Bro Gross was Elected modr
for the day. the Church was called in Session to Elect a Clerk and to appoint a delegation
to the Assosiation J.M. Roark was Elected Clerk and Bro Jeff Stulce Bro Joe Roark and Sister
Lillie Roark Bro Hoge was Elected Deligates. it Being the time for our Protracted meeting
the meeting was carried on for a few days Then Closed

     J.M. Roark Clerk   T.J. Hoge Modr

Saturday, October 24, 1903

4th Saturday in Oct 1903
Salem Baptist Church met for buisiness the Pastor presiding
after Devotional Exesise. The minnets of the Previous meeting were red and approved.
Bro Charley Pendergrass s Case was disposed of on motion and Secon The Church withdrew
Fellow Ship from Bro Pendergrass and Bro Bill Taley [Talley] and Sister Eliza Priddy.
Sister Elizabeth Eldridge Called for her letter the same was granted Committie appointed
to take collection for the Pastor consisting of Bro Burk Roark & Bro Berrie [F.A.B.] Roark
Bro J.P. Talley and Bro Johnie Cross.
no other Business adjourned to meet Sunday the Pastor being Sick haad no preaching on
Sunday

     J.M. Roark CC   T.J. Hoge Modr

Sunday, November 8, 1903

Salem Nov 8th 1903
The Church mjet for buisness at E11 Oclock The Pastor Presiding after devtional exercise
The minutes of the previous meeting were red and approved. No other business comeing
before the Church adjourned to meet Sunday.

Saturday, December 12, 1903

Salem Church met the Second Saturday in Dec 1903
Preaching by the Pastor. Red and approved Previous minute of Saturday. Then took up the
case of Bro Dike Eldridge and Bro Key [s] Bro Wm Roark was appointed to See Bro Eldridge
and the Clerk was ordered to write Bro Key [s] in regard to his Charges. Bro Key [s] and
Sister Key [s] Called for letters the Church did not grant the letters their was Charges
against Bro Key [s] and Sister Key [s] is not a member of This Church. On motion and

Secon the following Deacons were appointed Bro Jack Eldridge Bro Jeff Stulce Bro Berrie
[F.A.B.] *Roark and J.M. Roark.*
No other buisniess adjourned to meet Sunday.
Met Sunday Preaching by Rev Tomie Lewis. Then Closed
   J.M. Roark Clerk   *T.J. Hoge Modr*

Bro Hoge Tendered the Church his resignation as Pastor.

1904

Saturday, January 9, 1904

Salem Church met the Second Saturday in Jany 1904 had preaching by Rev Tomie Lewis by motion and Second Bro Lewis was Elected modr for the Day. Adopted previous minuets. and on Request of Bro Dike Eldridge through Bro Talley The Church withdrew Fellow ship from Bro Dike Eldridge. laid Bro Keys Case over till next meeting. The Church agreed to ordain deacons Sunday. Met Sunday the Pastor Presiding and ordained the following Decons Bro Jeff Stulce Berrie [F.A.B.] *Roark and J.M. Roark. On motion and Second the Church changed the meeting from the 2nd Sat to the 4th Saturday. Adjourned*
   J.M. Roark CC   *T.J. Hoge Modr*

Saturday, January 23, 1904

Salem Church met the 4th Saturday in January for buisiness at 11 oclock the pastor Presiding after devotional Exercises The following business was transacted. Red and approved minutes of previous meeting. Bro Keys Case was laid over another month. The following comittie was appointed to See Some of the Members J.M. Roark S.J. Stulce Joseph Roark The Deacons was requested to collect the Subscription on last years [Pastor's] *sallery and Report at the February meeting*
No other buisiness adjourned to Meet Sunday. Met Sunday had preaching by the pastor made way for Reception of members and Recd none. Then Closed.
   J.M. Roark CC   *T.J. Hoge Modr*

Saturday, February 27, 1904

Salem Church Met the 4th Saturday in February 1904 for buisiness at Eleven O clock Preaching by the Pastor.
No buisines transacted on Sat Then Closed to meet Sunday
Met Sunday Preaching By the Pastor. Red and approved minnets of Previous meeting On Motion and Second Bro Keys
was granted more time to Satisfy the Church

the committie was granted more time to see Bro Defriese.
No other Business then Closed

    J.M. Roark CC   *T.J. Hoge Modr*

Sunday, March 27, 1904

Salem Church Met the 4ᵗʰ Sunday in March Preaching by the Pastor No business transacted.
had no meeting on Saturday on the account of Bad weather.

    J.M. Roark Clerk   *T.J. Hoge Modr*

Saturday, April 23, 1904

Salem Church Met the Saturday in April 1904 for busines at Eleven O Clock the pastor being
absent Bro [illegible] *was Elected Modr for the day The following business was transacted*
Opened the door of the Church and Recd Sister S.E. Alison [Allison] *by letter*
No other business adjourned to meet Sunday.
Met Sunday the Pastor being absent had no meeting.

    J.M. Roark Clerk   *T.J. Hoge Modr*

Sunday, May 28, 1904

Salem Church Met the 4ᵗʰ Sunday in May 1904 for buisiness at Eleven Oclock the Pastor pre-
siding after Devotional Exresise approved minuets of Previous Meeting also Extended the
hand of Church fellowship to sister Alison [Allison] *and agreed to a communion Servise*
at the next meeting. No other Buisiness adjourned

    J.M. Roark Clerk   *T.J. Hoge Modr*

Saturday, June 25, 1904

Salem Church Met the 4ᵗʰ Saturday in June the Pastor Pesiding
Their being but few presint had no Preaching. Met Sunday and had a communion Servise
then adjourned

    J.M. Roark Clerk   *T.J. Hoge Modr*

[No record of Church meetings July and August 1904]

Saturday, September 24, 1904

Salem Church Met the 4ᵗʰ Saturday in Sept, 1904 for buisness pastor presiding after an
excellont Sermon was delivered the church was considered in conference And elected
bro Rowlond [Rowland], *for pastor F.A.B. Roark as clerk, Bro. Burke Roark, Sister Ellen*
Stulce, Berry [F.A.B.] *Roark, as delegates to attend the Ocoee Babtist Association.*

Bro Jeff Stulce Lilly Roark Joe Roark Alternates
there being no other Business adjourned to meet Sunday.

    J.M. Roark Clerk   *T.J. Hoge Mod.*

Salem Church Met the 4ᵗʰ Sunday in Sept, 1904 after a general review of the Sunday School
there was peaching by T.J. Hoge.
then the church was considered in conference. there being no other buisness the Deacons
agreed to collect the pasters salary
Then adjourned

    F.B. [F.A.B.] Roark Clerk

1905

[No record of Church meetings January through May 1905]

Saturday, June 10, 1905

Salem Babtist Church met on Saturday Jun 10ᵗʰ 1905 for buisness after a sermon by Rev L.E.
Rowlande the Church was in consideration of the following buisness Bro. J.E. Eldridge was
elected tres. The former effort of inter taining the Ocoee Assocation was withdrawn The
pastors salary was taken into consideration the Church agreeing to pay her said pastor L.E.
Rowland $36.00 a year. The clerk was appointed to see each member how much they would
pay. Therer being no other buisness omitted the serveses for Sunday
then by motion and second the Church adjourned to meet on
Saturday before the second Sunday in July.

    F.A.B. Roark Clerk   *L.E. Rowlande Mod*

Saturday, July 8, 1905

Salem Church Met on Sat. July 8ᵗʰ 1905 for buieness preaching by the moderator after which
the Church was considered in conference. There being no other busness except the report of
the tres. The previous minute was red and approved. Then adjourned to meet Sunday

    F.A.B. Roark Clerk   *L.E. Rowlande Mod*

July 9ᵗʰ 1905 Met Sunday preaching by the Mod. there being no buisness before the Church
The Congregation was dismissed

    F.A.B. Roark Clerk   *L.E. Rowlande Mod*

Saturday, August 12, 1905

Salem Baptist Church met Aug. 12, 1905 for buisness preaching by the Moderator, after
which the Church was considered in conference. There being no other buisness, before the
Church, except an effort was made toward repairing the Church house. The matter was

put before the Church and without farther investigation agreed to repair the Church house. The previous minutes was read and approved There being no other business by motion and second adjourned to meet Sunday.

      F.A.B. Roark clerk   *L.E. Rowlande Mod*

Met Sunday preaching by the moderator there being no busness before the Church adjourned

      F.A.B. Roark clerk   *L.E. Rowlande Mod*

Saturday, September 9, 1905

Salem Church met Sept 9th 1905 for buisness preaching by the moderator after which the Church was considered in conference The Church appointed S.J. Stulce and F.A.B. Roark as delagates to the Ocoee Baptist Association made a collection of $100, one dollar for minutes of the Association. The delegates was appointed as committemen for the general benovelence funds for the ensuing year. Collection was also made for the orphans house of .38 cents. Then by motion an second adjourned to meet Sunday

Met Sunday preaching by the mod. There being no other buisness except the reelection of the pastor. adjourned

      F.[A.] B. Roark clerk   *L.E. Rowlande Mod*

Saturday, October 7, 1905

Salem Baptist Church met Oct. 7 1905 for buisness preaching by the mod after which the Church was considered in conference there being no other buisness except the services for Sundy was omitted by motion and Second adjourned to meet 2nd Sunday in Nov.

      F.A.B. Roark clerk   *L.E. Rowland mod.*

Saturday, November 11, 1905

Saturday, November 11, 1905

Salem Baptist Church met Sat. Nov. 11th 1905 fo buisness preaching by the mod. after which the Church was considered in conference. The business was as follows. Report of the Tres. and more members was appointed on the mission committe there being no other business by motion and second adjourned to meet Sunday. Met Sunday after preaching the Church looked after any business or any unfinished business there being none adjourned.

      F.A.B. Roark C.C.   *L.E. Rowland Mod*

Saturday, December 9, 1905

Salem Baptist Church met Dec 9th 1905 for business. preaching by the mod after which the Church was considered in conference. The tres. made his report and there were more mem-

bers appointed on the mission committe there being no other business by motion and second adjourned to meet Sunday.

Met Sunday preaching by the mod there being no business

the Church decided to protract a series of meetings but withdrawn the idea on Monday night.

F.A.B. Roark C.C.   L.E. Rowlande Mod

1906

Sunday, January 14, 1906

Salem Church met Sunday Jan. 14 1906 preaching by the pastor there being no business before the Church adjourned

F.A.B. Roark Clerk   L.E. Rowlande Mod

Saturday, February 10, 1906

Salem Church met Feb. 10. 1906 for business preaching by the pastor of which the Church was considered in conference.

Some of the members was charged with dancing some for non attendance a committee was appointed to investagate the matter. The committee was composed of the following members Bro. John Cross, Berry [F.A.B.] Roark Sister Mamie Smith Ellen Stulce. The clerk was appointed to communicate with the non attendees. There being no other business by motion and second adjourned to met Sunday. Met Sunday preaching by the pastor no business except the Church meetings were changed from the 2nd to the 1^t. Then adjourned

F.A.B. Roark clerk   L.E. Rowlande Mod

Saturday, March 3, 1906

Salem Baptist Church met Mar 3, .06 for business preaching by the pastor after which the Church was considered in conference. Read and approved the previous minutes

then the report of the committe on the non attenders and dancers. Bro S.J. Stulce gave in his resignation which the Church granted and prefered charges against Bro Frieland Defriece [Freeland Defriese] for pub. drunkness and non attendance. Bro Jack Roark and Bro A.L. Stulce was appointed to talk with him there being no other business by motion a second

adjourned to meet Sun. at 10 oclock.

Met Sun. preaching by the pastor no business adjourned.

F.A.B. Roark C.C.   L.E. Rowlande Mod

Saturday, April 7, 1906

Salem Church met Mar 3 1906[37] for business preaching by the pastor. Read and approved the previous minutes. Bro Jack Roark and A.L. Stulce as a committee on Bro Freiland Defriece's [Freeland Defriese's] *Case reported their request non attended to. Bro Defriece was withdrawn fellowship from. More members was appointed on the committee to talk to and investigate the dancing charges the members was Bro Jack Roark Bro. A.L. Stulce Sister Nannie Allisson* [Allison].

No other business by motion and second adjourned to meet Sunday. Met Sun. preaching by the pastor no business adjourned

        F.A.B. Roark clerk   L.E. Rowlande Mod

Saturday, May 5, 1906

Salem Church Met May 5. 1906 for business.

Read and approved the previous minutes after which the committe on the conduct of members reported Their business being non attended to. By Motion and second the charges against the members charged with dancing or any other act was withdrawn on their statment either written or oral up to the previous meeting that is those who gave in their statment to the Church or to any of its representities.

No other business By Motion and Second adjourned to meet Sun. Met Sun. preaching by the pastor no business Adjourned.

        F.A.B. Roark c clerk   L.E. Rowlande Mod

Saturday, June 2, 1906

First Sat. in June no meeting on account of pastor couldnt be present. The Church met Sun. but no business came before the Church. After preaching Adjourned.

        F.A.B. Roark c clerk   L.E. Rowlande Mod.

Saturday, August 4, 1906

Salem Baptist Church met Aug. 4th 1906 for business preaching by pastor. No business came before the Church. by motion and second adjourned to meet Sun. Met Sun preaching by the pastor after prayer and song adjourned.

        F.A.B. Roark C.C.   L.E. Rowlande Mod.

[No record of Church meetings September through December 1906]

---

[37]   It is possible that the date was written incorrectly. From the minutes, it is obvious that this is the next meeting which would have been on April 7.

1907

[No record of Church meeting in January 1907]

Saturday, February 2, 1907

Salem Baptist Church met Sat. Feb 2ⁿᵈ 1907 preaching by the pastor from Exodus 14–15 after an interesting sermon an invertation was extended to any who might wish to join the Church there being none preperations was made for Baptizing at 10 oclock a.m. Sun. No other business adjourned to meet at the waters edge Sun. Met Sun. At the waters edge eleven were baptized after the baptizing met at the Church house preach by the pastor text The origin of the Church.
Adjourned to meet next regular meeting day.

        F.A.B. Roark clerk   *Rev. Robert Phelpps Mod. &Pastor*

Saturday, March 2, 1907

Salem Baptist Church Met Sat. March 2ⁿᵈ 1907 preaching by the pastor. A very intersting sermon was delivered. Following the sermon, the Church was considered in conference. All visitors who might wished to take a part in transacting any business were invited to seat with the brethern but no business came before the Church. Adjourned to meet at 10 A.M. Sun.
Met Sun. After an interesting lecture on Sunday School work the pastor presided. Then a collection on pastors salary was made No other business adjourned.

        F.A.B. Roark clerk   *Robt Phelpss Mod*

Saturday, April 6, 1907

Salem Baptist Church Met April 6 1907 preaching by the pastor. After preaching the Church was considered in conference. An invitation was extend to any visitors who might wish to help transact any business to seat with the brethern.
The Church Covenant and Rules of Decorum was Read also the previous minutes was read and approved.
No other business adjourned to meet Sun.
Met Sun. preaching by the pastor no business adjourned to meet the 1ᵗ Sat. And Sun. in May.

        F.A.B. Roark C.C.   *Robert Phelpps Mod*

Saturday, May 4, 1907

Salem Baptist Church Met Sat. May 4 1907 preaching by the pastor from St. John, 13..34 Following an excellent sermon the Church was considered in conference. All visitors was invited to seat with the brethern. An invatation was extended to any who might wish to join the Church there being one the Church excepted [accepted] her statement and confession of excepting [accepting] Christ as her Saviour and she was extended the hand of fellowship. A collection of $1.30 was made on pastors salary. The pastor called for all contemplating being Baptized to make it known No other business adjourned to meet at the waters edge Sun. At 9.00 A.M. Met Sun. at waters edge

Baptized 8 eight persons and then congregated at the Church house. preaching by the pastor then gave fifteen minutes intermission after which the Church met and instituted the Lord's supper Then adjourned to meet 1ᵗ Sat. in June 1907

   F.A.B. Roark clerk   Robt. Phelpps Mod.

Saturday, June 1, 1907

Salem Baptist Church Met 1ᵗ Sat. in June 1907 for business, the body was called to order by song then prayer. Preaching by the pastor. No business came before the Church, Adjourned to meet Sun. Met Sun. after Sunday School the pastor gave a lecture on S.S. work. After a short interval of intermission the pastor preached an excellent sermon. Adjourned to meet 1ᵗ Sat. in July.

   F.A.B. Roark C.C.   Robert Phelpps Mod

Saturday, July 6, 1907

Salem Baptist Church Met Sat. July 6. 1907 preaching by the pastor. The Church was considered in conference the previous minutes was read and approved. The Church elected Bro. J.A. Shropshire treasurer of the Church. No other business came before the Church adjourned to meet Sun. at 10. oclock a.m. Met Sun. preaching by the pastor. Adjourned till the 1ᵗ Sat. and Sun. in Aug.

   F.A.B. Roark C.C.   Robert Phelpps Mod

Saturday, August 3, 1907

Salem Baptist Church Met the 1ᵗ Sat. in Aug. for business preaching by the pastor. The Church was considered in conference. Any members of churches of the denomination was envited to seat with the brethern. No business came before the Church adjourned to meet Sun. at 10. o clock A.M. Met Sun. At 10. o clock the pastor presiding. The Church decided to continue the meeting.

   F.A.B. Roark C.C.   Robt. Phelpps Mod

Saturday, August 31, 1907

Salem Baptist Church Met Aug. 31. 1907 for business the pastor preached from Sameul 13. 29. after preaching the

Church was considered in conference to transact any business that might come before the body. Bro Owen and Floyd Smith, J.W. and Berry [F.A.B.] *Roark were elected delegates to the Ocoee Baptist Association No other business came before the body motion was made and second to adjourne.*

F.A.B. Roark C.C.   Robt. Phelpps Mod

Saturday, September 7, 1907

Salem Baptist Church met Sept. 7. 1907 for business preaching by the pastor. After preaching the Church was considered in conference. The Church elected delegates to the Ocoee Baptist Association. The delegates were F.A.B. Roark Owen Smith, Joe W. Roark and Floyd Smith. No other business the Church decided to protract the meeting.

F.A.B. Roark C.C.   Robt. [Robert] Phelpps Mod.

Saturday, October 5, 1907

Salem Baptist Church Met Oct. 5 1907 for business preaching by the pastor after sermon the Church was considered in conference but no business transacted the Church adjourned to meet Sun. at the waters edge At 9:30 oclock a.m. Met and baptized six which were added to the Church. After baptizing the congregation met at the Church house for preaching

F.A.B. Roark C.C.   Robt Phelpps Mod

Saturday, November 2, 1907

Salem Baptist Church Met Nov. 2nd 1907 for business the pastor presiding after preaching the Church was considered in conference but no business came before the body Adjourned to meet Sun. Met Sun. at 10.30 o clock for preaching.

F.A.B. Roark C.C.   Robt Phelpps Mod

[No record of Church meeting in December 1907.]

1908

[No record of Church meetings from January through May 1908]

Sunday, June 21, 1908

Salem Baptist Church met June 21..08 for preaching. Rev. E. Eddwards [Edwards] *pre-sided following preaching the Church had a business conference and granted sister Pheobe* [Phoebe] *Cannon a letter of dismission*

F.A.B. Roark clerk   E. Eddwards Mod.

[No record of Church meeting in July 1908]

Saturday, August 1, 1908

Salem Baptist Church Met Sat. Aug. 1ᵗ .08 for a business session F.A.B. Roark was elected Mod. For the day. Rev. Robert Phelpps was elected pastor. A committee was organized for the work of Missions. Bro Will Stulce, Sister Martha Ellen Allison, Owen Smith Nettie Smith constitute this committee

F.A.B. Roark   Mod. and clerk.

Sunday, August 23, 1908

Salem Baptist Church Met Aug. 23, 08 preaching by the pastor from St John 19. 30. After preaching the Church considered its self in conference and enrolled sister Jennie Eldridge by letter as member in full fellowship.
By Motion adjourned

F.A.B. Roark clerk   Robert Phelpps Mod.

Saturday, September 12, 1908

Salem Baptist Church Met Sept. 12 08. preaching by the pastor
No business came before the Church.
Adjourned to Meet Sun. Met Sun. pastor presided

F.A.B. Roark clerk   Robert Phelpps Mod

Saturday, November 7, 1908

Salem Baptist Church held a conference Meeting Sat. Nov 7 .08
after a few days of revival services. By request Sister Mattie Darharty [Daugherty] *was granted a letter of dismission.*
There being no other business adjourned to Meet Sun.

F.A.B. Roark clerk   Robert Phelpps Mod

Nov. 8 Sun. No preaching.

Sunday, December 20, 1908

Salem Baptist Church Met the 3ʳᵈ Sun. in Dec. 1908 for the purpose of electing a pastor. F.A.B. Roark was elected mod. Protem. Rev. J.B. Trotter was elected pastor for the year 1909 No other business came before the Church.

F.A.B. Roark   Mod. and C.C.

1909

Sunday, January 17, 1909

Salem Baptist Church Met Jan. 17ᵗʰ 1909. Preaching by Rev.
J.B. Trotter. After Preaching the Church was considered in conference to transact any such
business that might come before the body. After some appropriate comment and suggestions
on Church business the Church decided to come to some conclusion as to their pastors salary
and report same at next regular meeting.

       F.A.B. Roark Clerk   *J.B. Trotter Mod.*

Saturday, February 13, 1909

Salem Baptist Church Met Sat. Feb. 13 1909 Preaching by the pastor from Psalm 23.1. A very
strong pointed and interesting sermon, following the sermon the Church was considered in
conference. Bro J.M. Roark was elected treasure of the Church. No other business came before
the body. By Motion and second adjourned to meet Sat night. Met Sat. night preaching by
pastor read and corrected the previous minutes The minute of Dec.'s conference meeting
not being on record the same was corrected and embodied in the record Adjourned to Meet
Sun

       F.A.B. Roark clerk   *J.B. Trotter Mod.*

Met Sun. preaching by pastor reread and approved the previous minutes But no business
came before the body.

       F.A.B. Roark clerk   *J.B. Trotter Mod.*

[No record of Church meeting for March 1909]

Saturday, April 10, 1909

The Baptist Church at Salem Met Sat. April 10ᵗʰ 1909 Preaching by the pastor after which
the Church was considered in conference, read and approved the previous minutes. By
request the Church granted Sister Rennie J. Hixon[38] a letter of dismission. Bro's John Cross
J.M. Roark and Owen Smith ware appointed as a committie to repair the Church house. No
other business came before the Church by motion and second adjourned to meet Sat night.
Met Sat. Night preaching by pastor adjourned to meet Sun. Met Sun. the pastor presided

       F.A.B. Roark clerk   *J.B. Trotter Mod.*

---

[38]   Rennie J. Hixon possibly refers to Rhoda Jane Hickson/Hixon on the Church rolls
with Rennie being a nickname. According to the rolls, Rhoda Jane was a long time
member of Salem Baptist Church and would probably have been referred to in
friendly terms, i.e., a nickname.

Saturday, May 8, 1909

The Baptist Church at Salem met Sat. May 8ᵗʰ 1909 for business,
preaching by Rev. George Trotter after preaching the Church was considered in conference
to transact any business that might come before the body there being none adjourned to
meet Sat. night. Met Sat. night preaching by moderater adjourned to meet Sun. Met Sun.
after Sun. school the Moderator presided.

      F.A.B. Roark clerk   *George Trotter Mod.*

Saturday, June 5, 1909

The Baptist Church at Salem met Sat. June 5ᵗʰ 1909 for business
preaching by the pastor, J.B. Trotter. After preaching the Church was considered in confer-
ence to transact any business that might come before the body. There being but few members
present no business came before the Church, A Motion was intertained to adjourne Motion
prevailed and adjourned to
meet Sat night Met Sat. night preaching by pastor
J.M. Roark one of the committee on repairing the Church stated the committee would be
ready to report next meeting July 10 adjourned to meet Sun. Met Sun. preaching by Pastor
adjourned to meet Sat July 10

      F.A.B. Roark clerk   *J.B. Trotter Mod.*

Saturday, July 10, 1909

The Baptist Church at Salem Met July 10ᵗʰ 1909 for business
preaching by pastor. Read and approved the previous minetes
The committee on repairing the Church house reported thet their decision was to call a
meeting Sat. July the 17ᵗʰ for the decission and calculation on repairing the house The
Church requested that all the members possible be present on next meeting day A Motion
was intertained to adjourn till Sat night. Met Sat. night preaching by pastor adjourned
to meet Sun, at eleven o'clock. Met Sun. the pastor presiding after preaching the Church
made a contribution of 1.90 to missions
By Motion and Second adjourned.

      F.A.B. Roark clerk   *J.B. Trotter Mod.*

Saturday, August 7, 1909

The Baptist Church at Salem met Sat. Aug. 7ᵗʰ 1909 for business
preaching by pastor read and approved the previous minutes an invitation was extended to
any visiting brethern. The committee on repairing the house asked for more time. A com-
mittee was appointed to look after the conduct of the members. The committee was com-
posed of the following members Bros Will Stulce, Grover Roark, John Cross, Nannie Allison,
Berry [F.A.B.] *Roark Mamie Smith. The Church*

authorized the clerk to write all the non attending members to attend their Church meet-
ings or ask for their letter. A motion was intertained to adjourn till Sat. Night. Met Sat.
night preaching by P.M. Pardue the meeting continued two weeks
on Friday morning the Church had a conference and
Discussed the matter of repairing the house or build a new one postponed the matter till
Sat. night elected Bros. J.M. Roark, Jim Allison, Jess Hindman, Berry [F.A.B.] *Roark del-*
egates to the Ocoee Association. On Sat. night the Church decided to build a new house. A
soliciting committee was appointed to solicit aid on building the Church house The com-
mittee was as follows Berry Roark, Will Stulce, Jess Hindman, Jim Allison, Floyd Smith,
Laura Moon, Sallie Cross, Jennie Stulce, Ether Eldridge Nettie Smith. A collection was made
for the preacher after which a motion was intertained to adjourn to meet at the waters
edge for the ardance [ordinance] *of Baptism Sun. morn. Met Sun. morning at waters*
edge and Baptized twelve then returned to the Church and had preaching by P.M. Pardue
the audience was dismissed till Sun. night. On Sun. night the revival closed with twenty-
two additions to the Church.

   F.A.B. Roark clerk   *J.B. Trotter Mod.*

**[The following two paragraphs were written sideways in the left
margin of the page either to conserve space or because they were
added after the next month's minutes had been written on the following page.]**

*On Sun. morning Aug. 15 met at the waters edge and baptized Lena Pendergrass Della
Pendergrass Jeff Cross Lilly Cross Willie Roark Grover Roark Will Pendergrass Jess Pendergrass
Arthur Hubbard Alex Smith.*

Baptized Aug. 20 [Friday] *Cordie Swafford, Charlie Swafford Essa Smith Bertha Smith
Dealthia Hindman Laura Smith Berkie Friddle Jane Friddle Buloh Pendergrass Sim
Eldridge Steve Allison Sim Williams J.C. Smith by Enrollment.*

Saturday, September 11, 1909

*The Baptist Church at Salem Met Sat. night Sept. 11 1909 preaching by pastor after which
the Church was considered in conference to transact any business that might come before
the body read corrected and approved the previous minutes. The committee on repairing
the house reported that nothing had been done owing to the committee failing to meet.
Bro. Owen Smith by motion and second was liberated to exercise himself as a minister of the
Gospel. The clerk was authorized to write a recomendation showing that he had been liberated by the Church. By Motion and Second adjourned to meet Sun. morning at 11 o'clock.*

   F.A.B. Roark clerk   *J.B. Trotter Mod.*

Met Sun. morning preaching by pastor after which there were new members added to the building committee and the Church decided to begin work on Thurs.

        F.A.B. Roark clerk   *J.B. Trotter Mod.*

Saturday, October 9, 1909

The Baptist Church at Salem Met Sat. Oct. 9th 1909 at the Conner Grave Yard for the purpose of cleaning and shrubbing off the Grave yard. At 11.30 o'clock had preaching by Pastor after services and dinner the crowd proceeded to work on the Graves. Met Sat. night at the Church house had preaching by pastor then read and approved the previous Minutes. Granted Sisters Harriet Roark Defriece [Defriese]*, Martha Runyans* [Runians]*, Elizabeth Henry letters by their request. By Motion and Second the Church excepted* [accepted] *the apportionment of the Ocoee Association and agreed to raise the amount and more if they could. By Motion and Second adjourned to meet Sun. morning. Met Sun. morning preaching by Pastor extended an invitation for the reception of members and took a collection of 1.35 for missions. Adjourned to meet on the next regular meeting day.*

        F.A.B. Roark clerk   *J.B. Trotter Mod.*

Saturday, November 13, 1909

The Baptist Church at Salem Met Sat. Nov. 13 1909 for business preaching by pastor after which the Church was considered in conference but no business came before the body. By Motion and Second adjourned to meet Sat. night. Met Sat. night preaching by Rev. George Trotter adjourned to meet Sunday
Morning at 11 oclock. Met Sunday Morning Preaching by Pastor it being in the month set apart by the State Board of Missions to contribute to the Orphans the Church made a collection of $1. By motion and second adjourned to meet the Second Sat. in Dec.

        F.A.B. Roark clerk   *J.B. Trotter Mod.*

Saturday, December 11, 1909

The Baptist Church at Salem Met Sat Dec 11. 1909 for business preaching by pastor after which the Church was considered in conference to transact any business that might come before the body it being the [time] *to elect a pastor the body went in to an election by ballot and reelected J.B. Trotter. No other business by common consent agreed to meet at the Salem School Building Sat. night. A motion was intertained to adjourne was second and prevailed till Sat night*
Met Sat. night preaching by pastor and agreed to meet back at the old Church house if the weather would admit Sun. morning. the weather was to bad and the Church failed to assemble.

        F.A.B. Roark C.C.   *J.B. Trotter Mod.*

Membership Activities of Salem Baptist Church from the Minutes 1900–1909

	1900	1901	1902	1903	1904	1905	1906	1907	1908	1909	Total
Excluded	1			5	1		1				8
Dismissed								3			3
Letter of Recommendation				1						3	4
Received by Letter					1			1			2
Received/ Experience											0
Enrollment				18			6			23	47
Baptized				9			25			35	69
Restored											
Dropped from the book											

Activities tabulated from the Minutes of Salem Baptist Church.

The Ordination of Owen L. Smith

The ordination of Owen L. Smith on September 3, 1911 was the only known ordination of a minister at Salem Baptist Church.

Chapter Six
Salem Baptist Church
1910–1915

Salem Baptist Church began the new year with no meetings in January and February, J.B. Trotter back at the pastoral helm, and the anticipation of a new church building on the horizon. At the March meeting of 1910, a motion was entertained to adjourn to meet Saturday night at the school building. They met Sunday morning at the church house. It cannot be ascertained whether they were building a new meeting house or heavily rebuilding the old one. The fact that they met back at the meeting house on Sunday morning would suggest that they had some sort of structure in which to meet.

Despite the adverse circumstances, the congregation of Salem Baptist Church did the best they could to continually conduct church business. Unfortunately, the income of the church was poor, and pledges made in good faith were not able to be kept. According to the minutes of the Ocoee Association, it was not a situation unique to a single small church. There is continuous mention in association minutes of churches being unable to meet their apportionment and pay their pastor's salary. At the July meeting of Salem Church the treasurer of the building committee requested that all who had subscribed to aid the committee pay the whole of their subscription. A collection of 75 cents was made on Salem Church's apportionment to the Ocoee Association. With the apportionment for Salem Church being $20, monthly payments would be $1.67 if the church met every month. In August, the pastor tendered his resignation until the church complied with their obligations.

There would be no meetings at Salem Baptist Church between September 1910 and July 1911. No mention is made of the church fulfilling its obligation to the pastor, but J.B. Trotter was once again pastor when the church met again in August 1911. It was an important month in the life of the church with the dedication of the new meeting house and it was fitting that J.B. Trotter was pastor at that time. It was the tenth year (although not successively) that J.B. Trotter had been pastor of Salem Baptist Church.

Although there were no meetings of Salem Church after August, Ocoee Association records, including Salem Baptist Church's Letter to the Association, show that F.A.B. Roark represented Salem Church at the Ocoee Association meeting in September. In the "Remarks" section of the form letter to the Association is written the following: "Dear Brethern the amount we send is what we have given on our apportionment fund of Twenty Dollars. Our mission funds are blank. We regret to say this year we have been building us a new church house and consequently we are behind."[1] Since the preceding minutes make no mention of a delegation being appointed to the Ocoee Association meeting, it would follow that the responsibility would go to the church clerk by default. J.B. Trotter was listed as pastor in the letter and F.A.B. Roark was listed as Sunday school superintendent as well as clerk.

At the August meeting, the building committee offered the church house to the congregation for dedication. The church accepted the building. It was agreed to dedicate the new church on the following Sunday. After the congregation accepted the church house, a motion was made and accepted to dedicate the building to the worship of God and his service and to bar it from picnics, ice cream suppers, or anything that would degrade its members or the property or yield a bad influence upon the community. Rev. J.B. Trotter preached the "dedicatoral sermon."

The members of Salem Baptist Church were proud of their new church building. They would take steps to keep it in good condition and make improvements. In May 1912 the church took up a collection to buy a lock for the church house, receiving $.23 on Sat. night and $1.45 on Sunday for a total collection of $1.68. At the June meeting, the church would elect a janitor to tend to the upkeep of the church house.

The first elected janitor was Grover Roark. According to the minutes, the amount of time a janitor would serve would vary, depending on circumstances. A specific amount of time would not be set in the minutes. The church would periodically take up a collection to pay the janitor. As with the term of service, no salary was set.

The Board of Deacons voted in February 1914 that the church and Sunday school would have entertainment at the next meeting and charge an admission fee at the door of fifteen cents for singles and twenty-five cents for a couple with proceeds to go toward buying an organ for the church house. A committee was appointed to arrange the program. It is not known from the minutes if the entertainment was ever held. However, the church was apparently earnest about getting an organ for the church and improving the church building. In February 1915 the church appointed two committees, one to look after the painting of Salem Church, and the other to raise money to carpet the aisle. In March, they would appoint another committee to look after the lighting of the church.

In 1911, Salem Baptist Church agreed to have a revival meeting to begin the fourth Saturday in August. On Wednesday night, August 30, Owen L. Smith asked the church to ordain him for the ministry. The church agreed and Smith was ordained on Sunday Sept. 3, 1911. He had spent the past two years preaching since Salem Church liberated him to exercise himself as a minister of the Gospel, had served his pastoral apprenticeship, and was ready to be ordained.

The minutes of the meeting on September 3rd include the ordination ceremony with J.B. Trotter, S.M. Sherrill, and L.E. Rowland constituting the presbytery. May 1912 would be the first and only time recorded in the existing minutes that Brother Owen L. Smith would preach at Salem Church as an ordained minister. In December 1914, Salem Church by motion and second would grant Owen Smith another letter of dismissal, the previous letter being lost or misplaced. It is not known if he preached at Salem Church after 1915.

At the meeting on September 9th Salem Baptist Church elected L.E. Rowland moderator for the day and then proceeded to elect him pastor and J.M. Roark clerk and treasurer. This was one of the few times that Salem Church would break with tradition. Ordinarily, a pastor could not be moderator at the meeting at which he was elected. The church then appointed delegates to the Ocoee Association. The church met Saturday night, gave an invitation, and received Millie Hixson [Hickson], Wilce Hixson Jr., Jeff Latham, Thomas Allison, and Rube Hubbard. The church extended the hand of Christian fellowship and adjourned the meeting to meet Sunday morning.

In October 1911, the clerk and treasurer began recording the financial report in the minutes. Amounts that were collected and the purpose for which they were collected were reported in the minutes of each meeting, as well as a list of how much each member had contributed to the pastor's salary. Outside of the pastor's salary, collections were made for missions and "incidental purposes." The apportionment for the Ocoee Association was not mentioned in the church minutes after July 1910. In the minutes of the Ocoee Association in September of 1910 it states that in "as much as the State Mission Board now does most effectively the work formerly done by our colporters…" indicating that the State Mission Board had accepted the responsibility of collecting and distributing mission funds. Fifth Sunday Meetings had been dropped in favor of church rallies. Fifth Sunday events and services would, however, be held by single churches and Christian organizations into the twenty-first century.

In December 1911, Salem Church began once again to take up a collection for missions. In the minutes for April 1912, the total collection for missions was $1.76. The amount was forwarded to W.M. Woodcock in Nashville, Tennessee. The total was the sum of collections from December to April. In January 1913 the total collection for missions of $8.65 was paid to J.W. Gillon, Secretary of the State Mission Board at Nashville, Tennessee.

This would lead one to infer that the payment of collections for missions was made to the State Mission Board quarterly, but not in every quarter, due to meetings not held or unsuccessful collections. Mission and Mission Finance committees would be appointed in October 1913. Appointing the two committees illustrates the faith and determination with which the members tried to conduct business at Salem Church on a level with her sister churches, some of which paid their pastor $1000 or more per year. In 1913, Salem had no more than 30 active members and through the end of the surviving minutes would not collect more than $5 for the missions at any one time, and usually no more than $10 for any given quarter. Certainly, it would not require a committee of four to manage these funds, in addition to the committee of three to manage collections.

The inclusion of the financial report in the minutes, primarily to report the contributions on the pastor's salary, was another attempt to get members, old and new, to attend church regularly and contribute to the pastor's salary, missions, and other church funds. In October 1911, the church read the Rules of Decorum and the Church Covenant, then called the roll. Then by motion and second agreed to enforce the two church documents. They met Sunday night and elected five deacons: Will Stulce, James Allison, Jess Pendergrass, John Cross, and Floyd Smith. The church organized a Sunday school and set the next Saturday for a prayer meeting and to organize a Board of Deacons. There is no mention of a meeting the next Saturday.

The members of Salem Baptist Church conducted no business in November except the financial report of a collection for the pastor's salary of $9.65. On Saturday of the December meeting, the church agreed by motion and second that the clerk should write the delinquent members. On Sunday the appointed deacons were ordained by L.E. Rowland. The newly formed Board of Deacons held their first meeting in January 1912 and requested that all members be present at the next meeting on Sunday. Those that were not present would have charges preferred against them for non-attendance. It would continually fall to the Board of Deacons to fellowship and discipline the church. The Board of Deacons would vote again in April that those not present next meeting without a good excuse would be dealt with according to the Rules of Decorum. In May, the Board voted for the pastor to appoint a committee of W.M. Roark (chairman), J.L. Roark, and

W.A. Stulce to adjust some business in the church. June would find the Board voting that the church, once again, prefer charges against all delinquent members.

In February 1913, Salem Baptist Church found itself not in fellowship. The church requested that the Board of Deacons fellowship and discipline the church if possible before the next meeting. In May, L.E. Rowland preached a "very interesting" sermon on the subject of repentance and then made a proposition to the church for all that would enter into covenant with him and each other to read one chapter of the Bible per day and pray one prayer a day. Quite a few members agreed to join the pastor in bible study. Despite the appeal to the congregation on repentance, and the first organized bible study at Salem Church, the Board of Deacons once again voted in the February 1914 meeting to prefer charges against all male members that missed attending and contributing for three meetings in succession without good cause.

At the March meeting of Salem Baptist Church, the Board voted to prefer charges against all members that failed to vote on all motions and for W.A. Pendergrass to keep a list of all members failing to contribute or to attend their church meetings. The church and the Board of Deacons would at times be over-zealous in their efforts to persuade members to attend church meetings and services. In May, by motion and second, the Board voted to drop 15 members from the rolls.

In November 1914, Salem Baptist Church would vote to adopt the Laymen's Missionary Movement following a lecture by Brother Powell on the movement, and appointed a committee to see what each member would contribute for the cause. The committee was called to report at the December meeting and the report that followed showed that total subscription (pledges) for the Laymen's Missionary Movement so far for the year was $130.80. The report also included resolutions to be added as amendments to the Church Covenant.

The increasing concern over church business and concentration on the conduct of the members was due in large part to events that led to the adoption by the church of the Laymen's Missionary Movement. The Laymen's Missionary Movement began in 1906 with a ten-day prayer meeting at the 100th anniversary of the foreign missions movement. The foreign missions movement began with the Williams College Haystack Prayer Meeting. The twentieth century had begun with the expectation among Christian believers of the coming of the Lord and the grave realization that world evangelization must precede that occurrence.

An executive committee had met in Philadelphia on January 9, 1907 to state the purpose of the movement. The statement included, "We earnestly recommend to the Foreign Mission Boards of all denominations that they secure groups of laymen to promote campaigns of intelligent and generous interest in foreign missions with special reference to the men of the churches. The expense of these movements to be borne, whenever possible, by such groups of men so that funds of the boards shall not be drawn upon."[2]

The first general meeting of the movement had been held in Chattanooga February 4–6, 1913, and was attended by 1,200 men. There is no evidence that a member of Salem Church was in attendance at the meeting. Resolutions adopted by the body included:

- laymen were called upon to give time to daily prayer and the development of family affairs
- laymen were encouraged to devote intense study to missions
- the use of a "businesslike system of giving" was urged in every Southern Baptist Church
- a laymen's Missionary Committee was to be appointed in every association
- churches were to adopt the tithe as the minimum gift of Christians to their church
- the convention deplored the absence of laymen from denominational meetings[3]

The Laymen's Missionary Movement became the Baptist Brotherhood of the South in 1926, shortened to the Brotherhood Commission in 1950, and changed to Baptist Men on Missions in 1997. As the movement was being organized between 1906 and 1913, the spirit of the movement began to spread, gaining momentum as it rolled along from church to church, and organization to organization.

With the Southern Baptist Convention (SBC) being the first denomination to respond, news of the movement would have filtered down from the SBC to the Ocoee Association to Salem Baptist Church (and sister churches) prior to the general meeting in 1913.

The effect of the coming movement was partially responsible for the earnestness with which Salem Baptist Church began conducting church business in the second decade of the twentieth century. The Ocoee Association would regularly plead with churches to comply with new associational decisions. Although Baptist associations were designed to be autonomous organizations, the member churches, as a general rule, would comply with the wishes of the association. Several Salem Baptist Church members over the years held positions within the association. Many of the changes that Salem Church made, such as the creation of a Board of Deacons, can be traced to previous minutes of the Ocoee Association.

The coming Laymen's Missionary Movement would provide the impetus behind the seeming revitalization of Salem Baptist Church in the last years of the surviving minutes.

On July 3, 1915, the "Board of Deacons had a call meeting, it being rumored that some of the members had been dancing." The Board recommended that the church take action and a committee was appointed. The Board also recommended that the church take action and drop from the roll those who had not complied with the Laymen's Missionary Movement and the resolutions that the church adopted. At the previous meeting in June, the church had voted by motion and second that the church take steps to help pay the small debt the church owed.

The last surviving minutes of Salem Baptist Church were of the August 1915 meeting. It was a fitting end to the surviving minutes. The meeting would be continued for a week. The church appointed delegates to the Ocoee Association. "Sister Lena Hixson [Hickson] made her acknowledgment to the Church and she was restored to full fellowship." As the meeting closed, the collection on the pastor's salary to date was $16.35. The minutes end with "yet due our pastor $8.20."

Minutes of Salem Baptist Church
1910–1915

[No record of Church meetings for January and February 1910.]

Saturday, March 12, 1910

The Baptist Church at Salem Met Sat. March 12 1910 for business preaching by pastor, after which the body was considered in conference to transact any business that might come before the church. By request Sister Jennie Priddy was granted a letter of dismission. A motion was intertained to adjourned to meet Sat. Night at the School Building
Met Sat night pastor presided no business came before the body
adjourned to meet Sun at the church House after an excellent sermon The church unanimously elected Bro. J.B. Trotter pastor for the ensuing year.

   F.A.B. Roark Clerk   *J.B. Trotter Mod*

Saturday, April 9, 1910

The Baptist Church at Salem Met Sat. April 9th 1910. for business preaching by the pastor, an invitation was extended to any visiting Breathern to seat with the body to receive or give instruction The building committee requested that those who had subscribed for building the house pay same in and authorized the lumber to be dressed. No other buisness came before the body a motion was intertained to adjourn the motion carried and the body adjourned till Sat. night.
Met Sat. night pastor presiding after which the church adjourned till Sun morning at 10.30 oclock. Sun morning the pastor lectured on the Sun. School. following he delivered his Sermon. The roll was called and the church was adjourned.

   F.A.B. Roark C.C.   *J.B. Trotter Mod.*

[No record of a church meeting in May]

Saturday, June 11, 1910

The Baptist Church at Salem met June 11th 1910 for business pastor presided. After preaching the Church considered it self in conference for the action of business. By request Sisters Martha Darghty [Daugherty] and Molly Rains were granted letters of dissmissal No other business came before the body a motion was intertained to adjourn, motion carried, the Church adjourned till Sat night. Met Sat. night preaching by pastor, Adjourned to meet Sun morning Met Sun. After Sunday School the pastor presided. Adjourned to met Second Sat and Sun in July.

   F.A.B. Roark C.C.   *J.B. Trotter, Mod.*

Saturday, July 9, 1910

Salem Baptist Church met July, 9. 1910. for business. The pastor presided the Church was considered in conference to transact business. Read and approved the previous minutes. The tresuar of the building committee requested that all who had subscribed to aid the committee to pay same in. No other business a motion was intertained to adjourn. Adjourned to meet Sat. night. Met Sat night preaching by the pastor. The audience was dismissed to reassemble Sun. morn Met Sun morn after sunday school the pastor delivered his sermon follow [following] *a collection of 75 cts was made on the Churches apportionment to the Ocoee Asso.*
Adjourned till Aug. Meeting
    F.A.B. Roark C C   *J.B. Trotter Mod.*

Saturday, August 13, 1910

The Baptist Church at Salem met Sat Aug 13 1910 Preaching by the pastor no business came before the body Adjourned to meet Sat night Met Sat night pastor presided. adjourned to meet Sun morning Met Sun morning after Sun School the pastor presided after preaching the church was considered in conference to transact any business that might come before the church. J.A. Shropshire and wife joined by letter following the
extension of the hand of fellowship The pastor tendered his resignation till the church compliad with their obligations
The Church adjourned
    F.A.B. Roark C.C.   *J.B. Trotter Mod.*

[No record of Church meetings September through December, 1910]

1911

[No record of Church meetings January through July, 1911]

Saturday, August 12, 1911

Salem Baptist Church met Sat Aug 13 1911[39] *for preaching*
Rev. J.B. Trotter presided after preaching the Church was considered in conference to transact any business that might come before the body. By request Sister Jerusia [Jerusha] *Campbell was granted a letter of dismission. The Building committee offered the Church the Church house for dedication. The Church accepted the house. It was agreed upon to*

---

[39] August 12 was actually the date for Saturday. The confusion may have been caused by the minutes being written later.

dedicate the house on Sun following. A motion prevailed to dedicate the house to the worship of God and his service and to bar it from picnics ice cream suppers or anything that
would degrade its members or the property or yield a bad influence upon the community.
No other business adjourned to meet Sun.

F.A.B. Roark C.C.   J.B. Trotter Mod.

Met Sun morning Rev J.B. Trotter preached the dedicatoral sermon. The Church agreed to
have a revival meeting to begin the 4ᵗʰ Sat in Aug. On Wed. Night of Aug. 30 by request of
Bro Owen L. Smith the church agreed to ordain him for the
ministry on Sun. Sept. 3. 1911
Rev. J.B. Trotter L.E. Rowland & S.M. Sherrill were chosen to constitute the Presbytery There
being no other business the body gave way for regular meeting

F.A.B. Roark CC   J.B. Trotter Mod.

Sunday, September 3, 1911

Met Sun morning to officiate to the ordainance of Bro Owen L. Smith The Presbytry which
was called by the Salem Church to officiate in the ordination of Bro Owen L. Smith to the
full work of the Ministry met on Sept 3 1911
The Presbytry organized with Rev J.B. Trotter Chairman S.M. Sherrill secretary, and L.E.
Rowland to pray the ordination prayer. The Chairman preached the ordination Sermon
The Secretary examined the candidate after which the laying on of hands by the prebytry.
Rev L.E. Rowland delivered the charge.

J.B. Trotter   }
S.M. Sherrill   }   Presbytry
L.E. Rowland   }
The hand of fellowship was extended to Bro O.L. Smith
and adjourned.

F.A.B. Roark C.C.

Saturday, September 9, 1911

Salem Baptist Church met Sat. Sept 9ᵗʰ 1911 it being the regular time for Church meeting.
Rev. L.E. Rowland was elected moderator for the day the Church was called in cession to
transact any business that might come before the body. went into an election for purpose
of electing a pastor and Clerk. Rev. L. E. Rowland was elected pastor. and J.M. Roark was
elected Clerk and Treas. The Church appointed Deligates to the Association The deligation
was Bro. J.W. Roark Grover Roark and James Allison. No other business, adjourned till Sat
night, Met Sat. night Preaching by Rev. L.E. Rowland then gave an invitation for membership and received Sister Millie Hixson [Hickson] Bro Wilce Hixson [Hickson] Jr, Bro
Jeff Latham,

Bro. *Thomas Allison* Bro *Rube Hubbard.* the Church extended the hand of Christian fellowship, then adjourned to meet Sunday at 10 oclock to attend to the ordinance of babtism and baptised

Bro. *Jeff Latham*

Bro. *Wilce Hixson* [Hickson]

Bro *Thomas Allison*

Bro. *Rube Hubbard.*

then met at the Church at 11 oclock and extended the hand of Church fellowship to those that were baptised then had preaching by Rev. S.M. Sherrill and adjourned.

   J.M. Roark Clerk   *L.E. Rowland Mod.*

Saturday, October 7, 1911

Salem Baptist Church met Saturday night before the first Sunday in Oct. 1911 preaching by the pastor then adjourned to meet Sunday. Met Sunday at 10 oclock. the Church was called in cession and transacted the following business Read the rules of Decorum and Church Covenant and called the roll. Motion and Seccon to inforce Rules of Decorum and Church Covenant. adjourned till Sunday night Met Sunday night and appointed five Deacons, Bro. Will Stulce James Allison Jess Pendergrass John Cross, Floyd Smith next business organized a Sunday School and then set the next Saturday for Prayer meeting and to organize a Board of Deacons

then preaching by the pastor and Closed

   J.M. Roark CC & Treas.   *L.E. Rowland Modr.*

Financial report for Oct.

T.A. Roark	.50	Essie Smith	.25
J.L. Roark & wife	.50	Manda Bare	.10
J.M. Roark	.25	W. M. Roark	.25
C.H. Hixson [Hickson]	.10	Mrs. W.M. "	.15
W.G. Roark	.50	Lilly Moon	.25
Floyd Smith	.50	W.A. Stulce	.15
W.A. Pendergrass	.15	Willie Roark	.10
Jess Pendergrass	.30	J.A. Shropshire	.50
Uyless [Ulysses] Cross	.11	Minnie Smith	.10
Sallie Cross	.25	L.H. Roark	.10
Johnnie "	.25	total	$5.36
			2.89[40]

---

[40] This number can neither be explained nor reconciled.

Saturday, November 4, 1911

Salem Baptist Church met Saturday night before the first Sunday in Nov. 1911 preaching by the pastor then adjourned to meet Sunday. Met sunday preaching by the pastor.
then read and approved minute of previous meeting and adjourned to meet Sunday night,
Met Sunday night preaching by pastor then Closed

   J.M. Roark Clerk   *L.E. Rowland Modr.*

Financial report for November
Collection for pastors salary

Minnie Smith	.10	Willie Roark	.10
Margret Smith	.10	Harry McCallie	.10
Lilly Moon	.25	W.A. Stulce	.10
J.M. Roark	.25	Jess Pendergrass	.25
W.M. Roark	.50	W.A. Pendergrass	.20
Mrs. J.L. Roark	.25	T.A. Roark	.25
J.L. Roark	.50	J.R. Allison	.25
W.B. Roark	.50	Della Allison	.10
Mrs. W.M. Roark	.25	Thomas Allison	.25
Nannie Allison	.20	J.R. Davis	.25
Lena Hixson [Hickson]	.10	A.B. Cross	.50
Jennie Eldridge	.30	John Cross	.25
L.H. Roark	.15	Grace Stulce	.10
S.E. Allison	.10	Jeff Latham	.10
C.H. Hixson [Hickson]	.10	Mrs. Jack Eldridge	.25
Sallie Cross	.25	James Posey	.50
F.A.B. Roark	.25	Wilson Hixson [Hickson]	.50
M.J. Bare	.10	Jennie Guinn	.10
J.A. Shropshire	.50	Jeff Smith	.50
T.J. Gowin	.25	total	$9.65

Saturday, December 2, 1911

Salem baptist Church met Saturday night before the first
Sunday in Dec. 1911 Preaching by the pastor the Church was
called in cession Motion and Second that the Clerk write the
delinquent members then adjourned to meet Sunday at 10.30
Met Sunday preaching by the Pastor, then ordained the
following Deacons John Cross, James Allison Floyd Smith Jess
Pendergrass William Stulce, ordained by L.E. Rowland paster
and Rev. S.M. Sherrill then took up collection for Mission and

received .75 cents contribution adjourned till Sunday night
Met Sunday night preaching by the pastor then Closed

   J.M. Roark Clerk & Treas.   *L.E. Rowland Modr.*

Financial report for December
Collection for Pastors salary.

Laura Moon	.50	W.A. Pendergrass	.25
Lillie Moon	.25	Jess Pendergrass	.25
J.R. Davis	.25	M.J. Bare	.10
Jennie Eldridge	.15	Minnie Smith	.10
J.M. Roark	.25	Lena Hixson [Hickson]	.10
W.G. Roark	.50	Mamie Smith	.10
W.M. Roark	.50	Louie Samples	.10
J.L. Roark	.25	C.H. Hixson [Hickson]	.10
Mrs. J.L. Roark	.25	James Allison	.25
T.A. Roark	.25	Nannie Allison	.10
W.B. Roark	.25	Thomas Allison	.10
J.W. Roark	.35	Joseph Hubbard	.50
John Cross	.25	W.A. Stulce	.20
Sallie Cross	.25	T.J. Gowin	.25
L.H. Roark	.15	J.A. Shropshire	.50
Mrs. W.M. Roark	.25	F.O. Smith	.50
T.J. Roark	.25	total	$8.40

1912

Saturday, January 6, 1912

Salem Baptist Church met Saturday night before the first
Sunday in Jan. 1912 Preaching by the pastor the Church was
called in cession and transacted the following business.
The Church decided that Bro. Sam Smith had severed his
relation from the Church by joining another Church and this
Church withdrew fellowship from Bro. Smith. then adjourned
to meet Sunday. Met Sunday preaching by Pastor then took
up collection for Mission and received 41 cents contribution.
then adjourned till Sunday night met Sunday night
preaching by the pastor The board of Deacons held a
conference and requested all members present at the next

meeting on Sunday and those that were not present prefer charges against them for non attendance.

J.M. Roark Clerk   L.E. Rowland Modr.

Financial report for Jan. Collection for Pastors salary.

Jennie Eldridge	.15	Minnie Smith	.10
J.M. Roark	.25	John Dungan	.10
W.M. Roark	.50	R.C. Dungan	.25
Mrs. W.M. Roark	.25	J.R. Allison	.25
John Cross	.25	Thomas Allison	.10
Sallie Cross	.25	Nannie Allison	.10
O.B. Cross	.15	C.H. Hixson [Hickson]	.10
Uyless [Ulysses] Cross	.10	Lena Hixson [Hickson]	.10
W. A. Stulce	.15	W.B. Roark	.25
J.R. Davis	.25	J.L. Roark	.25
		Mrs. J.L. Roark	.25
		F.A.B. Roark	.25
		L.H. Roark	.15
		total	$4.55

[No Church record of a meeting for February, 1912]

Saturday, March 2, 1912

Salem Baptist Church met Saturday night before the first Sunday in March. the pastor presiding after preaching gave an invitation for membership and recieved none then adjourned to meet Sunday on account of bad weather had no service on Sunday. Met Sunday night preaching by the pastor and then Closed

J.M. Roark Clk & Treas.   L.E. Rowland Modr

Financial report for March Collection for pastors salary.

Alec Smith	.25	J.L. Roark	.25
Floid [Floyd] Smith	.50	Mrs. J.L. Roark	.25
M.J. Bare	.20	Mrs. W.M. Roark	.25
W.G. Roark	.50	L.H. Roark	.10
Thomas Allison	.10	W.M. Roark	.50
Nannie Allison	.10	J.M. Roark	.25
J.R. Allison	.25	John Cross	.25

W.B. Roark	.25	Sallie Cross	.25
Lilly Moon	.25	total	$4.65
W.A. Stulce	.15		

Saturday, April 6, 1912

Salem Baptist Church met Saturday night before the first
Sunday in April 1912 the pastor presiding after an interesting sermon the Church was
called in cession read and approved minutes fo previous meeting. Sister Daugherty called
for letter this was laid over and a motion and second that our pastor see Bro. Baldwin of
Highland Park and find out whether or not the Sister is in full fellowship or not. Motion
and second that all members of this church be present at our next meeting those that are
not present without a good excuse the Church will deal with them according to Rules of
Decorum.
then adjourned to meet Sunday at an early hour to organize a
Sunday school. Met Sunday and organized a Sunday school.
preaching by the pastor then took up collection for Mission
and received .60 cts. then adjourned till Sunday night.
Met Sunday night preaching by pastor the church decided to
have an all day service and a communion at its next regular
meeting. then Closed.

> *J.M. Roark Clerk & Treas.   L.E. Rowland Modr.*

Financial report collection on pastors salary.

Alec Smith	.10	Mamie Smith	.10
W.G. Roark	.20	Minnie Smith	.25
L.H. Roark	.10	C.H. Hixson [Hickson]	.20
W.M. Roark	.50	Lena Hixson [Hickson]	.20
J.M. Roark	.25	J.R. Davis	.25
Mrs. W.M. Roark	.25	W.A. Pendergrass	.25
W.B. Roark	.25	Jess Pendergrass	.25
J.L. Roark	.25	John Cross	.25
Mrs. J.L. Roark	.50	Sallie Cross	.25
T.A. Roark	.50	Otis Cross	.25
M.J. Bare	.10	Joe Hubbard	.10
Thomas Allison	.10	A.L. Smith	.25
Nannie Allison	.10	W.A. Stulce	.15
J.R. Allison	.25	Lilly Moon	.25
Jennie Eldridge	.10	B.F. Moon	.10
		total	$6.65

*Total collection for Missions up to present one dollar & .76 cents
this amount has been forwarded to W.M. Woodcock, Nashville,
Tenn.*

Saturday, May 4, 1912

*Salem Baptist Church met Saturday night before the first
Sunday in May 1912 the Pastor presiding after devotional
exercise the Church was called in cession and transacted
the following business read and approved minute of previous
meeting the Board of Deacons voted for our pastor to appoint
a committe to adjust some business in the Church the
committe is W.M. Roark — Chairman J.L. Roark and W.A. Stulce
then took up a collection to buy a lock for the Church house
and received .23 on Sat. night and on Sunday received $1.45
total collection $1.68 adjourned till Sunday
Met Sunday Preaching by Bro. Owen L. Smith and then took
the Lords supper and adjourned till 3 p.m.
preaching by the pastor then Closed.*

        J.M. Roark clerk & Treas.   *L.E. Rowland Modr*

Financial report for May contribution for pastors salary.

Manda J. Bare	.10	Roscoe Bower	.10
W.G. Roark	.50	Joseph Hubbard	.10
T.A. Roark	.25	Lelan Samples	.10
F.O. Smith	.25	C.H. Hixson [Hickson]	.10
W.A. Pendergrass	.10	Lena Hixson [Hickson]	.10
F.A.B. Roark	.25	A.B. Cross	1.00
John Cross	.25	J.H. McCallie	.15
O.B. Cross	.25	Sallie Cross	.25
Dike Eldridge	.50	Thomas Allison	.10
T.J. Cross jr.	.25	Nannie Allison	.10
Jess Pendergrass	.25	Arthur Hubbard	.10
Jennie Guinn	.10	Mrs. J.L. Roark	.30
W.T. Davis	.10	J.L. Roark	.25
Mrs. Jack Eldridge	$1.00	W.B. Roark	.25
Mr. W.M. Roark	.25	W.H. Roark	.20
W.A. Stulce	.25	Minnie Smith	.10
Louie Samples	.10	L.H. Roark	.10
Lillie Moon	.25	J.M. Roark	.25

J.R. Allison	*.25*	*total*	*$9.10*
Jennie Eldridge	*.20*		

Saturday, June 1, 1912

Salem Baptist Church met Sat. night before the first Sunday in
June 1912 the pastor presiding after devotional exercise the
Church was called in cession to transact any business that
might legally come before the body read and approved
minute of previous meeting the Church granted Sister Dolly
Daugherty a letter of reccommendation.
Motion and second that the case of Bro. Shropshire and Bro.
Berry [F.A.B.] *Roark be investigated by the board of Deacons*
and take proof in the case and recomend to the Church for
action at its next regular meeting motion and second that
the Church prefer charges against all delinquent members.
Bro. Grover Roark was elected janitor for this Church then
adjourned till Sunday. Met Sunday preaching by pastor
then took up collection for incidental purpose and recd. .90 cts
also .25 cts from Bro. Rowland for janitor and then closed.

    J.M. Roark CC & Treas.   *L.E. Rowland Mdr*

Financial report collection for pastors salary.

Jane Fann	*.50*	*Mrs. W.M. Roark*	*.25*
W.B. Roark	*.25*	*Lilly Moon*	*.25*
George Gooden	*.10*	*Laura Moon*	*.25*
J.R. Allison	*.25*	*Jeff Latham*	*.15*
O.B. Cross	*.10*	*Rosa Latham*	*.10*
John Cross	*.25*	*T.J. Gowin*	*.10*
S.C. Allison	*.25*	*Nannie Allison*	*.10*
W.M. Roark	*.50*	*Minnie Smith*	*.10*
Sallie Cross	*.25*	*F.A.B. Roark*	*.25*
J.L. Roark	*.50*	*Jennie Eldridge*	*.15*
Mrs. J.L. Roark	*.25*	*C.H. Hixson* [Hickson]	*.10*
J.M. Roark	*.25*	*Lena Hixson* [Hickson]	*.10*
M.J. Bare	*.10*	*W.A. Pendergrass*	*.25*
Grace Stulce	*.10*	*L.H. Roark*	*.10*
W.A. Stulce	*.25*	*F.O. Smith*	*.20*
W.G. Roark	*.50*	*Jeff Roark*	*.50*

| Mamie Smith | .20 | Jess Pendergrass | .13 |
| Joseph Hubbard | .25 | total | $8.40[41] |

Saturday, July 6, 1912

Salem Baptist Church met Saturday night before the first
Sunday in July 1912 after devotional exercise the Church was
called in session to transact any business that might legally
come before the body it being the time for the committee to
report on Brother Shropshire and Bro. Berry [F.A.B.] Roarks
case the committee was not ready. So it was suggested that
they meet on Sunday at 2.30 and invistigate the case and
report to the Church. Motion and second that the roll be
called at our next meeting the Church adjourned till 10.30
Sunday met Sunday preaching by the pastor then adjourned
till sunday night Met sunday night after a very interesting
sermon the committee was ready to report on the case of Bro.
Shropshire and Bro. Berry [F.A.B.] Roark the report was
accepted by the Church we found that the Brethern were due
each other an acknowledgement the same was made to the
Church and accepted the Church then Closed its present session

J.M. Roark C. And Treas.   L.E. Rowland Modr.

Financial report collection on pastors salary.

Jennie Eldridge	.25	Sallie Cross	.25
J.L. Roark	.50	Laura Moon	.25
Mrs. J.L. Roark	.25	James McCallie	.05
W.B. Roark	.25	Jim Allison	.25
W.H. Roark	.20	John Cross	.25
Wilson Hixson[Hickson]	.25	Jess Pendergrass	.25
J.M. Roark	.25	F.O. Smith	.25
Mrs. W.M. Roark	.25	J.R. Davis	.25
F.A.B. Roark	.25	N.N. Roark	.15
Lillie Moon	.25	Emma Roark	.10
A.B. Cross	.25	Nannie Allison	.10
W.A. Stulce	.25	Thomas Allison	.10
L.H. Roark	.15	W.M. Roark	.50
Otis Cross	.25	Charlie Swafford	.15

---

[41]   The Treasurer total does not reconcile with the actual total of the individual contributions.

Mrs. Wrinkle	.25	C.H. Hixson [Hickson]	.10
Lena Hixson [Hickson]	.10	total	$7.20
W.G. Roark	.25		

Saturday, August 31, 1912

*Salem Baptist Church met Sat. night before the first Sunday in
Sept 1912 the Pastor presiding read and approved minute of
previous meeting gave an invitation for membership and
received none. Sister Martha Lovell called for her letter the
same was granted and the Clerk was authorized to write her
letter. then adjourned till Sunday. Met Sunday preaching by
the Pastor the Church decided to hold a revival the meeting
was continued till the following Sunday. On Saturday the
Church was called in cession to appoint deligates to the
Association the following Brethern were appointed Bro.
Shropshire Bro. John Cross Bro. Berry [F.A.B.] Roark and
Bro. Floid [Floyd] Smith also to elect a Pastor and Clerk Bro.
Rowland was elected by a unanimous vote and J.M. Roark was
reelected Clerk on Sat. night gave an invitation for membership
and received Sister Martha Holder by letter and
Bro. A.L. Smith and wife as by letter also Clara Roark and
Maggie Smith by experiance for Baptism. then extended
the hand of Church fellowship to Sister Holder and Bro. Smith and
wife also the hand of Christian fellowship to Clara Roark and
Maggie Smith. Met on Sunday preaching by the Pastor
agreed to meet at the creek to attend to the ordinance of
Baptism and baptized Sister Maggie Smith and Clara Roark
then extended the hand of Church fellowship to those that were
Baptized.*

       J.M. Roark Clerk   *L.E. Rowland Mdr.*

*The Financial report shows that our Pastor has been paid up
for his years work in full.*

Saturday, October 5, 1912

*Salem Baptist Church met Saturday night before the first
Sunday in Oct. the Pastor presiding. The minute of last meeting
was read and approved no other business*

adjourned till Sunday met Sunday preaching by the Pastor then adjourned till Sunday night. Met Sunday night preaching by the Pastor then Closed.

J.M. Roark clerk & Treas   L.E. Rowland Modr.

Financial report for Oct Collection on Pastors salary

Jennie Eldridge	.15	Laura Moon	.25
F.O. Smith	.25	John Cross	.25
C.H. Hixson	.10	Sallie Cross	.25
Lena Hixson	.10	Mrs. W.M. Roark	.25
J.L. Roark	.50	F.A.B. Roark	.25
Mrs. J.L. Roark	.25	Minnie Smith	.10
W.B. Roark	.25	L.H. Roark	.15
W.A. Pendergrass	.20	Mrs. Samples	.25
Jess Pendergrass	.25	Willie Roark	.25
O.B. Cross	.10	J.R. Allison	.25
W.A. Stulce	.25	total	$4.65

Saturday, November 2, 1912

Salem Baptist Church met Saturday night before the first Sunday in Nov. 1912 the Pastor presiding after preaching the Church was called in cession to transact any business that might legally come before the body. read and approved minnutes of previous meeting motion and second that this Church ask the State Board to pay our Pastor one hundred dollars $100.00 per year in addition to the $100 that this Church is to pay Said Pastor for one fourth of his service for the present year. Motion and Second to Elect a Janitor motion carried and Bro. T.W. Allison was elected by a unaminous vote then adjourned to meet Sunday met Sunday preaching by the Pastor adjourned till Sunday night Met according to appointment preaching by the Pastor then closed

J.M. Roark Clerk   L.E. Rowland Mdr.

Financial report for November contribution on Pastors salary by

J.R. Davis	.25	J.R. Allison	.25
Laura Henry	.25	Floyd Smith	.25
Mrs. W.M. Roark	.25	Maud Bare	.25
W.A. Pendergrass	.25	Minnie Smith	.10
Joe Hubbard	.50	Steve Allison	.10
F.A.B. Roark	.25	W.B. Roark	.25
L.H. Roark	.15	W.H. Roark	.50
Clara Roark	.20	Mrs. J.L. Roark	.30
J.M. Roark	.50	J.L. Roark	.50

Willie McCallie	.05	*W.G. Roark*	.50
T.W. Allison	.10	*C.H. Hixson* [Hickson]	.10
Nannie Allison	.10	*total*	$6.00
Lena Hixson [Hickson]	.10		

Contribution through envelopes $1.15 for Missions.

Saturday, November 30, 1912

Salem Baptist Church met Sat. night before the first Sunday in December the pastor presiding approved minutes of previous meeting then adjourned to meet Sunday at eleven met Sunday according to appointment preaching by the pastor then Closed.

J.M. Roark Clerk & Treas.   L.E. Rowland Modr.

Financial report contribution for pastors salary by

Grace Stulce	.10	*T.J. Roark*	.10
Ellen Stulce	.05	*W.A. Stulce*	.25
Mary McCallie	.10	*J.H. McCallie*	.25
J.M. Roark	.25	*Minnie Smith*	.10
Clara Roark	.10	*W.A. Pendergrass*	.25
J.R. Davis	.25	*Mrs. W.M. Roark*	.25
A.L. Smith	.25	*Joe Hubbard*	.25
F. O. Smith	.25	*J.R. Allison*	.25
Johnnie Smith	.05	*T.A. Roark*	.50
Sam Davis	.10	*W.G. Roark*	.25
Jess Pendergrass	.50	*J.W. Roark*	.25
Lena Hixson [Hickson]	.10	*W.B. Roark*	.50
C.H. Hixson [Hickson]	.10	*W.H. Roark*	.25
John Cross	.50	*J.A. Shropshire*	1.00
Sallie Cross	.50	*Nannie Allison*	.10
Mrs. J.L. Roark	.40	*Steve Allison*	.10
Maggie Smith	.10	*T.W. Allison*	.10
Mammie Smith	.25	*F.A.B. Roark*	.25
L.H. Roark	.15	*total*	$9.50
Mrs. Eldridge	.25		

Mission money .40 cents col—for Janitor $1.15

1913

Saturday, January 4, 1913

Salem Baptist Church met Saturday night before the first Sunday in January 1913 preaching by the pastor the Church was called in cession read and approved minutes of previous meeting no other business coming before the Church adjourned to meet Sunday met Sunday preaching by the pastor then adjourned to meet Sunday night met Sunday night after a very interesting sermon Bro. Rowland tendered his resignation as pastor and asked the Church to think over the matter till our next meeting

J.M. Roark clerk   *L.E. Rowland Modr.*

Financial report. total collection for Missions during four months $8.65 which amount has been paid to J.W. Gillon at Nashville, Tenn. Secetary of state Mission Board.
collection on Pastors salary in January By

F.O. Smith	.25	Jess Pendergrass	.25
J.R. Davis	.75	Lillie Moon	.25
J.M. Roark	.25	Mrs. W.M. Roark	.25
Clara Roark	.10	C.H. Hixson	.10
A.L. Smith	.25	Lena Hixson	.15
W.G. Roark	.25	F.A.B. Roark	.25
John Cross	.25	W.B. Roark	.50
A.B. Cross	.75	Mrs. J.L. Roark	.40
J.L. Roark	.50	Louie Samples	.10
J.R. Allison	.25	Minnie Smith	.10
W.A. Pendergrass	.15	total	$6.10

Saturday, February 1, 1913

Salem Baptist Church met Saturday night before the first Sunday in February 1913 the pastor presiding after devotional exercise the Church was called in cession.
Read and approved minutes of previous meeting. Called for the fellowship of the Church finding the Church not in fellowship. The Board of Deacons was requested to fellowship and discipilen the Church if possible before the next meeting. then adjourned till Sunday met Sunday preaching by the pastor then adjourned to meet Sunday night met according to appointment preaching by pastor then Closed

J.M. Roark clerk   *L.E. Rowland Mdr.*

Financial report for February

Manda Bare	.30	Mrs. J.L. Roark	.50
W.A. Stulce	.15	Jess Pendergrass	.25

W.M. Roark	1.00	Mamie Smith	.25
Willie Roark	.25	Liddia Stulce	.25
Ether Kincannon	.10	Willie McCallie	.10
Sallie Cross	.50	F.O. Smith	.25
Minnie Smith	.10	A.L. Smith	.25
J.R. Allison	.25	W.A. Pendergrass	.25
John Cross	.25	Harrison Roark	.50
W.B. Roark	.50	Mrs. W.M. Roark	.25
J.M. Roark	.25	Lillie Moon	.25
Clara Roark	.10	Lena Hixson	.10
C.H. Hixson	.10	total	$7.05

[No record of Church meeting for March, 1913]

Saturday, April 5, 1913

Salem Baptist Church met Saturday night before the first
Sunday in April the pastor presiding after devotional exercise the Church was called in ces-
sion. No Business of importance comeing before the Church adjourned till sunday. preach-
ing by the pastor then adjourned to meet sunday night Met sunday night preaching by the
pastor then closed

   J.M. Roark clerk   *L.E. Rowland Mdr.*

Financial report for April

T.A. Roark	$1.00	John Cross	.25
Jess Pendergrass	.25	W.G. Roark	.25
Mrs. J.L. Roark	$1.00	A.L. Smith	.25
W.B. Roark	$1.00	C. H. Hixson	.10
J.L. Roark	$1.00	Lena Hixson	.10
F.O. Smith	.25	Sallie Cross	.25
Jennie Eldridge	.25	Mrs. W.M. Roark	.25
J.R. Allison	.25	W.A. Pendergrass	.15
J.M. Roark	.20	Minnie Smith	.10
Clara Roark	.10	W.M. Roark	.50
W.H. Roark	.25	J.R. Davis	.25
Louie Brown	.10	J.A. Shropshire	.75
Ether Kin Cammon	.10	Lillie Moon	.25
[Ether Kincannon]		total	$9.20

public collection for home mission $4.08

Saturday, May 3, 1913

Salem Baptist Church met Saturday night before the first Sunday in May 1913 Preaching by the Pastor after which the Church was called in cession. red and approved minnets of Previous meeting no business comeing before the Church adjourned till Sunday morning met Sunday morning after Preaching the Lords Supper ws administered then Closed to meet Sunday Nite

Met Sunday nite after a verry interesting Sermon on the Subject of repentance our Pastor then made a Proposition to the Church for all that would inter into covenant with him and each other that they would read one chapter Per day and Pray

one Prayer a day quite a number intered into this covenant, then Closed.

J.M. Roark clerk & Treas.   L.E. Rowland Modr.

Financial report for May contribution on Pastors Salary by

Mandy Bare	.30	*W.G. Roark*	.50
Lillie Moon	.25	*W.H. Roark*	.50
Jennie Eldridge	.20	*Mrs. W.M. Roark*	.25
Lener [Lena] *Hixson*	.20	*Willie Roark*	.50
C.H. Hixson	.10	*Mrs. Samples*	.10
F.O. Smith	.50	*A.L. Smith*	.35
J.M. Roark	.25	*Grove McDade*	.10
Clara Roark	.10	*Mrs Stulce*	.10
W.M. Roark	.25	*Minnie Smith*	.25
J.L. Roark	.50	*Ether Kincannon*	.10
Mrs. J.L. Roark	.50	*total*	6.70
W.B. Roark	.50	*We are Yet due our Pastor*	
F.A.B. Roark	.25		*$8.45*

Saturday, May 31, 1913

Salem Baptist Church met Saturday night before the first Sunday in June 1913 the pastor presiding the Clerk being absent no business was transacted adjourned to meet Sunday Met Sunday preaching by the pastor the Church was then called in cession read and approved minutes of previous meeting then Closed the present cession.

J.M. Roark Clerk & Treas   L.E. Rowland Modr.

Financial report for June contribution on pastors salary.

F.O. Smith	.25	*Nannie Allison*	.10
A.L. Smith	.25	*Mrs. Samples*	.10
J.M. Roark	.25	*W.M. Roark*	*$1.00*
Clara Roark	.10	*Grace Stulce*	.10

W.A. Stulce	.10	Laura Moon	.25
E.P. Smith	.25	Minnie Smith	.10
Lilly Moon	.25	Sarah Stulce	.25
J.L. Roark	.50	total	$4.60
Mrs. J.L. Roark	.50	yet due our pastor	$12.10
Jane Fann	.25		

Saturday, July 5, 1913

Salem Baptist Church met Saturday night before the first Sunday in July 1913 preaching by the pastor the Church was called in cession read and approved minutes of previous meeting no other business coming before the Church adjourned till Sunday met Sunday preaching by our pastor then adjourned till Sunday night met Sunday night preaching by our pastor then Closed.

J.M. Roark Clerk   L.E. Rowland Modr.

Financial report contribution on pastors salary by

W.A. Pendergrass	.25	W.B. Roark	.50
Lillie Moon	.50	Jess Pendergrass	.45
Thomas Allison	.10	M.J. Bare	.15
C.H. Hixson	.10	Willie McCallie	.05
Sarah Stulce	.10	J.R. Davis	.10
J.M. Roark	.25	W.H. Roark	.30
S.C. Allison	.25	R.C. Dungan	.25
Arnold Pendergrass	.10	F.A.[B.] Roark	.25
J.L. Roark	.50	W.G. Roark	.50
Mrs. J.L. Roark	.50	W.A. Stulce	.10
W.M. Roark	$1.00	Minnie Smith	.10
Mammie Smith	.10	Nannie Allison	.10
Willie Roark	.25	L.H. Roark	.20
T.A. Roark	.25	Roscoe Bower	.10
Bertha Smith	.25	Mrs. W.M. Roark	.50
Ether Kincannon	.10	Maggie Smith	.10
Rosa Smith	.10	A.L. Smith	.25
Bertha McCallie	.25	Jennie Eldridge	.20
Nettie Smith	.25	Clay Monger	.10
		total	$9.50
		yet due our pastor	$10.85

[No record of Church meeting in August, 1913]

Saturday, September 6, 1913

Salem Baptist Church met Saturday night before the first Sunday in September 1913 The pastor presiding afer Devotional exercise. read and approved minutes of previous meeting. It was agreed upon to hold a revival. The meeting was continued day and night till Thursday night. On the first Monday of the meeting a motion and second was made to elect a pastor and Clerk. Reverend L.E. Rowland was reelected by a unanimous vote and J.M. Roark was reelected Clerk. Motion

and second that the Church appoint a delligation to represent us in the Association consisting of Bro Berry [F.A.B.] *Roark Bro. James Allison and W.B. Roark. on Tuesday motion and second that the Church withdraw fellowship from Bro. Jeff Latham and Bro. S.C. Allison. On Thursday night Sister Laura Moon called for a letter of recomendation. The same was granted the meeting then Closed.*

   J.M. Roark clerk   *L.E. Rowland Mdr.*

Financial report contribution on pastors salary by

C.H. Hixson	.25	Jess Pendergrass	.25
Louie Brown	.10	Thomas Allison	.10
J.L. Roark	.50	J.R. Allison	.50
Mrs. J.L. Roark	.50	J.R. Davis	.25
W.B. Roark	.50	A.L. Smith	.25
J.M. Roark	.50	Jeff Roark	.50
W.M. Roark	.50	total	$4.95
Mrs. W.M. Roark	.25	public col	$1.02
			$5.97

recd. for missions in Sept. By

W.G. Roark	.50	H.E. White	.25
Lilly Moon	.25	W.A. Pendergrass	.15
J.M. Roark	.50	L.H. Roark	.25
		total	$1.90

Saturday, October 4, 1913

Salem Baptist Church met Saturday night before the first Sunday in October 1913 the pastor presiding. After preaching the Church was called in cession. read and approved minutes of previous meeting. Motion and second that the Church appoint a finance committe on Mission also. The finance committe consist of Bro. John Cross, Will Stulce and James Allison. The Mission committe was Ether Kincannon Clara Roark, Floid [Floyd] *smith and W.B. Roark. No other business motion and second to adjourn till 10.30 on Sunday Met Sunday preaching by the pastor then closed.*

   J.M. Roark Clerk & Treas.   *L.E. Rowland Modr.*

Financial report contribution on pastors salary by

C.H. Hixson	.25	Nannie Allison	.10
J.M. Roark	.25	W.M. Roark	.50
W.A. Pendergrass	.25	J.A. Shropshire	.25
W.B. Roark	.50	Mrs. W.M. Roark	.25
J.L. Roark	.25	Manda Bare	.25
Mrs. J.L. Roark	.25	F.A.B. Roark	.50
John Cross	.25	total	$3.85
		yet due our pastor	$12.50

Saturday, November 1, 1913

Salem Baptist Church met Saturday night before the first Sunday in Nov. 1913 the pastor being present After preaching by Bro. Sprague the church was called in cession read and approved minutes of previous meeting new business Bro. J.W. Roark had .30 cents on hand that was collected some time ago for the Ladies Aid Society and was not used. Motion and second that it be turned over to the Treasure for Missions. it was agreed to carry on the meeting for the following week on

Thursday our Pastor was called home on account of sickness and the meeting was carried on by Bro. Sprague till Sunday our Pastor before leaving appointed a committe to get up some money to pay Bro. Sprague for his service. The committe was

Bro. John Cross turned in .10 cents W.A. Pendergrass turned in .30 cents J.M. Roark turned in $6.10 Total $6.50

On Saturday night gave an invitation for member ship and received Sister Mary McCallie Lillen [Lilly?] Roark, Emma Smith, Bessie McCallie, Willie Roark, and Lou Hixson. Also on Sunday received Sister Stella Dungan for Baptism. extended the hand of Christian fellowship to those that had joined the Church then closed the meeting By Bro. Sprague.

J.M. Roark, Clerk & Treas.   L.E. Rowland Modr.

Finance collection for church expence .60 cts.
Contribution on pastors salary total $2.25
Yet due our Pastor $18.50

Sunday, December 7, 1913

Salem Baptist Church met the first Sunday in December 1913.
preaching by the pastor then closed to meet Sunday night
Met Sunday night the pastor presiding the Church was called in cession read and approved minutes of previous meeting then closed.

J.M. Roark clerk & Treas.   L.E. Rowland Modr.

Financial report contribution on pastors salary by

W.M. Roark	1.00	Willie Roark	.10
Mrs. W.M. Roark	.25	Sarah Stulce	.25
Jennie Eldridge	.10	W.A. Pendergrass	.25
J.R. Davis	.25	J.M. Roark	.50
Joe Smith	.10	Lellen [Lilly?] Roark	.10
C.H. Hixson	.25	Clara Roark	.10
F.A.B. Roark	.50	Jess Pendergrass	.15
Roscoe Bower	.50	J.L. Roark	.50
W.G. Roark	.50	Mrs. J.L. Roark	.50
Thomas Allison	.15	T.A. Roark	.25
W.B. Roark	.50	J.R. Allison	.25
Mrs. Samples	.10	total	$7.15
		Yet due our pastor	$19.60

1914

[No record of Church meeting in January, 1914]

Saturday, January 31, 1914

Salem Baptist Church met Saturday night before the first Sunday in February 1914 preaching by the pastor after preaching the Church was called in cession read and approved minutes of previous meeting motion and second that we prefer charges against all male members that missed attending and contributing three meetings in succession without a good cause. Motion and second to elect a Janitor and Bro. John Davis was elected. Motion and second to adjourn till Sunday at eleven oclock met Sunday preaching by the Pastor then closed till Sunday night. met Sunday night preaching by the pastor. motion and second to begin service at 10:30. motion and second that the Church and Sunday school have an intertainment at our next meeting and an admission fee be charged at the door .15 cents single or .25 cents for a couple the proceeds to go for the purpose of buying an organ for the Church a committe was appointed to arrange the program for the same committee W.H. Roark-Ch [Chairman]—*Ether Kincannon and L.H. Roark then closed the present cession.*

J.M. Roark clerk & Treas.   L.E. Rowland Modr

Financial report contribution on Pastors salary by

T.W. Allison	.25	T.J. Gowin	.25
F.A.B. Roark	.25	J.L. Roark	.50

Mrs. W.M. Roark	.25	Mrs. J.L. Roark	.50
R.C. Dungan	.25	W.B. Roark	.50
W.A. Pendergrass	.50	W.H. Roark	.25
J.W. Roark	5.00	Jess Pendergrass	.25
Grover Roark	.25	J.R. Allison	.50
Lillian Stulce	.10	W.A. Stulce	1.00
Ether Kincannon	.20	J.M. Roark	.50
Lilly Moon	1.00	C.H. Hixson	.25
W.M. Roark	1.00	Roscoe Bower	.50
Joe Smith	.10	Wilson Hixson	.20
Mrs. Allison	.10	Sarah Stulce	.20
Willie Roark	.50		$15.15
		public collection	2.45
			$17.60
		yet due our pastor	$10.25

Saturday, February 28, 1914

Salem Baptist Church met Saturday night before the first Sunday in March 1914 the Pastor presiding after devotional exercise the Church was called in cession read and approved minute of previous meeting. motion and second the Church grant Bro. C.A. Smith a letter of dismission. motion and second that we prefer charges against all members that fail to vote on all motions motion and second that W. A. Pendergrass Keep a list of all members that fail to contribute or to attend their Church Meetings. motion and second to adjourn till 10.30 Sunday.

Met Sunday preaching by the Pastor then adjourned to meet Sunday night on the account of cold bad weather no meeting Sunday night.

    J.M. Roark Clerk & Treas.   L.E. Rowland Modr.

Financial report contribution on pastors salary by

W.A. Pendergrass	.25	J.M. Roark	.50
Mrs. W.M. Roark	.25	W.G. Roark	.50
W.M. Roark	.50	M.J. Bare	.25
F.A.B. Roark	.25	W.B. Roark	.25
Joe Smith	.10	J.L. Roark	.50
Ether Kincannon	.20	Mrs. J.L. Roark	.50
		total	$4.05
		Bro. S.J. Stulce	.75
			1.00
		yet due our pastor	$12.70

Saturday, April 4, 1914

Salem Baptist Church met Saturday night before the first Sunday in April 1914 the pastor presiding. After preaching the Church was called in cession read and approved minutes of previous meeting. case of Bro. Sim Williams was then taken up and Bro. Williams was excluded from our Church. We found that he had severed his relation from us by joining another Church motion and second to adjourn till 10:30 Sunday.

Met Sunday preaching by the pastor On Sunday morning the Board of Deacons were called togather. motion and second before the Board to prefer charges against all members that fail to pay .15 cents per month or .45 cts every 3 months motion carried. this amount to be turned into the Treasury to pay on our Pastors salary. on account of sickness our Pastor was called home and the present cession was closed.

J.M. Roark clerk & Treas.   L.E. Rowland Modr.

Financial report contribution on pastors salary by

T.A. Roark	$1.00	W.A. Stulce	.25
J.M. Roark	.25	W.G. Roark	1.00
Mrs. W.M. Roark	.25	John Cross	.30
W.M. Roark	.50	J.R. Allison	.25
F.A.B. Roark	.25	Jess Pendergrass	.25
W.A. Pendergrass	.25	O.B. Cross	.15
J.L. Roark	.50	A.B. Cross	.15
Mrs. J.L. Roark	.50	Willie Roark	.25
W.B. Roark	.50	T.W. Allison	.15
R.C. Dungan	.25	Pearl Smith	.25
Nettie Smith	.25	J.W. Roark	.25
		total	$7.75
		Yet due our pastor	$13.45

Saturday, May 2, 1914

Salem Baptist Church met Saturday night before the first Sunday in May 1914 the pastor presiding. after devotional exerice the Church was called in cession read and approved minutes of previous meeting. motion and second that we drop the following Brethern from the roll for non attendance Bro. T.A. Roark — C.A. Smith — W.T. Heaton — Jack Eldridge, James Shelton, Joseph Conner, Enoch Hardin, Andy Hardin, W. H. Hixson, Bill Hardin, Jeff Cross jr., Arthur Hubbard, Alec Smith, Sim Eldridge, Rube Hubbard. motion and second that the Church withdraw fellowship from Bro. Jim Posey charged with swearing. Motion and second to adjourn till 10.30 Sunday.

Met Sunday preaching by the pastor then Closed.

J.M. Roark Clerk & Treas.   L.E. Rowland Modr.

Contribution on pastors salary by

Berry [F.A.B.] Roark	.25	Ether Kincannon	.10
John Cross	.15	L.H. Roark	.25
T.W. Allison	.15	Mrs. J.L. Roark	.50
Mag Davis	.15	W.H. Roark	.50
J.R. Allison	.25	Jess Pendergrass	.25
J.M. Roark	.25	R.C. Dungan	.25
Mrs. W.M. Roark	.25	W.B. Roark	.50
C.H. Hixson	.50	W.G. Roark	.25
J.L. Roark	.50	O.B. Cross	.15
W.A. Pendergrass	.25	W.M. Roark	1.00
J.W. Roark	.25	J.R. Davis	.25
			$7.15
		from others	2.00
		total	$9.15
		Yet due our pastor	$12.55
		May by cash	7.00
			$5.55

Saturday, June 6, 1914

Salem Baptist Church met Saturday night before the first
Sunday in June 1914 the pastor presiding, after devotional exercise the Church was called
in cession, read and approved minutes of previous meeting motion and second that the
Church reinstate Bro T.A. Roark motion and second to
adjourn till Sunday, met Sunday, preaching by the pastor Then adjourned to meet Sunday
night met Sunday night, preaching by the pastor then closed,
　　　J.M. Roark clerk & Treas.　　*L.E. Rowland Modr.*

Financial report contribution on pastors salary by

T.W. Allison	.20	W.A. Pendergrass	.25
J.L. Roark	.50	W.G. Roark	.25
Mrs. J.L. Roark	.50	J.M. Roark	.25
Mrs. W.M. Roark	.25	Mrs. White	.50
John Cross	.50	W.H. Roark	.25
W.B. Roark	.50	Roscoe Bower	.50
T. J. Gowin	.10	L.H. Roark	.75
Jeff Roark	.25	R.C. Dungan	.25
W.M. Roark	.50	A.L. Smith	.25

W.A. Stulce	.10	F.A.B. Roark	.25
J.W. Roark	.25	total	$7.15

Saturday, July 4, 1914

Salem Baptist Church met Saturday night before the first Sunday in July 1914 the pastor presiding after devotional exercise the Church was called in cession read and approved minutes of previous meeting there being no other business adjourned till Sunday met Sunday preaching by the pastor then closed.

J.M. Roark Clerk & Treas.   L.E. Rowland Modr.

Financial report contribution on pastors salary by

W.B. Roark	.25	Sallie Cross	.30
C.H. Hixson	.30	C.H. Swafford	.25
T.W. Allison	.15	Mrs. W.M. Roark	.25
Ether Kincannon	.10	A.B. Cross	.40
F.A.B. Roark	.25	O.B. Cross	.30
W.M. Roark	.50	John Cross	.25
L.H. Roark	.25	J.A. Shropshire	.50
J.L. Roark	.50	J.R. Davis	.25
Mrs. J.L. Roark	.50	A.L. Smith	.25
W.H. Roark	.50	total	$6.10

Saturday, August 1, 1914

Salem Baptist Church met Saturday night before the first Sunday in August 1914 the pastor presiding after devotional exercise the Church was called in cession read and approved minutes of previous meeting motion and second that we appoint Deligates to the Association Deligation W.G. Roark J.R. Allison W.A. Pendergrass F.A.B. Roark motion and second to adjourn till 10.30 Sunday Met Sunday preaching by the pastor Then Closed.

J.M. Roark clerk   L.E. Rowland Modr.

Collection on pastors salary	$6.50
By others	$2.25
total	$8.75
yet due our pastor	$8.30
	2.50
	5.80

[No record of Church meeting in September, 1914]

Saturday, October 3, 1914

Salem Baptist Church met Saturday night before the first Sunday in October 1914 the pastor presiding motion and second to adjourn till Sunday met Sunday preaching by the pastor then Closed.

        J.M. Roark clerk   L.E. Rowland Modr.

Sunday, October 17, 1914

Salem Baptist Church met in call cession on the 3rd Sunday in October for the purpose of electing a pastor and Clerk Bro. L.E. Rowland was elected pastor by a unanimous vote and J.M. Roark was elected Clerk then adjourned

        J.M. Roark Clerk   F.A.B. Roark chairman

Saturday, October 31, 1914

Salem Baptist Church met Saturday night before the first Sunday in November 1914 The pastor presiding after preaching by the moderator the Church was called in cession read and approved minutes of previous meetings Bro. Powell being present it was announced that he would lecture to the Church at 10.30 Sunday motion and second to adjourn

met Sunday at 10.30 Bro. Powell delivered a good lecture adjourned till Sunday evening Met Sunday evening and Bro. Powell delivered a lecture on the laymans movement next the Church was called in cession motion and second that our

Church adopt the laymans movement and a committee was appointed to see the membership of this Church and see what each member would contribute for the cause The committee as follows Bro. John Davis Arch Smith J.R. Allison F.A.B. Roark, W.A. Pendergrass W.B. Roark, John Cross J.M. Roark

then adjourned till Sunday night

met Sunday night preaching by the pastor then closed

        J.M. Roark Clerk & Treas.   L.E. Rowland Modr.

Contribution on pastors salary $6.75

Saturday, December 5, 1914

Salem Baptist Church met Saturday night before the first Sunday in December 1914 preaching by the pastor there being but few present had no conference adjourned till

10.30 Sunday Met Sunday preaching by the pastor the Church was then called in cession read and approved minutes of previous meeting. then adjourned till Sunday night

Met Sunday night preaching by the pastor the Church agreed to continue the meeting for a few days on Monday night the committee on the Missionary laymens movement was called on to report and the same was made and adopted by the Church the report as follows total

subscription so far for the year $130.80 with the following requests asking for letters of dismission. Hattie Rains asked to be dropped from the roll. the
Sister being a nonaffiliated member she was excluded from the Church for nonaffiliation. motion and second that the Church grant Bro. S.J. Stulce a letter of dismission in full fellowship. motion and second that the Church grant Sister Elizabeth Eldridge a letter of recomendation motion and second the Church grant Sister Sarah L. Stulce a letter of dismission in full fellowship. motion and second that the Church grant Bro. Owen Smith another letter of dismission on account of the previous letter being lost or misplaced.

also adopted the following resolutions that the committee suggested. Brethern as we have each and all of us who have here to fore added ourselves to the Missionary Baptist Church at Salem and have believed and accepted, and agreed to comply with our Church covenant and believing as we do that same is in conformity and compliance with the Bible and that its principals are well founded and believing that the Laymens Missionary Movement is in strict compliance with our covenant do hereby resolve to adopt the following resolutions. Be it resolved that we organize the Laymens Missionary Movement and carry same faith to the limit of its intentions and purposes and that we strive to make this the best year of work and service for our master that has gone on record of our Church.

And be it resolved that we solicit each member to cooperate in the work of our Church by and with their means, presents and influence.

And be it farther resolved that when any member or members refuse to do so that we discontinue our relationship with them.

And be it farther resolved that we as a Church assume the leadership, directorship, and responsibility of our Sunday school. By directing its work and electing its officers.

And be it farther resolved that we be more zealous in our work, setting an hour to begin our work on said hour.

And that we elect and pay a janitor to keep our house clean and lighted as best of his ability.

And be it farther resolved that we take such steps or adopt some means where by we may get our young people to reading the Bible and such religious literature as will feed their minds on the subject of Christian Education.

motion and second that the Church retain those that are not able to pay and give the non-affiliated members till our next meeting to make their excuse to the Church.
motion and second to adjourn the present cession.

J.M. Roark clerk & Treas.   L.E. Rowland Modr.

Contribution on Salary $9.55

1915

Saturday, January 2, 1915

Salem Baptist Church met Saturday night before the first Sunday in January 1915 the pastor presiding after preaching the Church was called in cession. Read and approved minutes of previous meeting. Bro. J.W. Roark agreed to serve as Janitor the Church agreed to assist Bro. Joe in his work as Janitor.
Motion and Second to adjourn till Sunday at 10:30.
Met Sunday according to appointment preaching by the pastor then closed till Sunday night Met Sunday night preaching by the pastor. The roll was then called of the affiliating members, Motion and second to receive the report of the committie on the Laymans Missionary Movement and releice the committie. The Non affiliation Members are Otis Cross, Thomas Conner, Floyd Smith, Maggie Hixson, Nettie Smith, Pearl Smith, Lilly Cross, Charles Swafford, Laura Smith, J.A. Shropshire, Laura Shropshire. The above brethern and sisters have severed their connection from the Church for non affiliation.
Then closed the present cession

J.M. Roark C.C. and Treas.   L.E. Rowland Modr.

Contribution on pastors salary $9.65
*   "   for Colledge   .59*
*   "   " the Home $1.84*

Saturday, February 6, 1915

Salem Baptist Church met Saturday night before the first Sunday in February 1915. the pastor presiding after preaching the Church was called in cession read and approved minutes of previous metting adjourned till 10:30 Sunday, met Sunday preaching by the pastor after preaching Bro. Amos Shoat joined the Church by letter from Mountain Creek Church. The church then extended the hand of Christian fellowship to Bro. Shoat. then adjourned till Sunday night. met Sunday night preaching by the pastor after preaching the following committies were appointed, committie to seat and look after the painting of Salem Baptist Church house J.R. Allison, C.H. Hixson and J.M. Roark. Also committie to raise money to carpet the isle [aisle] of Salem Baptist Church House. Nannie Allison, Willie Roark, Ether

Kincannon, Maude Talley, Jennie Eldridge, it was also requested that the Subscription be paid in at March meeting. Then Closed the present cession.

J.M. Roark, Clerk & Treas.   L.E. Rowland Modr.

Contribution on pastors salary $10.60

Saturday, March 6, 1915

Salem Baptist Church met Saturday night before the first Sunday in March 1915 the pastor presiding after preaching The Church was called in cession. read and approved minutes of previous metting. It was suggested that the pastor appoint a committie to look after the lighting of our church. Committie,
J.W. Roark, A.L. Smith, and Sister Sallie Cross. Motion and Second to adjourn till 10:30 Sunday met Sunday preaching by the pastor then closed till Sunday night, met Sunday night preaching by the pastor then closed.

J.M. Roark Clerk & T.   L.E. Rowland Modr.

Financial report on pastors salary. $7.45. public collection for the home $1.35.

Saturday, April 3, 1915

Salem Baptist Church met Saturday night before the first Sunday in April 1915 the pastor presiding, after preaching the Church was called in cession read and approved minutes of previous meeting motion and second that the Church meet at 9:30 Sunday and organize a Sunday school. no other business motion and second to adjourn till Sunday, Met Sunday and organized Sunday School and then had preaching by the pastor then adjourned till Sunday night
Met Sunday night preaching by the pastor. On motion and second the Church granted Sister Lilly Moon a letter of dismission at her own request and the Clerk was authorized to write the same. Then closed.

J.M. Roark Clerk   L.E. Rowland Mdr.

Contribution on pastors salary $9.15

Saturday, May 1, 1915

Salem Baptist Church met Saturday night before the first Sunday in May 1915 the Pastor Presiding after preaching Red and approved minuets of Previous meeting motion and sec to adjourn till Sunday night
met Sunday night Preaching by the Pastor then Closed the Present cession

J.M. Roark C & Treas.   L.E. Rowland Modr

Wheat	*$3.00*
Contribution on Pastors Salary	*$7.35*
	$10.35

Saturday, June 5, 1915

Salem Baptist Church met Saturday night before the first Sunday in June 1915 The Pastor Presiding the Clerk being absent had no conference adjourned to meet Sunday met Sunday at 10:30 the Church wsa called in cession red and approved minuets of Previous meeting communication from the Secretary of the home was red to the church asking the Church to give June 10ᵗʰ as work day for the home only four bretheren responded to the call. Motion and Sec that this Church take some steps to help pay the small debt that this church owes. the Sunday night Servis was called in
then adjourned.

       J.M. Roark Clerk and treas   *L.E. Rowland Modr*

contribution on Pastors Salary   *$8.65*

Saturday, July 3, 1915

Salem Baptist Church met Saturday night before the first Sunday in July 1915 the Pastor presiding. After devotional exercise the Church was called in cession read and approved minutes of previous meeting. On June 13ᵗʰ the Board of Deacons had a call meeting it being rumored that some of the members had been dancing, the Board recomended that the Church take some action. A committe of investigation was appointed. W.A. Stulce Ch. W.G. Roark, Sister Jennie Eldridge, Sister Jane Cross. the board also recomended that the Church take action and drop from the roll those that have not complied with the Laymens Missionary Movement and the resolutions that this Church adopted motion and second to adjourn till 10:30 Sunday. Met Sunday at 10:30 Preaching by the Pastor then closed to meet Sunday night on the account of bad weather had no Serviss Sunday night

       J.M. Roark Clerk and Treas.   *L.E. Rowland Modr*

Financial report contribution on Pastors Salary $8.65

Saturday, July 31, 1915

Salem Baptist Church met Saturday night before the first Sunday in August 1915 the pastor presiding after devotional exercise the Church was called in cession read and approved minutes of previous meeting the committee of investigation reported that Sister Lena Hixson and sister [Ether] Kincannon had been dancing. They making no acknowledgement they were excluded from the Church the committee was granted till our next meeting to report in full. Motion and second to adjourn till 10:30 Sunday met Sunday preaching

by the pastor then Closed till Sunday night met Sunday night preaching by the pastor Bro
T.A. Roark requested a letter of dismission the same was granted it was announced that
our pastor would begin a revival on Saturday night before the fourth Sunday in August,
then closed the present cession.

> *J.M. Roark clerk & Treas.   L.E. Rowland Modr*

Financial report contribution on pastors salary $7.90
contribution for mission By L.H. Roark .25 cents for the home and .25 for state mission
yet Due our Pastor on Last year $5.80
Due on this year $8.75

Saturday, August 21, 1915

Salem Baptist Church met Saturday night before the 4th Sunday in August 1915 the pastor
presiding the meeting was continued till August the 30th. during this time the Church was
called in cession motion and second to appoint deligates to the association the following
brethern were appointed J.R. Allison, W.B. Roark and W.G. Roark. also sister Lena Hixson
made her acknowledgement to the Church and she was restored to full fellowship
then closed the present cession.

> *J.M. Roark clerk & Treas.   L.E. Rowland Modr.*

Financial report on contribution on pastors salary $16.35
yet due our pastor $ 8.20

Membership Records of Salem Baptist Church from the Minutes 1910–1915

	1910	1911	1912	1913	1914	1915	Total
Excluded	0	0	0	0	2	2	4
Dismissed	3	1	0	0	4	2	10
Letter of Recommendation	0	0	2	1	1	0	4
Received by Letter	2	0	3	6	0	1	12
Received/ Experience	5	0	2	1	0	0	8
Enrollment	0	0	0	0	0	0	0
Baptized	4	0	2	0	0	0	6
Restored	0	0	0	0	1	1	2
Fellowship Withdrawn	0	0	1	2	16	0	19

Activities tabulated from the Minutes of Salem Baptist Church

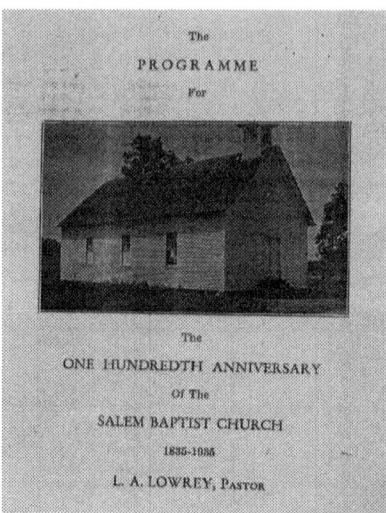

The

PROGRAMME

For

The

ONE HUNDREDTH ANNIVERSARY

Of The

SALEM BAPTIST CHURCH

1835-1935

L. A. LOWREY, Pastor

BRIEF CHURCH HISTORY

When a group of God-fearing men and women assembled in this community to organize Salem church, Andrew Jackson was president of the United States, Victoria was a sixteen-year-old girl being prepared to become queen of England. The Church of the Holy Sepulchre, which was the occasion of a great war, had not been erected in Jerusalem. Cleveland and Chattanooga had not yet appeared on the map. Birchwood was a spring and a birch tree or two. There were only scattering white families here and there in this part of the country which was still in possession of the Cherokee Indians. These pioneers, however, while striving to establish homes for themselves and their children in the wilderness thought it also well to plant and propagate the religion of their fathers.

In the year of 1835 the settlers of the Gardenhar community decided to organize and build a church. On the fourth Saturday of May, 1835, they met and organized Salem church. They erected a log building near the Gardenhar Spring, now the Dyke Eldridge Spring. More settlers came and settled along the Birchwood road. Among these were the Roarks and Connors and others. These were large families and inclined to be religious. Sometimes between 1850 and 1860 they decided to move Salem church. They selected and built a log house on the plot of ground where Salem church now stands. This was deeded to the church by Mr. Roark.

The log house stood on the present site for many years and was finally destroyed by fire, destroying all records of the church. After the erection of a new frame building the church met in conference and the surviving pioneers drew up a brief sketch giving dates of the organization of the pioneer church.

About twelve or fifteen years ago this building was torn down and the same building which now stands was erected.

This information was furnished by Mr. Friddell of Salem community and Mr. Jackie Roark of Georgetown.

PROGRAMME

Sunday, May 26, 1935

9:00 a. m.	Sunday School.
10:00 a. m.	Baptizing.
10:30 a. m.	Announcements.
10:35 a. m.	Song.
10:40 a. m.	Devotion by J. W. Linkous.
10:50 a. m.	Song.
10:55 a. m.	Recognition of former pastors and visitors.
11:10 a. m.	Quartette.
11:15 a. m.	Sermon by Rev. Jimmie Johnson.
11:50 a. m.	Song and prayer.
12:00 m.	Basket lunch.
1:00 p. m.	Song and prayer.
1:05 p. m.	Reading by Julian Snyder.
1:10 p. m.	Quartette.
1:15 p. m.	"Church History" by T. J. Campbell.
1:45 p. m.	Song by congregation.
1:50 p. m.	"Future of Church" by Beery Roark.
2:00 p. m.	Prayer.
2:05 p. m.	Singing.
2:15 p. m.	Sermon by Dr. T. S. McCallie.
2:45 p. m.	Singing.

Program for the One Hundredth Anniversary of Salem
Baptist Church
Held Sunday, May 26, 1935 at Salem Church

Chapter Seven
Salem Baptist Church 1915–1941

Salem Baptist Church would continually decline in membership into the 1930s when it would be reduced to a few families, despite the efforts of its members in conducting the business of the church. According to the minutes of the Ocoee Association, D.S. Kellum was listed as pastor of Salem Church in 1917, S.N. Fitzpatrick in 1918, and J.W. Linkous in 1924. C.H. King was pastor from 1925 to 1928, and L.A. Lowry from 1934 to 1935. In the missing years, Salem Baptist Church was either not represented or not listed.

The Program for the One Hundredth Anniversary of Salem listed as "Former Pastors Now Living:" J.W. Linkous, C.H. King, J.G. Blassingame, S.J. Lawrence, and T.J. Latham. The current pastor was L.A. Lowry. It is not known for sure which years Blassingame and Lawrence were pastors of the church, other than that, most likely, their terms would fit into the years not represented or not listed in the association minutes.

As the church membership dwindled, the women, young and old, of the church became more and more important to, and involved in, church business. In the minutes of the Ocoee Association from the 1926 associational meeting, Miss Reba Shropshire, at 16, was Senior President of the Baptist Young Peoples Union, Mrs. S.A. Mathis was the Superintendent of Sunday Schools, and Miss Martha Smith was church clerk. The total membership was listed as 40 members.

With a steady reduction of its membership in the 1930s, Salem Baptist Church began a slow decline to complete abandonment as families moved to urban locations. In 1934 T.J. Latham was pastor of Salem Church when he and an undetermined number of members left Salem to form New Liberty Baptist Church. L.A. Lowry became pastor of Salem following Latham's departure. Sometime after the One-Hundredth Anniversary celebration of Salem Baptist Church in May 1935, and before 1938, L.A. Lowry left unexpectedly. Rev. Clifford Owenby served as pastor from 1938 to 1939. Rev. Robert Lanham was called as pastor in 1939 and served until 1941. By the late 1930s the church was unable to pay its dues to the Ocoee Association. In late 1938, church clerk Velma Roark read a letter to the church from the Association stating that "without payment of dues the Salem Church could no longer be considered a member of the Association."

After Rev. Lanham left as pastor in 1941, the few remaining members of the church continued to hold lay services in the church building. Membership had been reduced to the Joe Roark, Thomas Allison, and Frank Scott families and, as in the first-century church at Philippi, dedicated women of the church. Members continued to meet in the church building for lay services in the summer of 1941 and Arlena Davis and Mrs. Frank Scott paid the deposit to maintain power so that lights were available for the lay services. Shortly thereafter the building was locked and all services of the church were terminated.[1]

The last known service in the church building was the funeral of Civil War veteran John Lewis Roark on July 15, 1941. Edgar Roark, grandson of the deceased, wrote of the cleanup effort at the church in preparation for the funeral service:

> The following is my recollection of the events surrounding my grandfather's last days and the final service held at the Salem Baptist Church. My grandfather, John Lewis Roark, lived with us for as long as I could remember. Grandfather was 90 years old when he fell and broke his hip. Dr. Friddell of Birchwood was his doctor. He treated Uncle Jack (Dr. Friddell always called him Uncle Jack) at home, and he made regular visits to our home to check on Uncle Jack. He recovered and could walk on crutches and then was able to use a cane. He lived on until he was 94 years old. He passed away July 14, 1941. At that time, I was 16 years old.
>
> When the funeral arrangements were made, they wanted to have the funeral in the old Salem Church, but there was a problem. The church had been closed for some time. We went over and looked at the church and decided we could clean it up and make it safe for the funeral service. Several of us gathered at the church to clean it up. We had to fight wasps and dirt dobbers, clean out spiders and webs, and sweep out leaves and trash of all kinds. All the benches had to be scrubbed, and of course the floors had to be scrubbed. Some repairs had to be made to the floor to make it safe, but after several hours of work it was presentable for the funeral.
>
> To the best of my knowledge, this was the last service that was ever held in the Salem Church. It is so sad to see a church that was dedicated to the Lord's work close its doors and rot down.[2]

After the last service, the church building was not maintained and its condition steadily deteriorated. By 1960, only the collapsed ruins of the once-proud meeting house remained. The church site is currently identified by a historical marker.

Appendixes

Appendix A

CHURCH ROLL
1872–1873[42]

List of the Members

1. M.H. Conner
2. Martha Conner
3. Joseph Cookson[43]
4. Sally Cookson[44]   *Died April 1874*[45]
5. Phebe C.Chambers
6. Silas Witt
7. Martha Witt
8. Thomas Conner
9. M.C. Conner
10. Margaret Conner
11. James Roark
12. Jerusha Roark
13. John B. Roark
14. Nancy Roark
15. Martha J. Roark
16. Juda Roark
17. Victoria Roark
18. John L. Roark
19. John W. Roark
20. James A. Roark

---

[42] This Church Roll was not dated. The dates of 1872–73 were developed based on the position of the roll in the pages of the Church Minutes ledger book and the dates from the Minutes on which certain members were accepted into Church membership.

[43] Joseph Cookston

[44] Sally Cookston

[45] Notes on the death of, or on Church actions on, certain members were obviously added at a later date and in a handwriting different from that of the Church Roll.

21. Merica Roark[46]	
22. Elizabeth Roark	Died 1892
23. James Conner	
24. Jane Conner	
25. Malinda Irwin	Died
26. M.M. Gross	
27. Latisha Gross	
28. John Gass	
29. Burton Holeman	
30. Sarah Holeman	
31. Robert Holeman	
32. Leander Lane	
33. Duke Kimbrough	Died
34. Mary J. Purcell	
35. James Cameron Jun [Junior]	
36. James Cameron Seign [Senior]	
37. Lina Dixon	
38. Sarah A. Dixon	
39. Elizabeth Baker	
40. Jacob Baker	
41. Rosa A.Gross	
42. Margaret Solomon	
43. Sarah J. Baker	
44. Betsey Baker	
45. William Curton	
46. Mary A. Curton	
47. Betsey J. Malone	
48. Samuel Smith	Lettered off
49. Eiza Smith	Lettered off
50. Wm.R. Haney	
51. Nancy Haney	
52. Isaac Haney	
53. F.M. Cookson	
54. Elizabeth Cookson	
55. Abner Stulce	
56. Leonard H. Stulce	
57. Sarah Stulce	
58. Marica C. Stulce	

---

[46]   America Roark, wife of James A.Roark

59. Mary J. Stulce
60. A.L. Stulce
61. Lucinda F. Stulce
62. Wm. J. Stulce
63. Nancy E. Stulce
64. John Campbell
65. Lucinda Campbell
66. Eliza Denson
67. Mary Denson
68. George Campbell
69. Susan Campbell
70. Martha Rains
71. ~~Betty Campbell~~
72. Elizabeth Brite   Dismist by letter
73. Martha J. Sampels
74. Sally Bly
75. Sarah Webb
76. Betsey J. Webb
77. Berrelda Kenner
78. James W. Taliefaro
79. Nancy Taliefaro   Dis by letter
80. Marand Taliefaro
81 Matter Taliefaro
82. Catharine Smith
83. Nancy Smith   Excluded
84. Betsey Killion
85. Orlena Killion
86. Susa Killion
87. Nancy Killion
88. Polly Smith   Excluded Restored Letterd off 1891
89. Nancy Smith
90. Ing Smith
91. Elizabeth Tally
92. Betsey A. Wilson
93. John S. McCormack   Dis by letter
94. Caroline Johnson
95. Jane Richey
96. Sarah McCormack
97. Wm. F. McCormack   Excluded

98. Mary McCormack	Dis by letter
99. Nancy Mcallie[47]	
100. A.A. Mcallie[48]	
101. Nancy Matthews	
102. Susa Matthews	
103. Margaret Franciscoe	
104. John Eppison	Dis by letter
105. Harriet Eppison	Died 1873
106. Manerva Blair	
107. Morris Howel	
108. Andrew Kingcannon	
109. Julia Moon	
110. Jane Tally	
111. Benjamin Tally	
113. Linda Sivels	
114. Herald Hays	
115. Jane Hardin	
116. Nancy Hays	
117. Jesse Ward	
118. Andrew Ward	
119. Tina Craighead	
120. Polly Gross	
121. Sebrena Monger	
122. Margaret Potter	
123. T.J. Leonard	
124. Will Eldridge	Excluded
125. Catty Mangrum	Col.[49]
126. Mary Moon	Col.
127. Isabel Eldridge	
128. Caldonia Eldridge	
129. Nancy Curton	
130. Nancy Carrel	
131. Nancy Cookson	
132. George W. Rodgers	
133. Rhoda Rodgers	
134. Catharin Gooden	

---

[47]   Nancy McCallie
[48]   A.A. McCallie
[49]   African-American members of the Church were referred to as "colored."

135. *Octava Harris*

136. *Hetty Williams*

137. *Charles Ford*

138. *Clementine Ford*

139. *Emly Millard*

140. *Jane Ward*

141. *Anna Smith*

142. *Mousira Aslinger*   *Leterd off 1892*

143. *Thomas Eldridg*   *Col*

144. *Mary Smith*   *Dis by letter*

145. *Sary A Talley*

146. *Mariam Haney*

147. *Elisabeth Day*   *Died*

148. *Hailey Smith*   *Died*

149. *Ann Hickson*

150. *Fanny Penney*   *Died*

151. *Betty Bear*

152. *Elizabeth Cross*   *by Baptism*

153. *Rhoda J. Killion*

154. *Margaret Pickens*

155. *Rebecca Campbell*   *by Baptism*

156. *Aaron Tucker*

157. *William E. Tucker*

158. *Davis Prada*[50]

159. *salie* [Sallie] *Scrovene*

160. *salie* [Sallie] *Moon*

[161.] *charly Moon*

[162.] *Bird Henry*

---

[50]   Davis Priddy

CHURCH ROLL
1874–1875

Roll for 1874 and 75

1 Aslinger Misouri	
163 Alexander Jane	Dismissed by Letter
2 Aslinger Mary	dismist by Leter
162 Bear Betty	dropt from the Book
3 Baker Elisabeth	
3 Bearns Margaret	Dropt from the Book
4 Bair [Blair] Manerva	Leter
5 Blythe Sarah	Died Jan 1878
6 Conner M.H.	
7 Conner Martha	Died June 1890
8 Conner Joseph H.	
9 Conner Thomas	
10 Cookston Joseph	
11 Cookston Salley	Died April 1874
12 Cookston Nancy	Letterd of [off] in June 1892
13 Campbell John	{Dismissed
14 Campbell Liucinda	{Sept 1877
15 Campbell David L.	Dropt from the Book
16 Campbell Suezann	
17 Denson Eliza	
18 Denson Mary	Dide September 1875
19 Denson James	
20 Day Elisabeth	Died
21 Eldridg Isibell	
22 Eldridg Caldonia	excluded
23 Elkins Thomas	Dismist by Leter 1877
24 Fridle Sarah	not Baptised dropt from the Book
25 Francisco Margaret	dismissed by letter
26 Ford Charls	Excluded
27 Ford Clementine	Dismisted by letter 1882
28 Gooden Luna	Dismist by letter
29 Gooden Catherine	
30 ~~Gooden Scott~~	Dropt from the Book

	Robert Gooden	Excluded April 1875
31	~~Gooden Birda~~	
32	Holman Sarah	{Gone to
33	Holman Robbert	{ Birchwood
34	Haney Wm R.	
35	Haney Nancy	
36	Haney Marinna	
37	Haney Isaac	Dismissed by lette Nov 1877
38	Haney John	
39	Haney Liza Jane	Dismissed by Leter Jan 1887
40	Henry Birda	Letterd off June 1892
41	Henry Julie	Letterd off June 1892
42	Henry James	Excluded
43	Howel Marion	Dis by Letter March 1887
44	Howel Nancy	by letter
45	Howel Mary	
46	Howel Hulda	by letter
47	Howel James	
48	Hayes Herald	
49	Hayes Nancy	
50	Hayes Wilson	Excluded January 1875
51	Hayes Martha	by Letter in March 1881
52	Harden Jane	
53	Harris Octavy	Dismissed by letter 1880
54	Hickson Ann	did died in 1876
55	Hickson Roda Jane	
56	~~Irwin Molinda~~	Dismist by Leter 1876 [Minutes date—1875]
57	Jonson Caroline	Dismissed by letter
58	Jonson Wm	Dismissed by letter
59	Jonson Rebecca	Dismissed by letter
60	Jonson Margaret	dismissed
61	Kenner Berrilda	lettered off
62	Killian Betty	
63	Killian Susa	
64	Killian Nancy	
	Killian Henry	Dis by letter 1874
65	Millard Emily	
66	Malone Betty	

67 McCanlie A.A.[51]		
68 McCanlie Jane [52]		
69 McCanlie Nancy [53]		
70 Mathews Susa	Dismist by leter in 1876	
71 Mathews Nancy		
Miller Emaline	Dismised	
72 McMillion Mathey [Mathew]	Dismissed by Letter Mar	
73 Moon Salley	Leterd of [off]	
74 Moon Charley		
75 Moon Mary		
76 ~~Moon George~~	Dismist by leter	
77 ~~Moon Emaline~~	Dismist by leter	
78 Monger Phronia		
79 Monger James		
80 McCormack Salley	Dismissed by Letter	
81 McCormack R.T.	Dismissed by Letter	
82 McCormack E.C.	Dismissed by Letter	
83 Newton Elisabeth	Died Sep. 1877	
84 Newton George	Excluded 1878	
85 Penny Fanney	Dismissed by Letter 1876	
86 Pickins Margaret		
87 Prada Davis[54]		
88 Potter Margaret	Died 1874	
Roark Joseph[55]		
89 Roark James	Died Sept 1877	
90 Roark Jerusha	Died May 1876	
91 Roark Joseph	Died February 1876	
92 Roark Juda		
93 Roark James A.	Dismissed by letter 1878	
94 Roark A.J.	Dismissed by Letter 1878	
95 Roark Jack		
96 Roark Victory		
97 Roark J.W.		

---

[51]   A.A. McCallie

[52]   Jane McCallie

[53]   Nancy McCallie

[54]   Davis Priddy

[55]   Name added at a later date. Probably refers to Joseph Roark, son of James and Jerusha Roark, sometimes referred to as "Joseph Roark, Jr."

98 Roark Permelia

99 Roark Elisabeth

100 Roark Wm. M.   Excluded

101 Roark Nancy   Dismissed for Constitution

102 Roark Marthy J.   Excluded

103 Rodgers G.W.   lettered of 4 Sabath in April 1876

104 Rodgers Roda   Lettered off

105 Rodgers Roof   letterd of & wife

106 Reno Wm.   dropt from the Book

107 Rains Marthy   Dismist by Leter September 1876

164 Rodgers Barney

165 Rodgers Caroline

108 Stults Abner [56]   Died July 1878

109 Stults A.L.   by letter in March 1881

110 Stults Lucinda   by letter in March 1881

111 Stults W.J.   Excluded 1879

112 Stults Nancy   Dismist by Leter Oct 1876

113 Stults Leonard

114 Stults Sarah

115 Stults Clementine

116 Stults Jane   Letered off

Stulce Sameul   by Letter March 1881

117 Smith Abner   Died June the 10th 89 [1889]

118 Smith J.C.

119 Smith Nancy   lettered off

120 Smith Mary   dismissed by letter

121 Smith Phebe   dropt not Baptised

122 Smith Ing

123 Smith Ann   Dismissed by letter

124 Smith Sameul   lettred off

125 Smith Liza   lettered off

126 Smith Haley   Ded

127 Solomon Margaret   Dismissed for Birchwood

128 Sivils Linda

129 Samples Marthy J.

130 Scrovene Salley   dismissed May 1874 returned continued

131 Short Wm.   lettered off Sept. 1878

132 Talley Elisabeth   Letterd off Aprile 1892

---

[56]   The spelling for the family name in the Minutes was almost universally "Stulce."

133 Talley Benny	Excluded
134 Talley A.J.	
135 Talley Jane	
136 Talley Benjaman	
137 Tally Ann	dismissed by letter in April 1874
138 Tucker Aaron	Died Sept 1887
139 Tucker W.E.	
140 Tucker Hetty	
141 Witt Silas	Leterd of [off]
142 Witt M.J.	Leterd
143 Witt C.H. [?]	Leterd
144 Ward Jessee	Died in 1876
145 Ward Andrew	{ Dismissed
146 Ward Jane	{ Feb, 1878
147 Wilson B.A.	killed July 1881
148 Webb B.J.	lettered off
149 Webb Sarah	leterd of [off] July 88 [1888]
(147) [Betsy Ann Wilson —	killed July 1881]
150 Cross James	Lettrd off Feb 1885
151 Cross Margaret	lettered off June 1877
152 Cross Elisabeth	
153 Cross Nancy	lettered off Jun 1877
154 Craighead Tina	Ded
155 ~~Campbell Rebecca~~	~~lettered off Rodgers~~
156 Chambers Phebe C	Dide June 1875
157 Carrell Nancy	
166 Carter Martha	by Baptism
Colard Members [57]	
158 Eldrage Thomas	Excluded in May 1875
159 Moon Mary	dided in 1876
160 Mangrum Arnold	lettered off Mach [March] 1877
161 Mangrum Caty	dismist by Leter October 1876
162 Isac Low[58]	Lettered off Sep 1884
163 Newtin Haney	Lettred off Apr 1892
164 Parilee Gooden	
165 Nancy Haney	

---

[57]   African-American members of Salem Church.

[58]   From this point in the Church Roll, the remaining members were listed with surname last rather than first as was previously the case.

166 Manthy [Marthy] *Jonson*	*dismmised*	
167 Jiney McCormack	*dissmissed*	
168 Sary McCormack	*Dismmissed*	
169 W.F. McCormack	*Dismmissed*	
170 Susan Johnson Smith	*Dismmissed*	
171 Elisabeth Rogers		
172 William White	*Dismissed by Letter*	
173 Thomas Quinn	*Dismist by Leter March 1875*	
174 David Quinn	*Dismist by Leter*	
175 Caroline Cane		
176 Jane Scott	*Letered off June 1877*	
177 Mary J. Scott	*Excluded Apr 1886*	
178 James P. Tally		
179 Caroline Talley		
180 Henry McDade		
181 James P. Moon		
182 Caroline McCain		
183 A.J. Barnes	*leterd of* [off]	
184 N.E. Barnes	*leterd of* [off]	
185 J.H. Samples		
186 Jane Samples		
187 Mary Allen		
188 John L. Carrell	*dismist by letter March 1881*	
189 M.M. Carrell	*dismist by letter March 1881*	
190 Jane Sisk	*Died Sept. 1882*	
191 James Rusk	*Lettered off Mar 1885*	
192 Mary Jane Rusk	*Lettered off Mar 1885*	
193 Siller Davis	*Ded*	
194 Julie Talley		
195 Sameul Stulce		

CHURCH ROLL
1876–1882 [59]

Aslinger Misourie	ltterd off 1892
Allen Mary	lettered off Feb. [Sept.-from Minutes] 1882
Baker Elisabeth	
Blair Manervie	lettered off Nov 1883
Barnes A.J.	
Barnes N.E.	
Barnett S.E.	Leterd off
Conner M.H.	
Conner Martha	
Conner Thomas	
Conner Joseph H.	
Cookston Joseph	
Cross James	Letterd off in June 1892
Campbell M.A.	
Campbell D.L.	
Carter Martha	
Carrell Manervie	
Carrell John L.	Letterd off Nov 1883
Carrell M.M.	
Denson Eliza	Leterd of [off] Dec 89
Denson James	
Davis Siller	
Day Elisabeth	Died apri[l] 1888
Eldridge Isabelle	
Eldridge George	Excluded Apr[il] 1886
Friddle Elisabeth	
Ford Clementine	Dismised by letter May 1882
Gooden Parville	lettered off March 1883
Haney Marinna	died April 1881
Haney W.R.	
Haney Nancy	

---

[59]   This Church Roll was not dated. The dates of 1876–82 were developed based on the position of the roll in the pages of the Church Minutes ledger book and the dates from the minutes on which certain members were accepted into Church membership.

Haney Nancy

Haney John

Haney Newton   *Letterd off Apr*[il] *(9) 1892*

Haney Liza Jane

Howel James

Howel Mary

Henry Byrd

Henry Julie

Hatfield Linch

Hayes Herald   *by letter May 1881*

Hayes Nancy   " " " "

Hayes Martha   *by letter March 1881*

Harden Jane   *Deid apr 1888*

Hixson Roda

Haney Thomas

Irwin A.G.   *Dismised by letter April 1883*

Lowe Isaac

Lowe Linda

Killian Elisabeth

Killian Nancy

McCain Caroline

Millard Emily

Malone Betty   *by Letter in March 1881*

McCallie A.A.

McCallie Jane

McCallie Nancy

McMillion Mathew   *Excluded Sept 1880*

Moon Sarah C.   *Leterd off*

Moon James P.   *Leterd of* [off] *May 1880*

Moon Sarah A.

Moon Charley   *Dismised by letter Decembr 1882*

Moon Mary Jane   *Dismised by letter Decembr 1882*

Martin Clementine

Monger Phronia   *letered off Nov 1883*

Monger James

Mop Marian   *lettered off April 1883*

Pickens Margaret

Parett William   *letered off May 1882*

Parett Amanda   *lettered* " " "

Priddy Davis	Died Feb. The 4th 1882
Roark Jerusha	lettered off Nov. 1883
Roark J.L.	
Roark Victory	
Roark J.W.	
Roark Permelia	
Roark Joseph	lettered off Nov 1883
Roark Elisabeth	" " " "
Rusk James	
Rusk Mary Jane	
Roark T.A.	
Roark Margret J.	
Roark Daniel	
Rodgers Barnie	
Rodgers Caroline	
Rodgers Elisabeth	Dead
Stults A.L.[60]	by letter in March 1881
Stults Lucinda	" " " " "
Stults L.H.	
Stults Sarah	
Stults Clementine	lettered off Nov. 1883
Stults Sameul	by letter in March 1881
Scott Mary Jane	Excluded Apr 86
Samples J.H.	letered off Feb 1882
Samples Jane	letered off Feb 1882
Samples Martha J.	
Smith Abner	Dead
Smith J.C.	Lettered off Mar. 1884
Smith Ing	" " " "
Smith Mohala [Mahala]	
Sisk Jane	Died Sept 15th 1882
Talley Thomas	
Talley J.P.	
Talley Caroline	
Talley Jane	
Talley Julie	
Talley Elisabeth	
Talley Benjamin	lettered off June 1883

---

[60]   The spelling for the family name in the Minutes was almost universally "Stulce."

Talley A.J.	*lettered off June 1883*
Tucker Aaron	*Died Nov 1887*
Tucker W.E.	*Excluded Sept 1880*
Tucker Hetty	
Witt Silas	*letterd off March 1882*
Witt Jane	*letterd off March 1882*
Witt Calvin B	*Leterd apr 1887*
Webb Sarah	*Leterd off*
Wilson B.A.	*killed July 1881*
Webb Lodemia	
Webb Martha J.	
Alexander Jane	
Bare Amanda	
Bare Reese	
Baker John	
Cooley S.M.	*Dismissed by leter May 1888*
Johnson Franklin	*Dismised by letter feb 1883*
Johnson William	
Johnson Hanner	
Johnson Angeline	
Johnson Sidney	
Samples Nancy	
Samples Jerusha	
Smith C.A.	
Simes Elizabeth	
Camon [Cannon] *Pheba*	
Smith Mary R. bell	
Eliza Priddy	
Elisabeth Priddy	
William Priddy	*Died feb 1887*
Bear, Jacob	
J.M. Roark	
Martha Roark	
Stults Hemma	*Died Jan the 30 1888*

CHURCH ROLL
1883–1890[61]

1 M.H. Conner	Died July 1898
2 Martha Conner	Died June 1890
3 Thomas Conner	
4 Joseph Conner	
5 Joseph Cookson [62]	
6 Elizabeth Baker	Died
7 Misouri Aslinger	Letterd off 1892
8 W.R. Haney	Died March 12 1894
9 Nancy Haney	Letterd off 1894
10 John Haney	Letterd off 1894
11 Thos Haney	Died 1893
12 J.L. Roark	
13 Victoria Roark	
14 J.W. Roark	Letterd off Sep 1893
15 Permelia Roark	Letterd off Sep 1893
16 Thos. A. Roark	
17 Margrett J. Roark	
18 Daniel Roark	Erased from Book
19 J. Mack Roark	
20 Martha Roark	
21 J.P. Tally	
22 Carline Tally	
23 Jane Tally	
24 Elisabeth Tally	Dismissed by Letter Apr 9 1892
25 Julia Tally	
26 Thomas Tally	
27 Caroline McCain	
28 Jane Elexander	
29 Manda J. Bare	
30 Rease Bare	Excluded 97

---

61   This Church Roll was not dated. The dates of 1883–90 were developed based on the position of the roll in the pages of the Church Minutes ledger book and the dates from the Minutes on which certain members were accepted into Church membership.

62   Joseph Cookston

31 Jacob Bare

32 Ing Smith

33 C.A. Smith

34 Eliza Priddy

35 Elizabeth Priddy

36 Elizabeth Sims

37 Nancy Hayes

38 Roda J Hickson

39 Elisabeth Killian

40 Nancy Killian

41 Linda Sivils

42 L.H. Stulce

43 Sarah Stulce

44 Barney Rogers

45 Carline Rogers

46 Martha J. Samples

47 Nancy Samples

48 Jerusha Samples

49 Jane McCallie

50 Nancy McCallie

51 Bird Bolen

52 W.M. Roark

53 Harrett [Harriet] Roark

54 A.L. Stulce

55 Lenora Stulce   Died Oct the 1 1891

56 Clementine Stulce

57 Stacy Stulce

58 Salley Irwin

59 Juda Roark [63]   Letterd off Sep 1893

60 Wesley Millard   Letterd off 1894

61 Johney Cross

62 Molley Rains

63 Hattey Rains

64 Lydda Smith

65 Sarah L. Stulce

66 S.J. Stulce

---

[63] This is Julia Roark, daughter of John W. Roark and Permelia Conner Roark. Named originally for her grandmother, Juda Carr Roark, she later was commonly known as Julia and used that name.

67 Arch Smith   Letterd off September 94

68 William Erwin [Irwin]

69 Ady Talley

70 Marthey Smith

71 Marthey Darhartey

72 B.F. Baker   Died Octo 96

73 Samuel Davis

74 Ema Rains

75 Matie Cross

76 T.J. Cross

78 D.J. Elixander

79 Ema Thomas

80 Mamie Smith

81 Charley Pendergrass

82 S.E. Allison

83 J.T. Allison

84 Salley Cross

85 James Davis

86 Matie Davis

87 Lisebeth Henrey

88 W.T. Heaton

CHURCH ROLL
1891–1908[64]

1 *Japhes* [Joseph] *Cookston*	*May 1898 deceased.*
2 *J.L. Roark*	
3 *Victora Roark*	
4 *Thomas Roark*	
5 *Martha Roark*	
6 *J.P. Talley*	
7 *Carline Talley*	
8 *Carline Mcaine* [McCain]	*Died 1901*
9 *Jane Alixander*	*Letterd off*
10 *Manda J. Bare*	
11 *C.A. Smith*	
12 *Eliza Pridy*	*Excluded*
13 *Elizabeth Pridy*	*Lettered off*
14 *Elizabeth Sims*	
15 *Elizabeth Killian*	*Died 1896*
16 *Nancy Killian*	
17 *L.H. Stulce*	
18 *Sarah Stulce*	
19 *Barnie Rogers*	*Died 1897*
20 *Nanie Samples*	
21 *Jane McCallie*	
22 *Nancie McCallie*	
23 *W.M. Roark*	
24 *~~Hariet~~ Roark*	
25 *A.L. Stulce*	
26 *Clementine Stulce*	*died June 1898*
27 *Stacy Stulce*	*Died Oct 1907*
28 *Johnie Cross*	
29 *Mollie Rains*	
30 *Hattie Rains*	*excluded*
31 *Lydda Smith*	

---

64   This Church Roll was not dated. The dates of 1891–1908 were developed based on the position of the roll in the pages of the Church Minutes ledger book and the dates from the Minutes on which certain members were accepted into Church membership.

32 Sarah L. Stulce	*lettered off*
33 S.J. Stulce	*lettered off*
34 W.T. Irwin	*Excluded*
35 Adda Talley	*Died 1901*
36 Martha Smith	*Died Dec 1897*
37 Martha Darty	
38 Samuel Davis	*Died Octo 96*
39 Mattie Davis	*Lettered off*
40 James Davis	*died March 21 07*
42 Mattie Cross	
43 T.J. Cross	
44 D.J. Alixander	*Letterd off*
45 Emma James	
46 Mamie Smith	
47 Charley Pendergrass	*Excluded*
48 S.E. Allison	*died*
49 Frank Allison	*Excluded April 1894*
50 Salley Cross	
51 W.T. Heaton	
52 Elizabeth Henry	
53 Mack Roark	
54 Jacob Bare	*Excluded April 1894*
55 Thos Talley	*Excluded*
57 J.W. Baker	*Excluded*
58 Salley Irwin	
59 John W. Smith	*Died March 1902*
60 Margret Smith	
61 Eller Smith	
62 Adda Smith	
63 J.W. Talley	*Excluded*
64 Alcey Talley	
65 Martha Runians	
66 Nancey Smith	*Died Sept 1902*
67 Dike Eldridge	*Excluded*
68 Liley McClanhane	*excluded*
69 Bessie Irwin	*excluded*
70 Rease Bare	*Excluded*
71 Johney Eldridge	

72 *Berrie Roark* [65]

73 *James Shelton*

74 *Jennie Predie*

75 *Jophes* [Joseph] *Roark* [66]

76 *Samey Smith*

77 *Old Bro. Keys*

78 *W.B. Roark*

79 *Odas Cross*

80 *John Davis*

81 *Ellen Stulce*

82 *Grace Stulce*

83 *Freelen Defriese*   *Excluded 1906*

84 *Wilkie Eldridge*

85 *Lillie Roark*

86 *Laura Roark*

87 *Rosa Wrinkle*   *excluded*

88 *Thomas Conner*

89 *Joseph Conner*

90 *Martha J. Samples*

91 *Jerusia Campbell*

92 *Arhur* [Arthur] *Cross*

93 *Jane Cross*

94 *Minie Smith*

95 *Owen Smith*   *lettered off*

96 *Floyd Smith*

97 *Enoch Hardin*

98 *Andy Hardin*

99 *Jim Posy*

100 *Maebell Low*

101 *Jessie Hindman*

102 *Jim Allison*

~~103 *Jim Davis*~~   ~~*Died March 24 1907*~~

103 *Bill Hixson*

104 *Maggie Hixson*

105 *Bill Hardin*

106 *Will Stulce*

---

[65] This is Franklin Asbury Roark, son of William M. and Virginia Conner Roark, who, in the Minutes, is referred to as F.A.B. Roark, or Berry.

[66] This is Joseph Walter Roark, son of William M. and Virginia Conner Roark.

107 Jennie Stulce		lettered off
108 Carrie Davis		died
109 Louie Samples		lettered off
110 Nettie Smith		
111 Eher Eldridge		excluded
112 Nola Eldridge		died
113 Martha Ellen Allison		
114 Ethel Allison		
115 Dollie Darharty		lettered off
116 Pearl Smith		
117 Jennee Eldridge		by letter

CHURCH ROLL
1909–1914[67]

(Recopied July 27, 1909.)

1 J.L. Roark

2 Victora Roark

3 Thomas Roark — *lettered off*

4 Martha Roark — *Lettered off*

5 J.P. Talley — *Died Sept 13 1911*

6 Carline Talley — *Died Sept 19 1909*

7 Manda J. Bare

8 C.A. Smith — *Nonafiliating*

9 Elizabeth Sims — *died May 1912*

10 Nancie Killian — *non* [affiliating]

11 L.H. Stulce — *Died Oct. 1909*

12 Sarah Stulce — *died 1915*

13 Mamie Samples

14 Jane McCallie

15 Nancie McCallie

16 W.M. Roark

17 Harriet Roark — *Lettered off Oct. 9 1909*

18 A.L. Stulce — *Died, Dec. 22, 1910.*

19 John Cross

20 Mollie Rains — *Lettered off June 11, 1910*

21 Hattie Rains — *excluded*

22 Lydda Smith

23 Sarah L. Stulce — *lettered off*

24 S.J. Stulce — *lettered off*

25 Martha Darty — *Lettered off June 11. 1910*

26 Mattie Cross

27 T.J. Cross — *died March 30 1912*

28 Emma Thomas

29 Mammie Smith

---

67   This Church Roll was not dated. The dates of 1909–14 were developed based on the position of the roll in the pages of the Church Minutes ledger book and the dates from the Minutes on which certain members were accepted into Church membership.

30 Sallie Cross	
31 W.T. Heaton	Excluded
32 Elizabeth Henry	Lettered off Oct. 9 1909
33 J. Mc. Roark	
34 Sallie Irwin	
35 Margeret Smith	
36 Eller Smith	excluded
37 Adda Smith	
38 Alcey Tally	
39 Martha Runian	Lettered Oct. 9 1909
40 Johnie Eldridge	Non [affiliating]
41 Berry Roark	
42 James Shelton	Non [affiliating]
43 Jennie Priddy	Lettered off 3/12/10
44 Joseph Roark	
45 Sameul Smith	Excluded Jan 1912
46 Old Bro. Key's	Died Jan 1913
47 W.B. Roark	
48 Otis Cross	non [affiliating]
49 John Davis	
50 Ellen Stulce	
51 Grace Stulce	
52 Wilkie Eldridge	non [affiliating]
53 Lillie Roark	lettered off
54 Laura Roark	Lettered off
55 Rosa Wrinkle	excluded
56 Thomas Conner	Non [affiliating]
57 Joseph Conner	Non
58 Martha J. Samples	
59 Jerusia Campbell	lettered off
60 Arthur Cross	
61 Jane Cross	
62 Minnie Smith	
63 Owen Smith	Lettered off
64 Floyd J. Smith	
65 Enoch Hardin	~~Dropped~~ Excluded
66 Andy Hardin	~~Dropped~~ Excluded
67 Jim Posy	Excluded
68 Maebel Lowe	non [affiliating]

69 Jessie Hindman	Non
70 Jim Allison	
71 Bill Hixson	Non
72 Maggie Hixson	
73 Bill Hardin	Non
74 Will Stulce	
75 Jennie Stulce	lettered off
76 Carrie Davis	Died 1910
77 Lonie Samples	lettered off
78 Nettie Smith	
79 Ether Eldridge	excluded
80 Nola Eldridge	Died June 1914
81 Martha E. Allison	
82 Ethel Allison	
83 Dollie Darharty	Lettered off
84 Pearl Smith	
85 Jennie Eldridge	by Letter excluded
86 Lena Pendergrass	
87 Della Pendergrass	
88 Jeff Cross Jr	Non [affiliating]
89 Lilly Cross	non
90 Willie Roark	
91 Grover Roark	
92 Will Pendergrass	
93 Jess Pendergrass	
94 Arthur Hubbard	Non [affiliating]
95 Alex Smith	Non
96 Carddie Swafford	non
97 Charlie Swafford	non
98 Essa Smith	
99 Bertha Smith	
100 Diathia Hindman	non
101 Laura Smith	
102 Berkie Friddle	excluded
103 Jane Friddle	excluded
104 Bulah Pendergrass	non
105 Sim Eldridge	excluded
106 Steve Allison	excluded Sept 1913
107 Sim Williams	excluded April 1914

108	J.C. Smith	by enrollment Died May 14 1910
109	J.A. Shropshire	by Letter non [affiliating]
110	Laura Shropshire	by Letter non
111	Jeff Latham	excluded Sept 1913
112	Rube Hubbord	Non
113	Thomas Allison	
114	Wilce Hixson Jr	non
115	Julie White	lettered
116	Roda J. Hixson	non [affiliating]
117	Elizabeth Eldridge	lettered off
118	Martha Holder	by Letter non
119	A.L. Smith	as by Letter
120	Rosa Smith	asby Letter
121	Maggie Smith	
122	Clara Roark	
123	Amous Shoat	

CHURCH ROLL
1914

[Recopied Nov. 23, 1914]

   Members

J.L. Roark

Victoria Roark

Thomas Roark   lettered off Aug 1915

Manda J. Bare

Nancy Killian   nonaffiliating

Sarah Stulce   Died March 21ˢᵗ 1915

Nannie Samples

Jane McCallie   nonaffiliating

Nancy McCallie   nonaffiliating

W.M. Roark

John Cross

Hattie Rains   Excluded Dec 1914

Lydia Smith   Nonaffiliating

Sarah L. Stulce   Lettered off Dec 1914

S.J. Stulce   Lettered off Dec 1914

Mattie Cross

Emma Thomas   nonaffiliating

Mammie Smith

Sallie Cross

J.M. Roark

Sallie Irwin   nonaffiliating

Margaret Smith

Eller Smith   nonaffiliating

Adda Smith   nonaffiliating

Alcey Talley

Berry Roark

Joseph Roark

W.B. Roark

Otis Cross   nonaffiliating

John Davis

Ellen Stulce

Grace Stulce

Wilkie Eldridge   nonaffiliating

Lilly Roark	Lettered off April 1915
Rosa Wrinkle	excluded Oct. 1915
Thomas Conner	nonaffiliating
Martha J. Samples	
Arthur Cross	
Jane Cross	
Minnie Smith	
Floyd Smith	nonaffiliating
Mabel Lowe	nonaffiliating
Jim Allison	
Maggie Hixson	nonaffiliating
Will Stulce	
Jennie Stulce	lettered off Jan 1916
Louie Samples	lettered off 1915
Nettie Smith	nonaffiliating
Ether Eldridge	excluded Aug. 1915
Martha E. Allison	
Ethel Allison	
Pearl Smith	nonaffiliating
Jennie Eldridge	~~Excluded~~ Reinstated
Lena Pendergrass	
Della Pendergrass	
Lilly Cross	nonaffiliating
Willie Roark	
Grover Roark	
Will Pendergrass	
Jess Pendergrass	
Cordie Swafford	nonaffiliating
Charlie Swafford	
Essa Smith	
Bertha Smith	
Dialthia Hindman	nonaffiliating
Laura Smith	
Berkie Friddell	excluded Oct 1915
Jane Friddell	excluded Oct 1915
Beulah Pendergrass	nonaffiliating
J.A. Shropshire	nonaffiliating
Laura Shropshire	nonaffiliating
Thomas Allison	

Wilce Hixson jr.	*nonaffiliating*
Julia White	*Lettered off 1916*
Roda J. Hixson	*nonaffiliating*
Elizabeth Eldridge	*Lettered off Dec 1914*
Martha Holder	*nonaffiliating*
A.L. Smith	
Rosa Smith	
Maggie Smith	
Clara Roark	

CHURCH ROLL
1915–1916

[recopied July 18 1915]

J.L. Roark

Victoria Roark

Thomas Roark   Lettered off Aug 1915

Manda J. Bare

Nancy Killian

Nannie Samples

Jane McCallie

Nancy McCallie

W.M. Roark

John Cross

Lydia Smith

Mattie Cross

Emma Thomas

Mammie Smith

Sallie Cross

J.M. Roark

Sallie Irwin

Margaret Smith

Eller Smith   Excluded Aug 1916

Adda Smith

Alcey Talley

Berry Roark

Joseph Roark

W.B. Roark

John Davis

Ellen Stulce

Grace Stulce

Rosa Wrinkle   Excluded Oct 1915

Martha J. Samples

Arthur Cross

Jane Cross

Minnie Smith

Mabel Lowe

Jim Allison

Will Stulce
Jennie Stulce   Lettered off Jan 1916
Louie Samples   Lettered off
Ether Eldridge   excluded Aug 1915
Martha E. Allison
Ethel Allison
Jennie Eldridge   Excluded Aug 1916
Lena Pendergrass
Della Pendergrass
Willie Roark
Grover Roark
Will Pendergrass
Jess Pendergrass
Cordie Swafford
Essa Smith
Bertha Smith
Dialthia Hindman
Berkie Friddell   excluded Oct 1915
Jane Friddell   excluded Oct 1915
Beulah Pendergrass
Thomas Allison
Wilson Hixson jr.
Julia White   Lettered off Aug 1916
Roda J. Hixson
Martha Holder
A.L. Smith
Rosa Smith
Maggie Smith
Clara Roark
Nettie Smith
Floid Smith
J.A. Shropshire
Laura Shropshire
Charles Swafford
C.A. Smith

Appendix B

Salem Baptist Church Delegates to Ocoee Association

1872—A.L. Stulce, John W. Roark, M.H. Conner, Silas Witt, W.R. Haney

1873—A.L. Stulce, M.H. Conner, John W. Roark, G.W. Rodgers—alternate

1874—A.L. Stulce, G.W. Rodgers, W.B. Haney, W.M. Roark

1875—Samuel Smith, William Roark, Joseph Cookston

1876—[M.] H. Conner, J. Cookston, A.L. Stulce, Davis Priddy, John Campbell—alternate

1877—A.L. Stulce, C.L. Moon, Joseph Cookston, Davis Prada [Priddy], James A. Roark

1878—A.L. Stulce, J.P. Talley, Joseph Cookston, C.L. Moon

1879—A.L. Stulce, J.P. Talley, W.R. Haney, J.W. Roark

1880—A.L. Stulce, J.P. Talley, C.L. Moon, James P. Moon

1881—J.P. Talley, A.G. Irwin, Isaac Lowe

1882—J.P. Talley, James Russ, James Moon, C.L. Moon

1883—John Roark, J.W. Roark, W.R. Haney, Thomas Talley

1884—J.P. Talley, J.L. Stults [Stulce]

1885—No record of delegates sent to the Association meeting.

1886—John W. Roark, S.M. Cooley, Lenard Stults [Leonard Stulce]

1887—J.P. Talley, Jacob Bair [Bare], L.H. Stulce

1888—L.H. Stulce, W.R. Haney, John Haney, Tomas [Thomas] Roark

1889—Joseph Cookson [Cookston], J.L. Roark, L.H. Stulce

1890—No delegates reported in minutes

1891—Bro. Thos. Roark, D.B. Roark, C.A. Smith

1892—W.M. Roark, J.P. Talley

1893—No delegates reported in minutes

1894—J.L. Roark, L.H. Stulce, J.P. Talley

1895—J.L. Roark, L.H. Stulce

1896—D.J. Alexander, T.J. Cross, A.L. Stulce

1897–1902 No delegates reported in minutes

1903—Bro. Jeff Stulce, Bro. Joe Roark, Sister Lillie Roark, Bro. Hoge

1904—Bro. Burke Roark, Sister Ellen Stulce, Berry [F.A.B] Roark Bro. Jeff Stulce, Lilly Roark, Joe Roark—Alternates

1905—S.J. Stulce, F.A.B. Roark

1906—No delegates reported in minutes

1907—Bro. Owen Smith, Floyd Smith, J.W. Roark, Berry [F.A.B.] Roark [at August meeting?]
F.A.B. Roark, Owen Smith, Joe W. Roark, Floyd Smith [at September meeting?]

1908—No delegates reported in minutes

1909—Bros. J.M. Roark, Jim Allison, Jess Hindman, Berry [F.A.B.] Roark

1910—F.A.B. Roark

1911—Bro. J.W. Roark, Grover Roark, James Allison

1912—Bro. Shropshire, Bro. John Cross, Bro. Berry [F.A.B.] Roark, Bro. Floid [Floyd] Smith

1913—Bro. Berry [F.A.B.] Roark, Bro. James Allison, and W.B. Roark

1914—W.G. Roark, J.R. Allison, W.A. Pendergrass, F.A.B. Roark

1915—J.R. Allison, W.B. Roark, and W.G. Roark

Appendix C

FORM OF ANNUAL CHURCH REPORT
to the
OCOEE BAPTIST ASSOCIATION

_____

The............Baptist Church, at.................to the Ocoee Baptist Association.
DEAR BRETHREN:—We report the following statistics since our last Association:

RECEIVED DURING THE YEAR:

By Baptism...... By Experience...... By Letter...... By Restoration......

LOST DURING THE YEAR:

By Letter............ By Death............ By Exclusion............
Membership last year............ Present Membership.................
Our Church is located in the County of...............................
The nearest Baptist Church to our house of worship is............miles.
Our Church was organized in...
Value of Church property $.................... Seating capacity......................
Days of preaching..
Prayer meeting, how often?...
Church meeting, when held?...
Pastor's name...
Pastor's P.O.,..
Clerk's name...
Clerk's P.O.,...

CONTRIBUTIONS DURING THE YEAR:

Pastor's salary.....................	State Missions.............................
Other Church expenses......................	Foreign Missions..........................
For Printing Minutes.........................	Home Missions.............................
Ministerial education........................	Ministerial Relief.........................
All other purposes...........................	Total.............................

SUNDAY-SCHOOL RECORD:

Name of Superintendent..
Postoffice address...
How often do you hold Sunday-School?...

Number of scholars...... Officers and teachers...... Average attendance......
Papers taken...... Vols. In library...... Members of School baptized during the year......
CONTRIBUTED DURING THE YEAR:
Sunday-School purposes.................. Ministerial education and relief..................
Foreign Missions............ State Missions............ Home Missions............
All other purposes $........................ Total........................

Names of Ordained Ministers:	Names of Licentiates:
....	....
Names of Delegates:	Names of Delegates:
....	....
Date....................................	....Clerk.

**Member churches of a Baptist Association were required to
present a report at the Association's yearly meeting.**

Notes

Chapter One: Salem Baptist Church 1835–1872

1. Folmsbee, Stanley J., Corlew, Robert E., Mitchell, Enoch L., *Tennessee A Short History*, Second Edition, 1981, The University of Tennessee Press, 145–149.

2. Ibid., 150.

3. Campbell, T.J., "The Centennial of Salem—Reminiscence," Speech delivered at the One Hundredth Anniversary Celebration of Salem Baptist Church, May 26, 1935.

4. Ibid.

5. Ehle, John, *Trail of Tears—The Rise and Fall of the Cherokee Nation*, Anchor Books/Doubleday, New York, 1989, 279–280.

6. G.W. Gardenhire deed

7. National Primitive Baptist Convention. *Discipline of the Primitive Baptist Church*. Huntsville, Alabama: National Primitive Baptist Publishing Board, 1960.

8. Hamilton County Baptist Association. *A History of Hamilton County Baptist Association, Formerly Ocoee Bapist Association*. Chattanooga, Tennessee: Hamilton County Baptist Association, 1980, 35.

9. DeBow, J.D.B., Superintendent of the United States Census, "The Seventh Census of the United States, 1850," Washington, D.C., 1853.

10. *History of Hamilton County Baptist Association*, 19–20.

11. Ibid., 16–17.

12. *History of Hamilton County Baptist Association*, 35.

13. Ibid., 15–16.

14. Based on the war records available for men on the church roll. Ages of members were taken from the 1870 census.

Chapter Two: Salem Baptist Church 1872–1879

1. Race was confirmed in the 1870 Census.

2. Hamilton County Baptist Association. *A History of Hamilton County Baptist Association, Formerly Ocoee Baptist Association.* Chattanooga, Tennessee: Hamilton County Baptist Association, 1980, 40.

3. Ibid., 62.

4. Burnett, J.J., *Sketches of Tennessee's Pioneer Baptist Preachers*, Press of Marshall & Bruce Company, Nashville, Tennessee, 1919, 242–243.

5. *History of Hamilton County Baptist Association*, 62.

6. Robert III, Henry M.., Evans, William J., Honemann, Daniel H., Balch, Thomas J., Robert's Rules of Order (Newly Revised, 10th Edition), Perseus Publishing, 2000. Additional information found at http://www.robertsrules.com, a website maintained by an organization of descendants of Henry Martyn Robert.

7. Wilson, John, *Early Hamilton Settlers*, Sheridan Books, 2001, 305.

Chapter Three: Salem Baptist Church 1880–1889

1. Hamilton County Baptist Association. *A History of Hamilton County Baptist Association, Formerly Ocoee Baptist Association.* Chattanooga, Tennessee: Hamilton County Baptist Association, 1980, 331.

2. Wilson, John, *Hamilton County Pioneers*, Sheridan Books, 1998, 200.

3. *History of Hamilton County Baptist Association*, 60.

Chapter Four: Salem Baptist Church 1890–1899

1. Hamilton County Baptist Association. *A History of Hamilton County Baptist Association, Formerly Ocoee Baptist Association*. Chattanooga, Tennessee: Hamilton County Baptist Association, 1980, 68.

2. Ibid., 67.

Chapter Five: Salem Baptist Church 1900–1909

1. Hamilton County Baptist Association. *A History of Hamilton County Baptist Association, Formerly Ocoee Baptist Association*. Chattanooga, Tennessee: Hamilton County Baptist Association, 1980, 100–101.

2. Ibid., 92–93.

Chapter Six: Salem Baptist Church 1910–1915

1. Salem Baptist Church Letter to the Ocoee Association, September, 1910, 1-1-1-1343.

2. Information found at http://www.namb.net, a website maintained by the North American Mission Board of the Southern Baptist Convention.

3. Ibid.

Chapter Seven: Salem Baptist Church 1915–1941

1. The history of the Salem Baptist Church during its last days was provided by Mr. Howard Scott, Cleveland, Tennessee, who was a member of the church during the period.

2. Edgar Roark, "Roark—Conner Family News," Issue 10, June, 1995.

Index

978-0-595-35657-7
0-595-35657-5